D1711725
P8-DFH-543

MIDNIGHT IN VEHICLE CITY

OTHER BOOKS BY EDWARD McCLELLAND

Folktales and Legends of the Middle West

How to Speak Midwestern

Nothin' But Blue Skies: The Heyday, Hard Times, and Hopes of America's Industrial Heartland

Young Mr. Obama: Chicago and the Making of a Black President

The Third Coast: Sailors, Strippers, Fishermen, Folksingers, Long-Haired Ojibway Painters, and God-Save-the-Queen Monarchists of the Great Lakes

Horseplayers: Life at the Track

MIDNIGHT IN VEHICLE CITY

GENERAL MOTORS, FLINT, AND THE STRIKE THAT CREATED THE MIDDLE CLASS

EDWARD McCLELLAND

BEACON PRESS
BOSTON

BEACON PRESS
Boston, Massachusetts
www.beacon.org

Beacon Press books
are published under the auspices of
the Unitarian Universalist Association of Congregations.

Printed in the United States of America

24 23 22 21 8 7 6 5 4 3 2 1

This book is printed on acid-free paper that meets the uncoated paper
ANSI/NISO specifications for permanence as revised in 1992.

Text design and composition by Kim Arney

Library of Congress Cataloging-in-Publication Data

Names: McClelland, Edward, author.
Title: Midnight in vehicle city : general motors, flint, and the strike
that created the middle class / Edward McClelland.
Description: Boston : Beacon Press, [2021] | Includes
bibliographical references and index.
Identifiers: LCCN 2020022064 (print) | LCCN 2020022065 (ebook) |
ISBN 9780807039670 (hardcover) | ISBN 9780807039687 (ebook)
Subjects: LCSH: General Motors Corporation Sit-Down Strike, 1936–1937. |
Labor unions—Michigan—Flint—History—20th century.
Classification: LCC HD5325.A82 1936-1937 M43 2021 (print) |
LCC HD5325.A82 1936-1937 (ebook) | DDC 331.892/8292220977437—dc23
LC record available at https://lccn.loc.gov/2020022064
LC ebook record available at https://lccn.loc.gov/2020022065

To Everett Ketchum

1914–2013

CONTENTS

MIDNIGHT IN VEHICLE CITY

INTRODUCTION

VEHICLE CITY

More than a hundred years ago, a series of wrought-iron arches were erected across Saginaw Street, the main drag of downtown Flint, Michigan. They spelled out, in white letters, Flint's nickname, its slogan, its reason for existence: "Vehicle City." Detroit may have built more cars than Flint, but Flint was the nation's transportation pioneer: first as a carriage maker, then as the birthplace of General Motors, the nation's leading automaker. By the mid-1930s, the Vehicle city was even more dependent on the auto industry than the Motor City: more than three-quarters of the workforce drew a paycheck from GM or one of its suppliers.

William Crapo Durant, the man who would one day found General Motors, the largest corporation in the history of the world, got into the transportation business by building horse-drawn buggies. Durant was a scion of the industry on which Flint, Michigan, had been founded: lumbering. His grandfather, Henry Howland Crapo, was a New England schoolteacher who gambled on the purchase of a $150,000 tract of Michigan pineland, won, and became so wealthy and respected that he was elected governor in 1864, only ten years after his arrival to the state. At the lumber industry's zenith, Flint's mills were sawing ninety million feet of virgin jack pine a year. By the end of the 1870s, though, the forests of the Flint River Valley were so depleted that the lumber kings began casting about for a new industry to save the town from economic devastation. They settled on horse-drawn vehicles.

Durant paid two thousand dollars to buy out a buggy maker. He moved the company to Flint, renamed it the Flint Road Cart Company, and was soon producing four hundred two-wheeled sulkies a day in a shop down by the Flint River. By the turn of the century, Flint was turning out more than a hundred thousand horse-drawn conveyances a year, more than any other city in the nation. The Vehicle City arches were erected to celebrate this distinction in 1901, just as the horse- and steam-powered nineteenth century was giving way to the gasoline-powered twentieth. Even as Flint was touting itself as the world's leading producer of buggies, wagons, and carriages, there was a feeling among its forward-looking citizens that the Vehicle City was building the wrong vehicles. Elsewhere in Michigan, Detroit's Henry Ford and Lansing's Ransom Eli Olds had already designed the cars that would bear their names, but the only motor car in Flint, assembled by a judge in his carriage house, was such a feeble machine that it stalled trying to drive over the raised wooden crosswalks of downtown intersections.

The Flint Wagon Works, a rival of Durant's, spent ten thousand dollars to purchase the creation of a Detroit tinkerer named David Dunbar Buick: the Model A, the first automobile with a valve-in-head engine. As part of the deal, both the Buick's assembly and Buick himself moved to Flint.

"Flint is the most natural center for the manufacture of autos in the whole country," the *Flint Daily Journal* wrote in an editorial celebrating the transaction. "It is the vehicle city of the United States and in order to maintain the name by which it is known from ocean to ocean there must be developed factories here for the manufacture of the automobile."

The buyers asked Durant to run Buick, impressed that he had built Flint Road Cart from a two-thousand-dollar investment to an enterprise bringing in two million dollars a year. The horse-and-buggy man was not a fan of automobiles, but a country drive in a Buick convinced Durant it was a capable machine, only rarely defeated by ruts or mud. Also, pedestrians wanted a closer look at the car, which appealed to his salesman's instincts. Believing it his civic duty to take part in Flint's next big thing, Durant signed on.

Setting up shop in the old Flint Wagon Works, Buick built forty cars that first year. By 1906, the automaker had outgrown the wagon shop and moved into a new three-story plant on an old North End farm, along a newly laid-out street named Industrial Avenue.

Durant, who loved the Big Deal, saw the automobile as his ticket to becoming an industrial titan as wealthy and influential as Andrew Carnegie. To achieve that goal, he decided to organize an "auto trust" of all the major manufacturers, based on the model of Carnegie's United States Steel. On September 16, 1908, the Buick and Oldsmobile companies merged by means of a stock swap to form the General Motors Corporation. Durant had also approached Henry Ford, but the cantankerous engineer wanted cash rather than stock. The ambitious Durant quickly acquired a third auto company, located in Pontiac; then, feeling he had to add a Detroit automaker to his portfolio, he paid $3.5 million for the Cadillac Motor Company. The classic GM five-brand lineup became complete in 1917, when Durant brought in a model founded by a mustachioed Swiss auto racer named Louis Chevrolet. The Chevrolet Royal Mail, a $750 four-cylinder roadster, was neither as cheap nor as popular as Ford's Model T, but the masses bought it nonetheless, and it established Chevrolet's future position as the bottom rung of GM's "price for every purse" brand ladder.

Flint, which had begun the first decade of the century with a single hand-assembled motorcar, was by that decade's end the Second City of the auto industry, behind only Detroit. In 1910, one out of every six automobiles sold in the United States was a Buick—a total of 30,525 cars.

The demand for Buicks meant a demand for workers to build Buicks. In the 1900s Flint's population tripled, from 13,103 to 38,550, making it the fastest-growing industrial city in the nation. The plants were so desperate for workers they dispatched agents to the rural South, offering train tickets to Flint (the offer was discontinued after hobos figured out it was a free ride). Flint was so overwhelmed with young men leaving their farms to build cars that the old sawmill settlement had nowhere to house them. Boarding house keepers rented beds in shifts—sometimes requiring men to sleep double—but even so, at least a thousand autoworkers were unable to find indoor accommodations. The homeless men set up camps along the river, or in the woods, within walking distance of the shops. They lived in piano crates, or railroad cars, or pitched tents, forking over a Liberty dime every week to shower at the Flint Vehicle Factories Mutual Benefit Association, where they could also amuse themselves in the gym, library, billiard room, or bowling alley. One well-to-do crate dweller had a four-hundred-dollar dining set delivered to his "residence."

With so much money flowing through the hands of so many single men, Flint was a Wild North boomtown. Saginaw Street's weekly highlight was no longer Saturday-morning market day but Saturday-night payday. Flint autoworkers earned an average of $2.61 a day, the highest industrial wage in Michigan, and plenty of them spent the checks as soon as they could cash them.

"Saginaw Street was a sight, with these electric arches lit up in many colors from Court Street to the bridge. Store windows incandescent, horses stamping at the curb, sidewalks overflowing with life," wrote *Flint Journal* reporter Frank Rodolf in his "Industrial History of Flint," written in 1949.

> Whole families filled the streets, packed the stores and recreation spots, the youngsters with peanuts, popcorn or crackerjack.
>
> They rushed the banks, too, until a stranger would suspect there was a run. All the plants paid the same night. Whether the pay was in checks or currency made little difference to the banks, for they also had to "break" big folding money into silver dollars and smaller change. In 1910, there were about 15,000 employees and a large percentage of them entered the few banks on those pay nights.

That year also saw the first stirrings of labor dissent in Flint. The only unionized workers in the city were cigar rollers, railwaymen, and builders, whose skills commanded high wages and made them difficult to replace. In 1901, the Flint Central Labor Council had attempted to form an "industrial union" for carriage shop laborers, who occupied an economic niche above the tradesmen, but it didn't catch on among workers who could easily be fired in favor of the next hungry farm boy who stepped off the train at the Flint Central Depot. Five years later, an attempt to organize the Buick engine factory fizzled when the company shut down the plant, citing a "material shortage." Two days later, the plant was back in operation—without a union. Thus, when the booming auto industry finally went bust, workers had no seniority to protect their jobs and no layoff pay to tide them through their sudden unemployment.

As the new century began its second decade, it appeared that Buick was only going to get bigger. Sales had doubled from the year before. On the first day of spring in 1910, Buick hired 200 employees, bringing the payroll to 6,500, which meant that one sixth of Flint's population worked for "the Buick," as they familiarly called their employer. But when sales began to slacken in midyear—a result of GM's having saturated the luxury market, while lacking an inexpensive car to suit the workingman's budget—Buick laid off thousands of workers.

"When Buick was closed for inventory and changeover to 1911 models it stayed closed so long there was widespread panic," wrote Rodolf. "Payroll figures were no longer good news. Most of Flint was jobless and could not understand why this swashbuckling boom town saw its gold mine closed and had a few weeks to wonder if it would reopen."

Business improved as the 1910s progressed. As the hometown of two of America's most popular cars, Buick and Chevrolet, Flint more than doubled in population for the second decade in a row, from 38,550 to 91,599. And after the World War ended, in 1918, GM finally took steps to house the workers stampeding the city and prevent the sanitary disaster of squatter settlements among the trees. First, Buick built military-style dormitories, known as "camps," to warehouse bachelor employees until housing construction caught up with demand. Then, GM came up with a permanent solution: a planned community designed for autoworkers. The company established a dummy developer, the Modern Housing Corporation, which set a goal of building a thousand houses in the first nine months of 1919. It wasn't just a profit-making enterprise; it was a personnel decision: GM was losing employees who couldn't find a place for their wives and children to sleep.

"In some homes that just rented sleeping rooms, there were many cases of four workers using one double bed," wrote the corporation's superintendent. "Two day workers would sleep in it in the night time and two night workers would sleep in it in the day time. When the new worker was unable to find any rentable space for his family, he would quit his job and go back to his family."

GM bought a plot of land two miles north of its Chevy complex and built a narrow-gauge railroad to haul rails and lumber to the site. Importing 1,600 carpenters, masons, and laborers for the project, the company almost reached its goal, building 946 five- or six-room workingman's cottages by the end of 1919. Selling for as little as $3,500, they would house generations of GM employees. Civic Park, as the development was known, established Flint as a company town, where General Motors both issued a man's paycheck and collected his mortgage.

General Motors did not control just its employees' working hours and home lives; it controlled the leisure hours in between as well. The Industrial Mutual Association, funded by workers' annual five-dollar contributions, built a seven-thousand-seat auditorium that became the recreational and entertainment center of the city, bringing in opera singers from New York; organizing bowling, basketball, and baseball leagues whose teams represented their shops; sponsoring a male glee club, a women's chorus, orchestras, bands, and a literary society. The association also managed GM's life insurance plan for workers, operated a summer camp, and published the *I.M.A. News*, which billed itself as "The Factory Worker's Own Paper" but published only material approved by management. In Flint, General Motors was all-powerful and paternalistic, like Pullman in Chicago and Carnegie Steel in Homestead, Pennsylvania. In the 1890s, workers in both of those communities had rebelled, unsuccessfully, against companies that controlled every aspect of their employees' lives and work.

As long as General Motors was growing and employment was steady, most of Flint was satisfied with this arrangement. In 1926, "the Buick" built its two-millionth car, in a year when it sold 266,753, a record that stood until 1940, after the Great Depression—an economic calamity that would devastate the auto industry and lead to changes in worker-employee relations everywhere. From its 1926 peak of 21,596 Buick employment dropped a third by 1930, to 14,960, even as the company tried to adapt to the nation's straitened finances by introducing an economy car, the Marquette. Unfortunately, the Marquette flopped. In 1931, Buick laid off another 3,500 workers, throwing them to the merciless conditions of the Depression.

Workers who remained received an hourly wage, but they depended on piecework bonuses to bring their earnings up to something they could live on. If a plant produced too many cars, GM cut the piece rate to keep wages down. Workers were paid only when the line was running. During layoffs or model changeovers, which might last five months, they were high and dry. To survive, laid-off workers took out loans from the company's Welfare Department, which were deducted from their checks, with interest, when they were rehired. General Motors offered no health benefits, pension plan, unemployment, vacation pay, or even job security. With so many men out of work, supervisors could afford to fire anyone who talked back, showed up late, or could not keep up with the assembly line. The hated line "speedup" left workers "too tired to eat after shifts"; the exhausted men were recognizable by their "pallid, gray skins from overwork."

The work was hot and dangerous as well as exhausting. In shops where grinding and metal finishing took place, metal dust clung to the skin and clogged lungs, causing respiratory problems. The Buick pressed-metal shop was so dangerous it was nicknamed "the slaughterhouse."

"There was a lot of sharp sheet metal, and they didn't provide heavy gloves," worker Kenny Malone recalled. "You brought your own or used cloth material to cover the edges."

Despite the low pay, the lack of job security, and the hazards of the shop, men trying to feed their families during the Depression would submit to any indignity to remain in the good graces of their capricious bosses. Workers did chores at their foreman's homes or farms. If a foreman dropped by your house, you were expected to throw him an instant party.

"It was not unusual for a foreman to have your wife," one worker claimed.

At General Motors in the 1930s, all the conditions were in place for a labor strike. In 1930 and 1934, workers staged failed strikes for better wages and working conditions. Then, in the summer of 1936, a new union, the United Auto Workers of America, sent an organizer to Flint.

CHAPTER 1

A STRANGER IN TOWN

THE HEAT WAVE BEGINS on the Great Plains, in the Dust Bowl, that dead, dry land whose barren fields have transformed it into a furnace. The summer of 1936 is the hottest anyone can remember. After killing the meager yield of crops in the farm states, the dome of heat spreads north and east, smothering the Great Lakes. In the second week of July, every afternoon, workers preparing for second shift at the General Motors plants in Flint, Michigan, look out the kitchen windows of their company-built Cape Cods and slope-roofed bungalows, at the thermometers bolted to the walls. The gauges fill with red mercury, measuring triple-digit temperatures: 108 degrees, 105 degrees, 102 degrees, 104 degrees, day after miserable day in the lush, humid Saginaw Valley.

It's so hot inside those brick factories. They were built to trap warmth during the hard winters, but they're kilns during this heat wave, even with all the windows cranked open. There are no fans to cool the workers, no air conditioning. Building automobiles is a strenuous, sweaty occupation, even during mild weather. The assembly line never stops moving, not once in eight hours. If the company needs more cars, it cranks up the speed. Men who can't keep up don't keep their jobs, so the workers go home exhausted, too tired to talk to their wives and children, too tired to do anything but eat and sleep.

They endure it, because every day, there's a line of men outside the personnel office, hungry for a job in this Depression.

Gilbert "Gib" Rose has one of the toughest jobs at General Motors, grinding crankshafts at Chevrolet Plant Number Four, called Chevy Four, the engine plant in the Chevrolet complex, a collection of factories that steams and smokes and clanks all day and night on the south bank of the Flint River. One of the plants in that complex is nicknamed "Chevy in the Hole," either because it lies in a depression alongside the river or because it's a hellhole—probably both. The crankshafts weigh a hundred and eight pounds, and Rose has to lift each one off the assembly line, set it on a grinding rack, then carry it back to the line when it's finished. By the end of a long shift, Rose will have lifted tons of metal with his bare hands and bare arms. Not even plowhorses pull so much weight during a day.

The men in the crankshaft department are the biggest and strongest at GM, men in the prime of their work lives. The company doesn't like workers over forty; it looks for reasons to fire them in favor of younger hires. But even the strongest are not stronger than this heat wave. On the day the thermometer spikes at 108, the hottest ever measured in Flint, four of Rose's coworkers faint on the assembly line. They're rolled onto stretchers and carried off the shop floor, but the crankshafts never stop coming.

"Get him on a stretcher and get him the hell out of here," a foreman shouts every time a man collapses. "And don't stop that line! If you miss one crankshaft, we'll fire you."

At General Motors, the workers come and go, but the assembly line never stops moving. It moves as fast as men can bolt seats and doors and crankshafts onto cars . . . and then it moves faster. The heat wave passes, but the despised "speedup," as the men call it, is an unceasing feature of factory life. Whenever there is a gap in the line, as a result of a parts shortage, the foreman speeds up the tempo for the rest of the day, to ensure the plant produces its quota. At the beginning of a shift, the line might move at forty cars an hour, but by the end, it can be cranked up to sixty. This is faster than the lines are engineered to run, so cars jerk forward under the stress of the speed.

A trim-line worker whose job is to tack head linings to an auto seat pounds a tack into his finger when a car lurches suddenly. His foreman tells him that lunch is coming in fifteen minutes, so he can go to the infirmary then. By the end of a day, the men are working so frantically that everyone is clustered at the end of the line because they haven't been able to keep up with the cars as they pass by. Workers arrive at the shop an hour early to lay out their parts—the only way to keep up with the pace of auto assembly and thus avoid getting fired. A factory wife complains that her wrung-out husband comes home so exhausted that "he throws himself on the floor, and he can't sometimes hold a fork in his hand afterwards."

A man whose job is to wipe down bodies at the end of the line with a gasoline-soaked rag doesn't have time to wring it out between jobs, the cars come at him so fast. He spatters gasoline on himself, burning his arms and legs. The unceasing approach of auto bodies drives him so mad he begins to hallucinate and hear bells ringing. His brother drives up from Detroit to take him home. Most men aren't driven crazy, but many are driven to drink. When the line is running, it doesn't just run fast, it runs unceasingly—nine hours a weekday and five on Saturday, Christmas Eve, New Year's Eve. You have to put in the time to save enough money for the next layoff. After work, men drown their exhaustion in beer gardens. Families come to know their fathers as drunk, tired, and surly.

"The man was so driven by the speedup inside the factory that he came home unable to be a decent companion either to his wife or children, and she had to take an awful lot of bad treatment from her husband," one worker's wife would recall. "When a person is driven beyond human endurance, you become so resentful inside yourself it's got to spill out somewhere."

Not only is the work exhausting, it's dirty and dangerous. Workers dare not step off the assembly lines, even to use the toilet. There are no fans, no ventilation, no dust masks, no safety glasses. A man named Neil Yaklin works half blind because a chip flies off a chisel when he's driving rails into car bodies—forty or fifty rails a minute—and lodges in his eye. He loses the eye but keeps working because there is no disability pay or unemployment insurance. There is no health insurance either, so it takes Yaklin four years and an appeal to the state labor board to get $1,800 for his missing eye.

Presses chop off fingers, hands, even a leg. In the nickel-plating department, where workers apply the finish to radiator grills with buffing wheels, the lye and lime dust settle in men's hair and depilates their heads. The dust is so thick that "sometimes all you could do was to stand there and cough for a couple of minutes," a worker later recalls. "If you had said anything to a foreman then about wearing a mask to protect your nose and mouth, he would have called you a sissy."

That sweltering summer, a labor organizer appears in Flint. Wyndham Mortimer, an autoworker from Cleveland and a member of the Communist Party USA, is the first vice president of the newly formed United Auto Workers of America (UAWA; later known as the UAW), which has recently broken away from the American Federation of Labor. At its first convention, held that April and May in South Bend, Indiana, the delegates agree that the only way to build the union's membership is to organize General Motors, the nation's number-one automaker. They want a strike between Christmas and New Year's. From a GM tool-and-die maker, they learn that two Fisher Body plants contain the dies that stamp out the body parts for all GM vehicles. (The Fisher Body Company was a carriage maker that shifted to building bodies for the automobile industry and was absorbed by General Motors in 1919.) Fisher One, in Flint, produces components for Buicks, Oldsmobiles, Pontiacs, and Cadillacs. Fisher Body, in Cleveland, produces components for Chevrolets. The Cleveland plant is already well organized, so Mortimer is dispatched to Flint, to persuade the workers there that joining the union and going on strike will end their misery.

On the morning of June 20, Mortimer parks his car in front of the green awning of the Hotel Dresden, a red-brick building with six tiers of cheap rooms at the corner of South Saginaw and Third. Mindful that the UAWA's treasury contains only $25,000, he asks the desk clerk for the simplest lodgings available, a bachelor's room costing twelve dollars a week. Signing his name in the register beneath the date, "June 20," he is handed a key from the rack behind the desk and follows the bellboy upstairs, where he opens the door to a bed, a sink, a pair of windows darkened by rolled-down shades.

Mort, as he is known to his union brothers, is making his first visit to Flint. A fifty-two- year-old man with thinning blond hair, round wire-framed spectacles, and the mild countenance of a schoolteacher or a pastor, he has grown up in Pennsylvania coal country, in the town of Bitumin, population five hundred, the son of a miner who immigrated to the United States from Wales. His father, Thomas Mortimer, was president of the local chapter of the Knights of Labor and led a strike that resulted in his blacklisting from the mines for years. Wyndham himself went into the mines when he was twelve, where he earned seven cents an hour as a "trapper boy," opening and closing doors for mule teams that hauled the coal. The family's straitened existence in the company town of Bitumen was "the nearest thing to peonage to be found anywhere in America," Mortimer would write in his 1971 autobiography, *Organize! My Life as a Union Man*. Eventually, as coal dust consumed Thomas's lungs, the Mortimers moved to Elyria, Ohio, where Wyndham found a job in a steel mill. While working there, he heard a campaign speech by Eugene Debs, during one of Debs's five campaigns for president on the Socialist Party of America ticket. The speech inspired Wyndham to join the Socialist Party, read Marx and Engels, and attempt to organize an International Workers of the World chapter in the US Steel tube mill where he was employed: "The intolerable drive for more and more production . . . had turned [it] into a madhouse." When US Steel discovered that he was a Wobbly, as members of the radical IWW union were called, Wyndham was fired. After that, he went through a period of itinerant labor, finding work as a teamster and railroad brakeman before finally catching on as a drill-press operator at the White Motor Company in Cleveland during the World War.

Wyndham Mortimer's organizing efforts were more successful at White Motors than at US Steel. During the Depression, with the aid of a group of Communist autoworkers who had organized two plants in Detroit, Mortimer collected union application cards from more than half the workers at White. In his autobiography, Mortimer will not admit to being a Communist but writes, "I have never been afraid of words or labels. I had seen what the Communists had done in the Small Home and Landowners [League], and calling a man or an organization 'Red' did not scare me at all." The new union was strong enough to win a fifty-cents-an-hour minimum wage in the plants and to force White to pay time and a half on Saturdays and Sundays.

Mortimer, who became chairman of his grievance committee and president of the Cleveland District Auto Council, was a successful organizer in his hometown, but in Flint, he is a stranger. Although he knows no one in this city he is expected to win over for the United Auto Workers of America, someone knows him, and knows why he's here. As soon as Mortimer shrugs off his suit jacket, the telephone on the nightstand rings.

"You had better get the hell back where you came from if you don't want to be carried out in a box," a voice threatens.

"Who is this?" Mortimer demands, to silence on the other end. "How would you like to go to hell?" says Mortimer, banging the receiver down into its cradle.

The next morning, Mortimer walks through the hotel lobby on his way to make a first tour of the Vehicle City. A man sitting in an armchair spots the new organizer, folds his copy of the *Flint Journal*, and follows Mortimer out the door. From then on, wherever he goes in Flint Mortimer finds a car full of men observing his movements. Pinkerton detectives, maybe. The Pinks had a history of breaking strikes, going all the way back to Homestead in 1892.

The Flint Common Council, which not surprisingly is under the influence of General Motors, has passed a number of ordinances intended to thwart union organizing efforts such as Mortimer's. It is illegal to hand out literature on the street. It is illegal to use an amplifier to broadcast a message or speech.

"To organize Flint, a town that was so completely dominated by the General Motors Corporation, would not be easy," he writes in *Organize!* "An indescribable cloud of fear hung over the city, and it was next to impossible to find anyone who would discuss the union, or who would be seen in my company, much less to help in building one. . . . I concluded that if Flint was to be organized, it would have to be done quietly, without publicity, and mostly at night."

Another obstacle, as Mortimer sees it, is that Flint's autoworkers have lost faith in unionism. Twice before they tried to strike for higher wages and better working conditions. Both efforts failed. In 1930, workers at Fisher One walked off the job after GM sped up the line and cut wages by 40 to 50 percent as a result of a model change. They called themselves the Automobile Workers Association of Flint, but GM claimed they were under the influence of "foreign agitators and communists from Detroit, Pontiac and Chicago," according to the *Flint Journal*. When the strikers picketed the plant, nightstick-wielding police shoved them around so badly that one man was sent to the hospital. When they held an outdoor meeting in the countryside south of town, the Flint police discovered the location and sent a corps of mounted officers to ride them down, scattering strikers into surrounding fields. Less than a week after abandoning their machines, most strikers walked back through the gates, lured by the company's promise that wages would return to the same rate as the year before. Not everyone was allowed to return, however: the strike committee members were fired and blacklisted. It would be long, penurious years before any of them built cars again.

The next time Flint's GM workers talked strike, in 1934, they had a union on their side, but they still didn't get what they wanted out of the company. The National Industrial Recovery Act, a piece of New Deal legislation passed in 1933 and signed by the new president, Franklin D. Roosevelt, granted workers the right to bargain collectively "through representatives of their own choosing." It also specified that "no employee and no one seeking employment shall be required as a condition of employment to join any company union or to refrain from joining, organizing, or assisting a labor organization of his own choosing."

Guaranteed the protection of the federal government, the American Federation of Labor, an umbrella organization of trade unions founded by Samuel Gompers in 1886, now recruited autoworkers into so-called "federal unions," using the slogan "The president wants you to join a union!"

The AFL chartered 183 federal auto unions. Of the 100,000 autoworkers it claimed to have organized, nearly half were in Flint's General Motors plants. They preferred the AFL to the "company unions" GM set up to comply with the new law.

When workers at Fisher One voted to strike, though, the AFL held them back.

The AFL submitted a list of demands to the company, including a 20 percent increase in basic rates, time and a half overtime after eight hours in a day, double time on weekends, and the abolition of the hated piecework bonus system. General Motors not only rejected the demands, it rejected the federation's right to make them. GM refused to bargain with a union claiming to act "on behalf of all employees, nor will it recognize such a union, even if a majority of employees vote to endorse it as a bargaining agent."

Dismayed by such obduracy, President Roosevelt stepped in. Fearing an automobile strike would imperil the industrial recovery on which his administration's success depended, the president invited representatives of GM and the AFL to the White House, where he personally mediated the dispute. Even though workers at Fisher One had already voted to strike, they agreed to hold off for FDR, who was almost unanimously popular in the shop.

Despite the workers' preference for the AFL over the company unions, many of them were disappointed with the deal AFL leaders cut to avoid a strike. The union dropped its demands for elections. Instead, it agreed to submit its membership lists to the government, to be compared with GM's payroll list, so that a three-member board could "allot representation of worker delegates for collective bargaining to A. F. of L. unions, company unions and others on the basis of membership in each plant." The employers agreed to bargain collectively and not discriminate against employees due to union membership. The National Recovery Administration, a New Deal agency established to write codes of fair wages and working hours, would set up a board to settle questions of representation, discharge, and discrimination. When the companies laid off workers, married men with families would be kept on first, followed by "seniority, individual skill, and efficient service."

The president was pleased.

"In this settlement there is a framework for a new structure of industrial relations—a new basis of understanding between employers and employees," Roosevelt said.

The auto companies were pleased, too. They preserved their company unions. The AFL couldn't claim to represent all their workers. To GM, that would be just a step short of socialism.

The autoworkers who placed their faith in the AFL were not so pleased. Attendance at union meetings had been seven or eight hundred when a strike was in the air. After the settlement, it dwindled to a dozen. Members stopped paying their dues and dropped off the rolls. Why support a union that had sold them out in Washington and left them every bit as much at the mercy of GM's caprice as they'd been before? By June 1935, only 22,687 autoworkers—5 percent of the national workforce—belonged to a federal union. In Michigan, membership was 3,610.

John L. Lewis, the president of the United Mine Workers of America, also was not pleased. Although he sat on the board of the American Federation of Labor, Lewis considered it a confederation of craft unions, an aristocracy of skilled tradesmen unsuited for representing workers in the growing industries of automaking and steel. In August 1935, the AFL finally chartered an international union, the United Auto Workers of America, but its membership did not include tool and die makers or skilled maintenance workers, who continued to belong to craft unions. At the federation's October 1935 convention in Atlantic City, New Jersey, Lewis backed a minority report favoring a campaign to organize mass-production workers into individual unions particular to their own industries. He called for a vote to accept the report's recommendations as official AFL policy. The time had come: that July, President Roosevelt had signed the Wagner Act, which guaranteed government protection for union elections. The convention voted to reject the report; it was defeated by craft unionists jealous of their membership rolls. In November, Lewis resigned as vice president of the AFL and formed the Congress of Industrial Organizations, a new labor movement that would seek to organize all factory workers, skilled and unskilled, into the same unions—and to win back the confidence of autoworkers who felt sold out by the AFL.

On January 10, 1936, Lewis addressed the Cleveland Auto Council, a federation of AFL locals preparing to launch an organizing drive in the auto plants. Speaking to a full house at the Cleveland Music Hall, he laid out the case for industrial unionism. Lewis was an imposing figure—tall, bulky, with a mane of gray hair and eyebrows the Fuller Brush Man would have envied. His profound, sonorous voice filled the auditorium.

> Not until the workers in the automotive, rubber, steel and other mass-production industries are organized effectively into industrial unions, will the American labor movement become a really significant factor in the economic and political life of the nation.

Employing a biblical allusion, which well suited his style of oratory, Lewis declared, "The harvest is ripe—all classes of individual workers are anxious to join an effective organization."

He then excoriated Ford and General Motors for their antagonism to labor, and for the enormous salaries and dividends their executives were collecting during the Depression, at the expense of their workers' well-being. In 1934, GM's chairman, Alfred P. Sloan, earned $201,000, more than one hundred times the average American worker's wage. Sloan prospered, Lewis declared, because his workers' labor was purchased as just another ledger expense, "like iron and steel, with no regard for human considerations."

Turning to American history, Lewis stated:

> Even the slave owners on Southern plantations prior to the Civil War, in time of depression, clothed, fed and sheltered their human chattels, but the Ford Company and General Motors, during the past

> six years, have made their employees a community burden, or abandoned them to public charity or relief. Even in normal times, because of irregularity of operations, automobile workers have not been able to earn annual incomes sufficient to maintain themselves and their families in decency and comfort.

Almost immediately after Lewis spoke in Cleveland, the United Auto Workers of America announced a convention in South Bend, Indiana, to plot an organizing drive, with the support of the CIO. Meeting from April 27 to May 2 at the Jefferson Plaza Hotel, the delegates voted out the union's AFL-installed president and replaced him with the more militant Homer Martin, a Socialist-turned-Baptist-preacher-turned-autoworker from Kansas City. While preaching at a church in Leeds, Missouri, Martin had declared from the pulpit his support for workers at the local Chevrolet plant, who were seeking higher wages: "The man who pays his workers less than a living wage takes advantage of the Depression, drives down the living standards. Then he comes to church on Sunday. He is no Christian but a carping hypocrite." The church's big donors forced Martin out, so Chevy workers who appreciated his sermon got him a job on the assembly line. He soon lost that, too, for attempting to organize his coworkers into an autoworkers' union. So the workers made him president of their federal union. Martin's personal choice for first vice president was Wyndham Mortimer.

As of summer 1936 there are still, officially, five AFL-chartered federal union locals in Flint, but their rolls contain only 122 active members. Mortimer visits headquarters in the Pengelly Building, a carriage works converted into a warren of offices, at the corner of Harrison and Third Streets, just across the river from downtown Flint. Using his authority as a vice president of the UAWA, he revokes their charters and recommends to the executive board that all of Flint be organized as a single local, Number 156.

Mortimer takes with him all the AFL locals' membership and financial records, which he will use in the next step of his quiet person-to-person campaign. He also purchases a hard-cover copy of the R. L. Polk & Co. City Directory, which lists the names, addresses, and occupations of every Flint resident. Along with the membership rolls, which include disillusioned workers who stopped paying dues in 1934, Mortimer builds a mailing list of five thousand workers, and posts a letter to each household. Mimeographed at and mailed from UAWA headquarters in Detroit, Mortimer's message attempts to appeal to its recipients' financial anxieties and class consciousness.

> Fellow Worker,
>
> What does the future hold for you as a worker in the automobile industry? Does it offer you security?
>
> Do you face the future unafraid? When your children come out of school, what are their prospects for the future? Do you think GM will be kinder to them than to you?
>
> What will become of your aged parents? Are they thrown aside to live as best they can after a lifetime of hard labor?
>
> Is the wife you promised to love, honor, and cherish able to enjoy the good things of life she's entitled to? And is she not as precious to you as the employer's wife is to him? And are your children not as sweet and lovable as his?
>
> Why, as an American, do you permit this intolerable discrimination against you and yours?
>
> You know that you and your family are being deprived of much that belongs to you, and the remedy is in your hands.
>
> Sign the enclosed card for membership in the United Automobile Workers, CIO, and join with many of your fellow workers who have decided that in unity there will be found the strength needed to right many wrongs.
>
> If you wish to speak to me personally, indicate this in the square provided for that purpose.
>
> Fraternally,
> Wyndham Mortimer

Mortimer's letter is passed around and read on the assembly lines. Little by little, workers respond, mailing back signed applications, along with invitations for personal meetings. Mortimer asks his respondents to arrange small, private house parties to which they invite a few other workers who might be persuaded to join the union.

Among Mortimer's first recruits is Berdine Simons, known to his Fisher One line mates as Bud. A young man with piercing, wide-set eyes and hair combed straight back from a widow's peak, Simons lives with his wife and their baby in a workingman's cottage in Floral Park, a neighborhood in the south end of Flint. The son of an itinerant farmhand from southern Indiana, Simons grew up so poor he couldn't afford to eat at fifty-cent church suppers. He was introduced to the labor movement as a teenager, after he ran away from home and found himself working alongside striking coal miners who had taken to shucking wheat and pitching grain on a farm north of Evansville to feed their families. The work was dawn to dusk, but one of the miners bragged to the kid that his union had guaranteed him an eight-hour day.

"What the hell?" Simons said. "If you guys are only workin' eight hours a day, why should we be workin' twelve out here shuckin' wheat?"

"You're not in the union," the miner told him.

"Well, dammit, we can act like union men anyhow."

So Simons did, knocking off work after ten hours, then demanding the farmer pay him two hours overtime. Instead, the farmer told him to get the hell off his land and take his Red notions with him.

"By God," Simons told himself, "someday I'm goin' to belong to a union, where I'll be protected. This thing of havin' to work sixteen hours a day is no damn good."

Only with a union, young Simons believed, could he obtain the money, the respect, and the leisure he and his father had never known working on other men's farms.

After he was kicked off that Indiana farm, Simons rode the rails. In Kansas he met a Wobbly who told him, "Look, you can't work in the harvest here if you don't join the IWW and have a red card, see"—a card identifying him as a member of the International Workers of the World. But when Simons tried to follow the harvest into South Dakota, he was told, "Nobody can come across the line that's got a red card." Rather than scab, Simons turned around and headed to Texas, where he spent a month fixing barbed-wire fences on a ranch, riding horses for days, sleeping and cooking beans under the stars, until deciding "this is not my way of livin', workin' from daylight to dark and half starved."

Simons made his way to Grand Rapids, Michigan, where he caught on at the Hayes Body Corporation, which produced bodies for Chrysler. With the help of the Communist-dominated Trade Union Unity League, he initiated a strike. The union lost. Simons and two other ringleaders were fired.

Simons first visited Flint in 1930, when he and two carloads of unionists from Grand Rapids drove across the state on Michigan Route M-50 and attempted to join the picket lines for that year's failed strike. Eventually, all three ended up working for GM in Flint. To get the job, Simons had to deny that he was a Communist, or knew any Communists—both lies. Hired in at Fisher One, he decided to keep his mouth shut about unions, because in Grand Rapids he'd been so broke that his wife had to cut up dead apple trees for firewood. When the AFL organized a federal union in Flint, though, Simons joined. He couldn't help himself, even after losing so many jobs for his labor activism. Once a militant, always a militant.

Bud and Mort already know each other because in 1935, Simons attended a conference of federal auto unions Mortimer organized at the Slovenian Hall in Cleveland. Mort figures he can trust Bud. Bud's not part of the old union leadership. In fact, Bud believes the local presidents are stool pigeons for GM, an opinion shared by many of his coworkers since the AFL forbade them from striking. That's why, in his letter, Mortimer specified he is affiliated with the CIO. The workers don't trust their old union. They do trust Bud, so Mort asks him to go around Fisher One—the target plant, the plant the UAWA has to shut down for its strike to succeed—to collect the addresses and telephone numbers of workers he thinks will sign a union card for the new Local 156. Like Mortimer, Simons belongs to the Communist Party, which has between sixty and a hundred members in Flint. They work in Fisher One and at the Buick and Chevrolet plants. Immigrants from

Finland, Bulgaria, Macedonia, Czechoslovakia, and Russia, the Communists give the organizers entrée with their ethnic communities.

"Mortimer started gatherin' up the pieces," Simons later recalled, "and findin' guys and gettin' us together. And then they had us getting more guys that we figured we could trust."

"Anybody ever say anything to you about how they'd like to have a union?" Mort asks Bud.

"Yeah."

"Well, get him and give me his name and address."

Simons marveled, "And then [he'd] go and see him. God almighty, Mortimer knocked on doors around that town for a year."

As he makes his rounds, Mortimer is still paranoid about being tailed by GM agents. He takes evasive measures that could inspire the author of a detective novel. One afternoon he drives to a movie theater in Saginaw, thirty miles north of Flint, buys a ticket, and steps out an exit door into an alley before the show even starts. Another time, he tells the desk clerk at the Dresden and the boys in the Pengelly Building that he's going down to Detroit for the day on union business. Then he drives out of town, drives back in on a dirt road, and spends the night at yet another cheap hotel.

When Mortimer visits a prospect's home, he asks the man to invite a few trusted coworkers to a "house party." On the night of the meeting, the shades are drawn, and Mortimer listens to workers and their wives talk about life in the plants while they drink coffee and eat doughnuts paid for by the UAWA. Then, in his quiet way, he pitches the benefits of the union: better pay, an end to the speedup, no more arbitrary firings. He's an autoworker, too, so he understands. On most nights Mortimer leaves with a handful of signed applications and one-dollar bills, for the initiation fee.

Most of the four thousand African American autoworkers in Flint toil at the Buick foundry, shoveling coal into coke ovens and forges. It's the sweatiest, dirtiest job at GM. Mortimer wants to organize these workers, too.

"Who should I contact among the Negroes?" he asks a man who has been his entrée to the white workforce.

"I don't want nothin' to do with the Black bastards," the man replies. "But you probably want to talk to Old Jim."

Mort finds white-haired Old Jim sitting out on the porch and introduces himself. Jim, now sixty, moved up to Flint from the South but has found almost as much racial prejudice here as down home. Not just in the plants but in the federal union too. Blacks are not invited to picnics or bowling nights. And the union has done nothing to get them out of the foundry and into assembly.

"But you talk to my son-in-law," Old Jim says. "Henry Clark. He work in the shop."

Mort visits Henry Clark's house the next evening. Invited to sit down for supper, he hands Clark a stack of application cards. "Take these to the foundry, get them signed, and collect the one-dollar initiation fee," he instructs Clark. "But don't take any chances with your job. I hope no one loses their job in building this union, but if anyone is to be fired, let it be a white man."

A few nights later, Mort finds a note under his door at the Dresden. Written on a sheet of paper smudged by a dirty hand, the note is difficult to read, but Mort deciphers it as "Tonight at midnight," followed by an address on Industrial Avenue near the Buick complex in the North End, where most of Flint's Black residents reside. At the bottom is a one-word signature: "Henry."

At midnight, Mort finds himself in front of a tiny Spiritualist church, no bigger than the homes of its ill-paid parishioners. No light is coming from inside. Mort knocks. The door opens. Inside are eighteen workers from the Buick foundry, sitting around a shaded candle that provides the sanctuary's only illumination. The scene looks like a séance, but Mort tells the people, "I came to Flint to improve working conditions and raise living standards."

"What's the union's policy towards discrimination?" asks a voice from the darkness. "Toward bettering the bad conditions of the Negro? You see, we have all the problems and worries white folks have, and one more. We're Negroes."

"The old A. F. of L. leadership is gone," Mort tells the workers. "The union has a new program, with new leadership that realizes none of us can advance unless all advance. Our program is to fight discrimination and Jim Crow. We have a much better chance of success if the Negro joins us, and adds his voice and presence on the union floor."

"Will we have a union of our own?" a man asks.

"We are not a Jim Crow union," Mort tells him, "nor do we have any second-class citizenship."

Since the meeting has been held in a church, it ends with a prayer. Mort leaves with eighteen application cards and eighteen dollars.

"Don't stick your necks out," Mort warns the newly enrolled members. "Just quietly get your fellow workers to sign the application cards. Let's meet here again next week."

Surreptitiously, Clark approaches his fellow foundry workers, asking them to sign union cards. "Man, you fool," one says. Another tells him, "We ain't goin' in no union." But others agree to attend meetings in the basement of a worker named Prince Combs, where they listen to recruitment pitches from members of the new Local 156's executive board. Those who join get for their dollar a receipt and a UAWA button, although no one is yet bold enough to wear it in the plant. General Motors not only provides the workers with their jobs, it owns many of their houses. GM controls the newspapers its workers read, and the politicians who make their laws. "The General," as later generations of locals call it, is the most powerful corporation in the world, and its power is magnified tenfold in its hometown. Nobody challenges General Motors in Flint, especially not to advertise membership in a union that's barely a year old.

CHAPTER 2

THE PERKINS BOYS

WYNDHAM MORTIMER STARTS the campaign to organize Flint, but he doesn't finish it. By the end of the summer of 1936, rumors of Mort's Communist affiliations have reached the Pengelly Building. The Local 156 executive board complains to the union's president, Homer Martin, that Mortimer is attempting to build a "Red Empire in Flint." Mort agrees to step down as Flint's lead organizer but only if he can name his successor. He chooses Bob Travis, an organizer from Toledo who has done a better job than Mort of concealing his Communist background. At the Chevy transmission plant in Toledo where he worked as a gear cutter, Travis led a nine-week strike that brought him into direct conflict with William Knudsen, the GM executive vice president in charge of the Chevrolet division. When Knudsen learned that Travis was collecting union cards, he drove sixty miles from Detroit to try to stop him.

"Knudsen, what the hell are you doin' down here?" Travis demanded when the executive confronted him inside the plant. "You've never been in this plant before. You come down here and we have to raise hell in order to get some recognition of what are the problems in this plant."

"Now, just a minute," Knudsen told his insubordinate employee. "Either you be quiet or you'll be fired."

"You can't fire me," Travis shot back. "I'm a member of the union now."

Knudsen motioned to a guard, then to Travis.

"Take this man out to the gate," Knudsen ordered.

"Nothin' doin'. No one takes me out to the gate."

When Travis's coworkers gathered around the bickering pair, Knudsen offered to discuss the situation in the office, with the plant manager. Travis refused.

"No," he said, "we won't come up to the office and talk. If you want to talk with me, talk with the committee. I'm not the problem in this plant."

The strike lasted nine weeks and resulted in GM's moving 1,600 jobs to Michigan and splitting Toledo's transmission production with a plant in Saginaw.

Despite the strike's disappointing outcome, the union's leadership is impressed with Travis's militancy and agrees with Mortimer to send him to Flint. At first, Travis thinks the job is too big for him. He drives a hundred miles north to the Vehicle City in his Willys-Overland "puddle jumper," parks outside the Chevy complex, and stands on a running board to watch the shift change. Then he parks outside Buick. He's never seen so many autoworkers streaming in and out of the gates. There are sixty-eight thousand in Flint, and he's expected to convince every one of them to join the United Auto Workers. Travis's next stop is UAWA headquarters in Detroit.

"You got the wrong guy," he tells Martin and Mortimer. "I come from a little shop with four thousand workers. They got more janitors in Flint than we have workers, you know. You need someone with experience to organize those people."

"Don't you know that we don't have anybody with experience?" Martin tells him. "Industrial workers? Nobody can do it. Nobody has been able to. You've done it in Toledo. You can do it in Flint."

Travis has already taken a day off from his job at Chevrolet, where he's president of the UAWA local. If he takes two more days off, he'll be fired.

"Don't worry," Martin says. "Go back up there and give it a try. The union will back you. You don't have to worry about a job."

At the beginning of October, Travis returns to Flint and checks into the Dresden, which will remain his private headquarters for now. Joining Travis in Flint is Roy Reuther, a Socialist Party member from Detroit. Reuther soon is followed by his brother Victor, who has recently returned to the United States after spending a year and a half working in an auto plant in the Soviet Union with their older brother, Walter, who will later serve as president of the United Auto Workers from 1946 until his death in a plane crash, in 1970. Even after his experiences among the Russian proletariat, Victor is shocked by the desperation he discovers in Flint.

"Flint was a GM town to the bone," he later writes in *The Brothers Reuther and the Story of the UAW*. "Eighty percent of Flint families were dependent for their living on Buick, Fisher Body, Chevrolet, or AC Spark Plug. The people were gaunt and seedy-looking; years of unemployment had left hollows in their faces and fear in their eyes. Their housing was more miserable than that in any other highly developed industrial town in the country. In a sense, Flint was a segment of the deep South transported North, for General Motors had primarily employed white Southern workers, who were lured up during the twenties by the growing automobile industry. A large number of them went south again in 1929; the rest suffered the Depression out—on the welfare lines."

Travis is so paranoid about company spies and anti-union foremen that he conducts his organizing efforts underground—literally. Among his hideouts for union meetings is the basement of a shoe store on Saginaw Street in downtown Flint. Leo Connelly, who supports a wife and five children working a drill press in a Chevy plant, attends meetings in that basement, as well as in the garage of a fellow worker in Burton Township, a Flint suburb populated by so many Ozark migrants that it will acquire the nickname Little Missouri. Everything is on the QT. Even after paying a dollar for his membership card, Connelly never mentions the union inside the plant, convinced he'll be fired if a foreman overhears. That's exactly what happens to a union brother bold enough to wear his UAWA button on the line at Chevy. When Mort, Travis, and Reuther hear about the firing, they go down to the plant to have a talk with Chevrolet's general manager, Arnold Lenz, and its personnel assistant, Henry Cohen. Lenz is aware of the organizing drive in his plants and intends to stop it. Earlier in May, he issued this directive to his foremen, in defiance of the Wagner Act: "We expect you to discharge anyone who is found circulating a [union] petition or soliciting names for a petition inside our plant." The anti-union campaign has been approved by the highest levels of GM leadership: a Senate investigation initiated by Robert M. La Follette Jr. of Wisconsin, the chairman of what comes to be known as the La Follette Civil Liberties Committee, discovers that the company has spent nearly $1 million on Pinkerton spies to infiltrate the workforce and report on union activity.

"How come," Roy Reuther asks the managers, "if you're a Mason, or a K of C, or a member of the Elks, it's okay to wear a button, but if you wear a union button you get fired?"

"Well, we just fired him," Cohen says brusquely. "Now what are you going to do about it?"

The UAWA delegation can't do anything about it. There are no committeemen in the plant. There is no grievance procedure. No seniority. No job security. Middle-aged husbands and fathers worn out by twenty years of labor are shunted out of the plant because they can no longer keep up with the assembly line, to be replaced by teenaged farm boys, like aging athletes making way for rookies. Nothing we can do about it *now*, thinks Reuther as he leaves the plant, having failed to save a man's job.

The national election on November 3, though, is a victory for the labor movement. Franklin D. Roosevelt, the New Deal president, is returned to office in a landslide, carrying every state except Maine and Vermont. Even more important, Michigan elects a New Deal governor, Frank Murphy, who has served as mayor of Detroit and governor of the Philippines. During the campaign Murphy made a point of speaking to even small gatherings of unionists. Murphy defeats the conservative Republican incumbent, Frank Fitzgerald, by just 49,000 votes, with labor providing his margin of victory. Tall, thin, and pale, with receding red hair and protruding red eyebrows, the bachelor politician lives an abstemious life, sharing an apartment in Detroit with his brother, his sister, and her husband. Since Michigan has no official governor's residence, Murphy rents a suite at the Hotel Olds in Lansing, across the street from the Capitol. The ambitious Murphy knows who put him in office, and he knows who can keep him there for two terms, until 1940, when Roosevelt surely will not break with George Washington's precedent by running for a third term as president. Beyond considerations for his political future, Murphy is a devout Catholic who genuinely believes it is his duty to ease the lot of the workingman. As an undergraduate at the University of Michigan, he wrote in a sociology paper, "If I can only feel, when my day is done that I have accomplished something towards uplifting the poor, uneducated, unfortunate, ten hour a day, laborer from the political chaos he now exists in, I will be satisfied that I have been worthwhile."

However, Murphy won't take office until January 1. The union leadership begins to wonder whether it can prevent its newly enrolled members from striking until then. Not only are the workers emboldened by the election results, but the annual fall model change is causing chaos inside the plants. The 1937 model year, which begins in September, is the first in which GM cars are built with all-steel bodies, rather than wooden trim and fabric roofs. Drills break, causing the line to shut down. And when the line shuts down, the workers can't make their piecework quotas. The company wants forty-five bodies an hour, but Fisher One can only turn out forty. So instead of earning eighty-five cents an hour for making quota, they're getting sixty cents. It's frustrating because the workers feel they're being penalized for the company's lack of planning. Adjusting to the new bodies is forcing them to work harder for less money.

"On a new model like that things don't fit, you know," Fisher One worker Raymond Zink later recalled. "And, of course, when you're building bodies, you know, putting moldings on and things like that, you got to make 'em fit. And you got to work at it until you get it and get a decent job out of it, so that, all in all, why, you were working really probably under peak pressure, you might say, and so fast as you could, but still and for all we were only getting sixty cents an hour."

After the speedup, the piecework pay system is the workers' greatest grievance. Weekly pay is determined by production figures, which are often manipulated by management to shortchange the workers. An assembly line worker might start with a flat rate of forty-seven cents an hour, with a productivity bonus. But he won't get paid for the hours when the line is down, and "scrap" or "repairs" are deducted from the bonus. Some workers complain of putting in long overtime hours to meet their quotas, then getting stiffed a hundred dollars for a two-week pay period.

In 1934, the National Industrial Recovery Administration hold a two-day hearing in Flint, whose results were printed in a report titled *Hearing on Regularizing Employment and Otherwise Improving the Conditions of Labor in the Automobile Industry*. Worker after worker testified to the insecurity and punishing pace of auto work during the Depression.

"Are they continuing to be paid on the piece work and bonus system rather than a flat rate?" an investigator asked Henry Simpson, a machine operator at Buick.

"Bonus system," Simpson replied.

"When you were working on the bonus system, had you any idea in advance of the pay day, what your earnings were going to amount to?"

"No we did not."

"Have you anything to say about that?"

"Our efficiency might be 104—we will say an efficiency of 104, on the last day of pay, but when we got paid off, we might get paid off at 100 efficiency, and how they figure it—I don't know if there is a man in that shop that knows how they figure it."

Another worker listed his earnings, going back to 1923. Throughout most of the Roaring Twenties he earned more than two thousand dollars a year. Once the Depression struck, his yearly wages declined:

1930—$1,242,26
1931—$1,293.25

1932—$698.61
1933—$965.02
1934—$1,060

"We averaged something like $1 an hour in 1923, and they cut us down sometimes to 90 cents or 85 cents and maybe sometimes 80 cents, and when we change models, for instance, they might work you as much as from one or two months at a straight rate, straight day rate, at 60 cents an hour, which there is no use in that."

Later, the investigator asked the worker if he had children.

"None," the man replied. "Why should I have any to make slaves of them?"

All the old complaints—the speedup and the piecework rate—are intensified by the advent of the steel-body car. Wildcat strikes break out all over Fisher One. The trim line quits an hour early, grumbling about "speedup and no pay." On an overburdened assembly line, workers halt their labors to demand an extra pair of hands. The foreman responds by reducing the speed from fifty auto bodies an hour to forty-five. Bud Simons is so worried the men will spontaneously stop working on their own initiative that he begs Travis to let him call a strike, with the union's blessing.

"Honest to God, Bob, you've got to let me pull a strike before one pops up somewhere that we can't control," Bud tells Travis when the organizer visits him at the end of second shift at Fisher One.

"You think they're as ready as that?" asks Travis, who has been working to get them ready but still wants to wait for the New Year and Murphy's inauguration.

"Ready? They're like a pregnant woman in her tenth month!"

To prepare for the moment when they do go on strike, Travis deputizes forty union members inside Fisher One as "volunteer organizers," giving each a card bearing the union's seal. If a disruption occurs inside the plant, they are to gather at a rally point where they can decide how to deal with the situation.

"Boys," Travis tells his deputies, "the whole future of the Flint workers depends on you. In fact, I can truthfully say that the fate of the autoworkers throughout the country rests on your shoulders. I know you're not going to let them down. Whatever happens, stick together. Don't leave the shop under any circumstances. And remember—*nobody gets fired*."

Three days later, two men sit down inside Fisher One—and both get fired. Bill and Frank Perkins, twenty-seven and twenty-nine years old, work on the line as "bow men" welding a support piece called a bow onto car roofs. They're small-town boys who commute from Columbiaville, in the Thumb region of mitten-shaped Michigan just east of Flint. That Thursday night, the foreman takes a man off the line, forcing the remaining bow men to weld more frantically. The men are also angry because the night before, management refused to tell them how much money they have earned. The Perkins boys have been reading in the *Flint Journal* about a strike at the Bendix Corporation, a brake manufacturer in South Bend, Indiana. Thousands of workers are occupying an unheated plant, dancing and playing cards to keep warm, refusing to leave until the company recognizes the UAWA as a bargaining agent.

Laborers have been sitting down on the job to protest working conditions since the beginning of the twentieth century. In 1906, the General Electric plant in Schenectady, New York, was hit with a sit-down strike. By the mid-1930s, sitting down as a form of labor rebellion has become an international movement. It's more effective than walking out of a plant, because if workers abandon their machinery, the bosses can hire scabs to get it running again. In 1933, meat packers at the Hormel Packing Company in Minnesota sit down for three days, until management agrees to slow down the line, cut hours, and raise wages. In Yugoslavia, Poland, Hungary, and Wales, coal miners occupy their pits and engage in hunger strikes until pay is increased. Hoping to win higher wages, sailors refuse to leave a ship in California's port of San Pedro. The greatest wave of sit-down strikes occurs in France, where in 1936 more than a million workers occupy metal shops, auto plants, shipyards, textile factories, and department stores, inspired by the election of a socialist prime minister, Leon Blum. Blum's government responds by passing legislation that mandates a forty-hour workweek and twelve days a year of paid vacation and guarantees unions the right to strike and bargain collectively.

"Sit-downs do not occur in plants where true collective bargaining exists," says Sherman H. Dalrymple, president of the United Rubber Workers of America. "Where management does not attempt to destroy unionism by financing company unions, by the formation of vigilante groups, and by placing other obstacles in the path of legitimate union growth, there is such a spirit of cooperation between the union and management that cessations of work do not occur." The United Rubber Workers leads a series of sit-down strikes at Akron rubber plants throughout 1936.

Thus, when Bill and Frank Perkins suddenly stop welding bows onto roofs, they're part of an international labor movement for which sucessation of work is a powerful tool. But their foreman and plant superintendent just see two loafing malcontents allowing auto bodies to slide by uncompleted—bodies that will have to be fixed at the end of the line. That is, if there are bodies there. Some disgruntled workers have been refusing to place them on the line.

"What's going on there, Frank?" demands the department foreman, Scotty McDonald. "How come there's a gap in the line?"

"Well, you'll have to talk to someone up there," Frank responds, "but I'll tell you one thing while you're right here, Scotty: we're gettin' sick of workin' without knowin' how much we made."

"That'll all be taken care of tomorrow night," McDonald promises. "Now, you go back to work and get these other men back to work and we'll get this thing straightened out."

After twenty minutes of arguing, during which the foreman points out that the day shift is getting by short-handed, the Perkins brothers go back to welding, with the idea that they'll get the day shift involved in asking for extra help, too.

Travis's deputies tell him all about the two-man strike. It's the talk of the plant. They all know how GM deals with insubordination, and they agree that this could be a chance for the union to take a public stand. If the Perkins boys are fired, all work will cease in the "body-in-white" department—as the department where welders and solderers put the car body components together is known.

Sure enough, when the brothers arrive for their Friday-night shift, their time cards have been replaced with red cards ordering them to report to the employment office. A red card means termination. Before the whistle blows, the brothers show the notices to Bud Simons and his deputies, who scatter throughout the department, spreading the word that the Perkins boys have been fired. Rather than report to the employment office, the brothers simply leave the plant. Since he won't be working that night, Bill decides to take his fiancée, Dorothy, on a date. The boys are well known in the department, and now, when the line clanks to life, their coworkers react by just watching the bodies go by.

"Don't do a tap of work until they're back to work," Simons instructs.

The foremen try slowing down the line, to give loyal workers an opportunity to weld or solder. When a few pick up their tools, they're confronted by Joe Devitt, one of Simons's deputies, who is patrolling the lines with an iron solder float, ready to enforce solidarity with a blow to the noggin.

"I'll give you just five seconds to get off of that line, or I'm gonna roll your head right down that aisle," Devitt threatens one of the workers, drawing his arm back to strike. The worker sits down, more afraid of losing his head than losing his job.

"Look," a plant superintendent threatens a union member named Walter Ananich, "you're gonna have to get off your butt and work or you're all finished."

Ananich jabs a finger into the boss's chest.

"You're not runnin' this plant anymore," he retorts. "You're going to listen to the union!"

The superintendent needs someone to blame for this sudden sit-down that has idled an entire shift of thirty-five hundred men. He corrals one of the Perkins brothers' fellow bow men, a diminutive Italian named Joe Urban, and marches him to the office. The two men pass Simons, who has set down his soldering torch.

"Hey, supe," Simon asks. "Where you going with that guy?"

The supe grabs Simons by the collar as if to take him into custody too. Wriggling free, Simons follows the supe down the line, shouting to his coworkers, "Come on, fellows, don't let them fire Little Joe!"

When a dozen men join the pursuit, the supe abandons Little Joe and runs to the office, returning shortly afterward with the assistant plant manager, the next rung up the chain of command. Seeing that no work is getting done, the assistant plant manager agrees to lead a delegation to the office of his own boss, Evan Parker, the plant manager.

"What seems to be the trouble here?" Parker asks, inviting the group of eighteen men to smoke or sit in his plush chairs.

"Mr. Parker, it's the speedup the boys are complaining about," Simons begins. "It's absolutely beyond human endurance. And now we've organized ourselves into a union. It's the union you're talking to right now."

Simons goes on to tell Parker that none of the men in his department will work until the Perkins brothers are working alongside them. Oh, well, that's fine, Parker finally agrees. Since the boys have already left the plant, they can come back on Monday.

Not Monday, Simons demands. Tonight. That's a ludicrous demand, Parker tells them. It could take hours to find those boys! Are thirty-five hundred men supposed to sit idle until they're hunted down? Parker orders the lines restarted, but as soon as the bodies begin lurching forward, Simons steps up on a bench.

"Wait a minute!" Simons cries. "What are we going to do, fellows, take the company's word and go back to work or wait till the Perkins boys are right there at their jobs? As many's in favor of bringing the Perkins boys back before we go to work, say 'Aye!'"

The ayes are nearly unanimous. When word gets back to Parker, he calls the state police and asks them to bring in Bill and Frank Perkins. It's the only way he can get his plant running again. Frank has gone home, so he's easy to find. But Bill is out with his fiancée.

After Bill picks up Dorothy in his Chevy Roadster, he drives toward the plant.

"Where we going?" Dorothy asks.

"I want to drive out past Fisher Body," Bill tells her. "Bud Simons said they were gonna close the line tonight because Frank and I got pink-slipped. We got fired."

"I can't believe they're strong enough they'll shut that line down," Dorothy says. "That line is a sacred cow to GM."

Bill's license plate number is radioed to all troopers patrolling the Flint area. A local radio station, WFDF, broadcasts bulletins imploring the young man to quit courting and return to Fisher One. The police finally track down the couple at Atherton Gardens, a beer hall on Atherton Road. Bill gets a ride to work in a squad car. Four hours after discovering red cards in place of their time slips, the Perkins boys have their jobs back. After Bill goes home to change out of his date-night clothes, he and Frank re-enter the plant to applause that's almost as loud as a clanking assembly line.

"Now the Perkins brothers are back," the supe announces, standing on table so the entire department can hear him. "They're goin' back to work, and so is Joe Urban. Now we'll go back to work."

Simons still has a bee in his bonnet, though.

"There's just one thing," he says, tapping the supe's leg. "We want pay for all this time that we've been sittin' here."

The supe is indignant. That's not how it works at General Motors. If the line doesn't move—for whatever reason—no one gets paid. And this goof wants to get paid for a boondoggle that shut down half a shift.

"No *way* are you gonna get any pay for that," he rages at Simons.

Simons shrugs.

"Well, that's all right with me," he says coolly. "And no way are you gonna get any work done either."

It takes an hour, and a series of phone calls that finally reach Parker's office, but GM agrees to pay the workers for their half-day sit-down strike. The line starts rolling again, with the Perkins brothers welding bows.

Word of the union's victory gets around all the shops—not just Fisher One, but Fisher Two, Buick, Chevy, AC Delco. On this Friday in November, the UAWA has won almost everything the beleaguered, overburdened, underpaid, insecure workers have been demanding from GM. The union has stopped the company from firing two guys just for getting on a foreman's bad side. It has slowed down the line. It has gotten the company to pay its employees for their time in the plant, not just the time the line is running—and it has done so through a show of solidarity on the shop floor, and a collective bargaining session in the plant manager's office, where Simons declared himself a representative of the union.

"The dark clouds of fear that had hung over Flint were rapidly disappearing," Mort writes later. "The auto workers were now feeling their strength and power. Fear of the boss had evaporated to the point where the workers were openly talking union. People were now crowding into the office to sign application blanks. Our plans to strike GM around January 1, 1937, were developing nicely."

Suddenly everyone wants to join the union. Emerging from their secret basements and garages, UAWA organizers open an office in a storefront on South Saginaw, across the street from Fisher One. Soon after the Perkins boys are rehired, the union holds a mass meeting of Fisher One workers there. When Travis visits a beer hall near the plant, he collects membership cards and dollar bills from fifty workers. Overall, the publicity from the Perkins boys adds five hundred members to the UAWA's rolls, but it still has only six hundred and thirty-eight inside Fisher One, out of a total of eight thousand workers across three shifts. Will that be enough to take over the plant and shut it down?

Everett Ketchum is a twenty-one-year-old trainee tool-and-die maker at Chevrolet, earning fifty cents an hour, when he joins the union at the urging of his supervisor.

"I said, 'What would you do, John?'" Ketchum later recalled. Supervisors' jobs were almost as insecure as assembly line workers', so his boss told him "'Join it. You need it.'

"The supervision, they had no control, either. You could come in to work today as a supervisor and have a desk and have a yellow slip on there that said, 'You're all done.'"

Keeping a job at GM requires staying in the good graces of the foreman, the shop floor laird who has the power to hire or fire any man for any reason. The simplest way to satisfy a foreman is to bring him food or perform chores at his house. Workers who live in the countryside and tend farms have an edge, because they can fill the boss's larder with bushels of potatoes, pork ribs, sides of beef. Feed a foreman well enough, and not only will he keep you on the payroll, he'll take you off the assembly line and put you in a cushy repair job. Farmers are also popular with the company because they're willing to work for low wages, since they can feed themselves off their land. Workers who don't have food to offer are forced to abase themselves in more personal ways. If the boss wants his house painted, you paint his house. If the boss wants a party, you throw him a party. If, at that party, the boss has too much to drink and flirts with your wife, why, you'd just better look the other way. General Motors foremen believe in the principle of *droit de seigneur*. The foremen hire attractive women willing to put up with petting, fondling, and even more intimate liberties to keep their jobs. One night-shift Chevy foreman has an employee transferred to the day shift so that he can pursue the man's wife during off hours. The alternative to giving in—collecting relief, not being able to feed, clothe, and house a family—is even more shameful to most men. Even religion plays a role in who works and who doesn't: most of the foremen are Masons, members of the all-Protestant fraternal order that meets in a temple on Saginaw Street. So it helps to be a Mason rather than a Catholic.

Although a few foremen are tolerant of the union's organizing efforts because they're just as sick of and exhausted by the speedup as the workers, the organizers still engage in subterfuges inside the plant so the bosses won't find out exactly who's in the union and who's not. One welder slips membership cards into his coworkers' heavy gloves, where a foreman's eyes can't see them. Even after the Perkins brothers' victory, it's still possible to be fired for joining the union, as Fisher One worker Robert Gibbs finds out.

Gibbs is no militant. After a fellow in his shop pesters him for a couple weeks, he ponies up a dollar, receiving a button and a carbon copy of his enrollment slip.

"You'll hear back from me when we need you," the recruiter tells Gibbs.

Gibbs never hears back from the UAWA, but he does hear from his foreman, who pulls him aside a few weeks later and shows him the original of his membership application.

"Hey, kid, is this you?" the foreman asks.

Gibbs sees his signature on the paper and admits that yes, it is him.

"Do you know what you done?"

"No, I don't know."

"Well, you joined the union, didn't you? Don't you know better than that?"

"No, I don't know better than that."

"Well, I ain't got time to talk to you now, but I'll be back for you later. We gotta go to the front end."

"The front end" is the personnel office, in the basement. Gibbs is ordered to lay down his tools and follow the foreman there. On the way they pass seventy-five job seekers lined up in the hallway.

"How come you joined the union?" the personnel manager demands. "Don't you like your job?"

Gibbs tells the personnel manager he does like his job.

"Well, this is a serious problem," the manager tells Gibbs. "Look at all these people trying to get a job here, and you join the union."

The personnel manager points an accusing index finger at Gibbs and bangs his fist on the table.

"You know, you done a very serious thing," he says. "You ain't got a job no more. You're fired, you son of a bitch."

Dumbfounded, Gibbs asked when he'll get his severance check.

"You don't get no pay," the personnel manager tells him. "You're fired. You see that door over there? You got about two minutes to get out that goddamn door."

Before he leaves the plant, Gibbs wants to collect his hat, his coat, and his tools: when he hired in, he'd been told to buy a claw hammer, a chisel, a Yankee screwdriver, and a tool box, all of which cost him thirteen dollars. But when he asks to retrieve them, he's told he has one minute to get out the door before he's guilty of trespassing on private property. He steps over the threshold into a twenty-degree wind blowing through his damp cotton shirt, still sweaty from the shop floor, and walks the mile and a half home in the snow. He never sees his tools again.

Gibbs is convinced he's been double-crossed by a stoolie who turned his membership application over to management. Roy Reuther and Travis are so concerned about stool pigeons that they ask the La Follette Committee to send an investigator to Flint, to root out company spies in the union ranks. The investigator uncovers a spy on the executive board of Local 156. During a local meeting in Pengelly Hall, Reuther stands up and announces that there's a stool pigeon in the room.

"Name him!" the workers demand.

Reuther tries to give a speech about the depths to which a man will sink for thirty pieces of silver, and the immorality of a company that would spy on its workers, but the unionists only want to hear the identity of the Judas in their ranks.

"Name him!" the cry goes up again. Reuther draws out the suspense.

"Perhaps by now, this lonely creature would prefer to rise and confess his sins before I am compelled to identify him publicly," he says. "I will count to ten, and if he has not by then risen to his feet, I will point him out."

Reuther counts to ten. No one stands.

"His name is John Stott," Reuther finally reveals, "and he is sitting in the center of this hall."

Exposed, Stott stands up and is escorted out of the room by a cadre of unionists who advise him to leave Flint for his own safety.

By the beginning of the snowy season, everyone in the union knows a strike is coming. The leadership in Detroit has set New Year's Day as the date, for three reasons: First, a strike during Christmas would be bad for the morale of workers and their families. Second,

GM, which obviously knows a strike is brewing, is planning to pay each worker a fifty-dollar bonus on December 18, as a way to win the loyalty of wavering workers. That money will help families buy food and coal throughout the cold, unpaid weeks that a strike might last. Finally, Governor-elect Murphy will be sworn in on January 1. The union is certain that the incumbent governor, Republican Frank Fitzgerald, would use the powers of his office to evict the strikers from Fisher One by force, but that Murphy will not. Having met the man, Wyndham Mortimer considers Murphy "a kindly, humane person" whose "sympathies [are] with the workers, the people."

"There are those who occupy positions of power, who will sit on the safety valve until an explosion occurs and its destructive force scatters debris far and wide," Mort later writes. "But Frank Murphy was not one of these. He knew the tremendous upsurge of the CIO, and the sit-down strikes were something more than just another labor dispute. He knew they were the result of a generations-long orgy of greed and exploitation resulting from a social system whose driving force was profit.

"Murphy unquestionably believed in and supported the profit system, but he also believed it must be controlled. Otherwise, like an engine without an operator, it would destroy itself. The best control was a strong labor movement, and Murphy was for it."

During the violent labor conflicts of the late nineteenth and early twentieth centuries, the authorities almost always took the side of capital, using force to subdue laborers if necessary. In 1892, Pennsylvania governor Robert Emory Pattison broke the Homestead Strike by dispatching 8,500 National Guardsmen to oust workers from US Steel's mill. During the 1894 strike against the Pullman Company, which manufactured railroad cars, President Grover Cleveland sent federal troops to Chicago to prevent strikers from blocking railroad traffic, on the grounds that they were interfering with mail delivery. An exception was President Theodore Roosevelt, who arranged a negotiated settlement of the 1902 Pennsylvania coal strike, winning the workers raises and shorter hours—but not a union.

Now, the UAWA feels it finally has, in Franklin D. Roosevelt and Frank Murphy, a president and a governor who will at least operate as disinterested arbiters in the union's dispute with General Motors.

As the New Year approaches and the UAWA's membership in Flint grows, the union's leadership becomes even more concerned about whether it can prevent a strike until Murphy's inauguration. In the weeks following FDR's landslide victory, emboldened workers begin sitting down and striking all over the country, sensing that never before in the history of labor-management relations has their cause been so favored by the powers that be. On November 18, six hundred workers at a Fisher Body plant in Atlanta stage a sit-down to protest the layoff of men wearing UAWA buttons. Since Fisher Atlanta only manufactures bodies for a nearby Chevrolet plant, though, the effects are merely local, not national, as a strike at Flint's Fisher One would be. In Kansas City, workers sit down after one of their fellows is fired for jumping over a moving conveyor belt. At Kelsey-Hayes Wheel Company, a Detroit manufacturer of brake drums for Ford, Walter Reuther leads a sit-down strike that results in a Christmas Eve settlement guaranteeing workers seventy-five cents an hour and a 20 percent slowdown of the production line. The Detroit authorities refuse to evict the strikers, judging that they entered their place of employment legally and have a right to remain there. Kelsey-Hayes is a rehearsal for Flint, but it will be a big step from beating a parts supplier that has to settle or lose its contract with Ford to beating the world's largest corporation. Around the country, glass workers are also on strike, causing UAWA organizers to worry that GM will run out of windshields and windows and be forced to shut down before the New Year. In mid-December, there's even an attempted wildcat strike in Flint's Chevy plant No. 6, when a worker who has recently been appointed a union steward is transferred to another department. At first his brothers refuse to work until he is reinstated, but they meekly return to their machines when the assistant plant manager begins filling out dismissal slips in all their names. Their surrender is actually not a bad outcome for the UAWA because it stops a premature strike from breaking out.

On the first day of winter, UAWA president Homer Martin begins building a justification for a New Year's strike by meeting with GM vice president William Knudsen at the General Motors Building in Detroit. Martin requests a meeting with Chairman Alfred P. Sloan to discuss four demands, on behalf of all 211,000 employees: "1. The present declared policy of General Motors with relation to collective bargaining, 2. Seniority rights, 3. The speed-up in the General Motors factory, 4. Rates and methods of pay—and also other conditions of employment." Martin knows he's not going to get any of it. Indeed, not only does Knudsen refuse to arrange a meeting with Sloan, he advises Martin that employees should take up their complaints with individual plant managers. After all, it has always been the company's policy that the best way to resolve issues in the workplace is through the collaboration of employees and managers on the shop floor. To Martin this is just more evidence that GM has no intention of abiding by the terms of the Wagner Act. At CIO headquarters in Washington, John L. Lewis feels the same way. Knudsen's response, he says, is "not collective bargaining, but simply an evasion of the responsibilities of General Motors."

After Knudsen's rebuff, the union announces a meeting of local officials from ten cities in Flint on January 3, "for the purpose of approving recommendations of the general offices concerning collective bargaining in General Motors." But before that meeting can happen, the sit-down strike starts.

CHAPTER 3

"THIS IS WHERE THE FIGHT BEGINS"

THE GREAT FLINT SIT-DOWN STRIKE actually begins in Cleveland. On the morning of December 28, a union delegation is scheduled to meet with management to hash out grievances at Cleveland's Fisher Body plant. They're planning to talk about piecework rate cuts during the model change from wood to steel—the exact same issue that has driven so many workers to join the union at Fisher One in Flint. When the meeting is rescheduled for the afternoon, the fed-up workers decide "to hell with all this stalling," and shut down the plant. First they cut the power to the assembly line's quarter-panel department. Then to the steel stock department. Then to the metal assembly department. Then to trim. By midafternoon no finished bodies are emerging from Fisher Cleveland. The mayor of Cleveland convenes a meeting between the plant manager and the president of the union local at City Hall, but UAWA first vice president Wyndham Mortimer is already on a train from Detroit to make sure this strike isn't settled locally.

Waiting for Mort at Cleveland's Union Terminal are newsmen with notebooks. They tell him the local president wants to cut a deal.

"Do you plan to meet with the mayor or the Fisher Body management?" the reporters ask.

"No!" Mort barks. "That is all out! The local president does not have the authority to settle this strike. The whole matter is now in the hands of the international union."

Settling strikes one plant at a time is exactly what GM wants—it's part of the company's plan to prevent the UAWA from becoming the bargaining unit for all its workers. This one's going to have to be talked out at the top, declares Mort—between GM vice president William Knudsen and UAWA president Homer Martin.

The occupied Fisher plant is surrounded by mounted police officers, so Mort can't get inside. He addresses the workers over a loudspeaker.

"The international union supports you all the way!" he tells the strikers. "Keep up the fight, fellows. We are going to win this one!"

Fisher Cleveland and Fisher One in Flint are the two plants the UAWA *must* occupy in order to shut down General Motors, since those plants contain dies that stamp out auto parts used in every GM facility. As soon as GM loses access to the Fisher Cleveland dies, the company begins disassembling dies in Fisher One and loading them onto trucks and trains bound for Grand Rapids. The unionists suspect it's a precaution to prevent their capture by another sit-down. On the evening of the thirtieth, Bob Travis is working at the Pengelly Building when he receives a frantic telephone call from Walter Ananich inside Fisher One.

"They're moving dies out, Bob!" Ananich shouts into the receiver.

"You sure?" Travis asks.

"Yeah! The boys in the press room working near the doors by the railroad dock say they got crank press dies on some trucks and they're loading a flock of freight cars!"

"Okay," Travis says, "they're asking for it. Tell the boys, 'Stewards meeting at lunch time.'"

Travis calls down to the UAWA office on Saginaw Street, across from Fisher One.

"Put the flicker on," he orders the woman who answers the phone.

"The flicker" is a 200-watt red light bulb above the door of the Saginaw Street office. When lit, it's a signal to the workers that a union meeting is about to take place. Adding to the urgency of capturing Fisher One is the fact that this morning, workers in Fisher Two in Flint have sat down on the job, shutting down production on the first shift.

Travis, Mort, Martin, John L. Lewis—the entire UAWA leadership wanted to wait until January 1, but GM is forcing the union to act *now*. If those dies get out of Fisher One, the plant will be a worthless prize because GM will be able to continue stamping out body parts somewhere else. The union boss decides that December 30 is close enough. Governor Fitzgerald's term has forty hours left to run. He won't be able to roust them from the plant in that short a time. At eight o'clock—second shift's lunch hour—Travis's deputies file across the street and into the spare, standing-room-only union office, furnished sparsely with a kitchen table and two wooden chairs.

"Boys, we'll make this snappy," Travis tells the stewards. "I understand there's something happening over there on the press room dock."

"That's right," a steward replies. "They're taking dies out of the press room. They got four or five cars lined up there."

"Well," Travis asks, "what are we going to do about it?"

"Them's our jobs," a worker responds. "We want them right here in Flint."

"That's right!" men shout in unison.

"I'm not going to tell you what to do," Travis says. "That ought to be plain enough to you if you want to protect your jobs. In my plant in Toledo, General Motors walked off with fifteen hundred jobs a year ago. In Cleveland, Fisher Body struck Monday to save theirs. What do you want to do?"

"Shut 'er down! Shut the goddamn plant!"

"Okay, fellows, that's what I wanted to hear you say. Now the important thing to remember from here on out is *discipline*. You can't have too much of it in a strike, especially at the beginning. Roy [Reuther] and I will come in after you've got the plant down and help you get everything organized. Bud [Simons] and the rest of the committee will be in charge. You'll have to enlarge the committee so as to get representation on it from all departments. Remember, obviously *no liquor*. And tell the girls in the cut-and-sew department [who stitch upholstery onto auto seats] to go home and come around to the Pengelly headquarters tomorrow morning. We'll have plenty of work for them to do. Now, everybody stays in 'til the warning whistle. We don't want any stooges tipping [off] the company ahead of time."

The men stream back toward the factory gate. Travis follows them outside as far as the sidewalk, where he paces back and forth on the ice, watching the windows for a sign from the workers inside that their plot has succeeded or failed. He thinks to himself, "This is where the fight begins."

Louis Strickland, the union's steward in metal finishing, returns from lunch and tells the men in his department, "This here's it. There's a sit-down strike. Everyone is to sit right here."

At nine thirty, the whistle blows, signaling the end of the lunch break and the resumption of work on second shift. The lines begin moving, but in every department, there's a steward who has just returned from the meeting across the street with instructions to order his coworkers to stop working. Bud Simons is in charge of the spot welders. In all of Flint the union has about 4,500 members, but it doesn't take that many to shut down a plant: earlier that day, 50 workers at Fisher Two sat down, halting the work of 1,000 and inciting an occupation of the plant. And plenty of workers sympathize with the union's aims but have been afraid to sign a membership card.

The sit-down doesn't happen all at once. When the trim line starts moving, none of the men move with it, having been told by their steward, "We're not going to work." Frozen on their benches, they stare at the bodies going by for a minute, five minutes, knowing that if enough of them break ranks they'll all have to work like blazes to get caught up. After ten minutes of inaction, the foreman comes running out of his office. He stalks up and down the trim line, giving each of the mutineers a death stare. But nobody breaks. Finally, the foreman shuts off the trim line himself.

In metal finishing, Joe Devitt, a close ally of Simons's, walks up and down the line, passing the word to stop working and step away from the machines.

For the strikers, silence is the sound of success. The press room, where the all-important dies stamp out body parts, is the best-organized department in the shop. Almost all the workers there are union. Once the press room gets the order to sit down, it happens so quickly that "in five minutes, you would have thought you were in a morgue but for the foremen as busy as little bees trying to get the men back on the job," as one worker later writes.

The stymied foremen head to the main office to ask for instructions on how to get the press room stamping out parts again. While they are gone, workers from the roof department and the quarter panel department arrive. They know how important it is to prevent the company from shipping out the dies.

By ten thirty, an hour after the whistle blows, every line in Fisher One has stopped running. Walter Ananich leans out a third-floor window, shouting and waving his arms to get the attention of Travis, who's still pacing the sidewalk across the street.

"Hooray, Bob!" Ananich cries. "She's ours!"

All across the glass grid on the factory's face, windows are popping open. Grinning faces of autoworkers appear in the frames.

"Was there any trouble?" Travis shouts back.

"Naw!"

Meanwhile, workers are occupying the railroad loading dock to prevent the company from removing dies. They're told that only one die is being shipped to Lansing, for repairs. The workers believe the company secretly intends to empty the plant by shipping out small panel–molding dies. They're convinced that after the night shift goes home, GM will load the bigger dies onto the railcars. If there's just one die going to Lansing, the workers wonder, then why are all these freight cars lined up at the loading dock? When a locomotive engine backs up to hook on to the train, workers gather beneath the cab.

"There's a strike on!" they call to the engineer.

The engineer understands. He steps out of his cab and signals to his brakeman to step down too. The train won't be going to Lansing, or Grand Rapids, or anywhere else, and neither will the dies.

Now that the workers have control of Fisher One, they have to figure out what to do with it. They start by sending home the women in the cut-and-sew department. The strikers want to spare the women from any violence, in case company goons or police attempt to retake the plant. They also want to prevent GM from undermining support from their wives at home—the so-called strike widows—with crude speculation on what might be going on between lonely husbands and working women.

Bud Simons stalks up and down the stilled assembly lines, carrying a pencil and a Blue Bird School Series Note Book in which he jots down memos and writes out orders. His first entry: "Women to have 5 mins. to leave plant." And so they stream out into the cold in their overalls and working caps. They're going home. The men are staying—for how long, they don't know.

At midnight, once the plant is safely under the union's control, Travis summons his stewards back to the Saginaw Street office.

"Well, now that we've sat down, what do we do?" one steward asks.

Travis distributes a sheet titled "What to Do in Case of a Sit Down." Compiled by a Communist Party activist named William Weinstone, it's based on the lessons learned from strikes in Poland, France, Akron, and Midland Steel in Detroit, where, a month earlier, workers sat down for union recognition. Weinstone's document recommends setting up a soup kitchen and figuring out a way to get food into the plant. The strikers will need a publicity committee, to put out a strike newsletter for fellow autoworkers. They should post guards at every entrance. Finally, they should elect a strike committee. Before the meeting breaks up, around three in the morning, the stewards elect Bud Simons strike committee chairman and set up subcommittees on food, security, cleanliness, and exercise.

Almost immediately the occupied plant is cut off from the rest of Flint. After evicting the managers and plant security and sending the women home, the strikers fire up their torches and begin welding the doors shut. As New Year's Eve dawns, the day shift arrives at Fisher One, only to be turned away by GM security, which has orders not to allow anyone into the plant.

From Detroit, Homer Martin sends a telegram to William Knudsen. Martin blames the plant takeover on General Motors's refusal to bargain with the international UAWA. He again demands that the company recognize the union.

"We feel the necessity of again calling to your attention the seriousness of the labor situation at General Motors," Martin writes.

> The international union has made every effort to effect an amicable settlement with plant managers of the various plants where strikes are in effect, but with absolutely no success.
>
> The officers and members of the International union recognize in this situation the truth of our contention that only through a national conference and negotiations with you and other officials of your organization can a satisfactory and permanent settlement be made.
>
> Why should General Motors Corporation longer avoid meeting representatives of their organized employees on a national scale for the purpose of entering into real collective bargaining?

At the time of the takeover, between 1,500 and 1,600 employees are inside Fisher One. That number dwindles quickly as men leave the plant through the windows. Some don't sympathize with the strike. Some want to go home to their families. Some just want to celebrate New Year's Eve. By the time 1936 turns into 1937, the plant's population is in the low three figures.

Those who stay realize they're disappointing friends and family who want to celebrate the holiday, but feel they've committed themselves to a fight for their livelihoods. Lawrence Taylor's wife shows up outside the plant to remind him that they've invited friends over for New Year's Eve.

"Tell them to accept my hospitality, but that I have some important work on," Taylor tells her. "You can tell them to save one toast for me. When I walk out of the plant, it will be through the front door."

That morning, Francis O'Rourke, a striker in Fisher Two, the other occupied plant, begins a diary that will turn out to be the most detailed document of the sit-down strike. After staying up until 4 a.m., kept awake by men snake dancing along the idled assembly lines, singing songs, and reciting poems, O'Rourke falls asleep on an auto seat. In fact, auto seats end up serving as beds for most the rest of the strikers throughout the occupation. When he awakes, O'Rourke is surprised to find himself still at the factory.

"Thinking of my party at home this evening," O'Rourke writes, "I wonder if the basement is decorated for the occasion. Wonder how Sweet (the wife) and the children are feeling. Bet Mother is worried about me."

At midnight, as the city outside the factory walls celebrates, O'Rourke picks up his pencil again: "There it is, twelve o'clock, whistles, cheers—1937. Peace on earth. Why must men in the world's most perfect democracy take such steps to survive? Well the wife and all my guests are out on the street celebrating with me . . . it's sure swell, but (somehow) a lump climbs into a guy's throat."

The men in the plant have shelter. They have heat. They're still in the warm clothes they wore to work on Wednesday night. Now it's Thursday and they have to figure out how to acquire the two other essentials of life—food and tobacco—and quickly.

"Send over some cigarettes at once," Simons writes in his Blue Bird notebook.

To feed their husbands, wives show up at the plant on New Year's Day with lunchboxes and buckets full of milk and sandwiches. They tie the buckets to clotheslines that they have tossed up to second-floor windows, so the men can hoist the food inside. Asked whether she's sending up a change of underwear, a woman tells a *Flint Journal* reporter, "No, just cigarettes." To entertain themselves the strikers listen to hot jazz on the radio and play low-stakes poker. Although the union has banned women and liquor from the plants, a story will later circulate that foremen smuggled in booze and prostitutes to tempt the strikers, with the result that some of them "got burnt."

Down at GM headquarters in Detroit, William Knudsen isn't taking the day off to celebrate the New Year. He's in his office, drafting an angry response to Homer Martin. Knudsen accuses the union of preferring strikes to negotiation and informs Martin that the company won't bargain until the strikers cease their lawless occupation of its plants. The vice president begins his letter by reminding Martin that it's company policy to bargain locally, not nationally. With 232,000 employees in 35 cities, GM is just too big to deal with a single union. Knudsen also reminds Martin that a meeting had been scheduled between Fisher One plant managers and union representatives for January 4, the first Monday of the new year. That's not going to take place, now that the sit-down is on.

"Sit-downs are strikes," he writes. "Such strikers are clearly trespassers and violators of the law of the land.

"We cannot have bona fide collective bargaining with sit-down strikers in illegal possession of plants. Collective bargaining cannot be justified if one party having seized the plant, holds a gun at the other party's head . . . No one can afford to bargain with sitdown strikers or with their representatives until the plants are cleared."

As the owner of Fisher One and Fisher Two, GM feels it has the law on its side. January 2 is a Saturday, but the company's lawyers are in Genesee County Circuit Court filing a motion for an injunction that will force the strikers to evacuate the plants. The UAWA's leadership has "conspired, confederated and combined for the purpose, as has been expressed in published newspaper reports, to injure and cripple, if possible, all of the General Motors Corporation operating units," the motion reads. "The defendants and the employees remaining in the plants aforesaid constitute an unlawful interference with the rights of the plaintiff and an unlawful interference with the rights of other employees of the plaintiff who desire to work."

Outside the militant Fisher Body plants, support for the sit-down strike among Flint autoworkers is far from unanimous. The American Federation of Labor orders its metal tradesmen to work in GM plants. In Flint's Chevrolet plants, which are still operating, half the

21,488 workers sign an anti-strike petition, drafted by GM. So do 8,000 Buick workers, almost all of the brand's workforce. As a luxury manufacturer, Buick produces fewer cars than Chevy and so does not drive its workers as hard. GM's court filing asks that the strikers be prohibited "from continuing to remain in said plants in idleness in a so-called 'sit-down' strike, as well as from picketing, blocking deliveries, or intimidating employees who want to work."

Judge Edward D. Black issues an injunction forbidding the strikers from "continuing to remain in said plants in idleness in a so-called 'sit-down' strike," or even from picketing on the sidewalk outside. Enforcing the injunction is the duty of the Genesee County sheriff, Thomas Wolcott. A New Deal Democrat, Wolcott is sympathetic to the labor movement, but the law is the law, the courts are the courts, and his job is his job. So late that afternoon, Wolcott heads over to Fisher One to read the injunction to the strikers, accompanied by a deputy sheriff and a Flint police captain.

Despite the authority of his office, Wolcott is hardly a man to intimidate hundreds of workers who have just won a skirmish with General Motors. A former butcher, the rotund sheriff wears a shapeless fedora and chews anxiously on an unlit cigar. The sit-downers escort him to the second floor, where strike meetings are held. Winded from climbing a flight of stairs, he steps on to the speakers' platform and asks to see the strike leaders whose names are listed on the injunction.

"Is Bud Simons here?" Wolcott asks.

"No, he's gone to church," a striker cracks, even though it's Saturday.

"Is Harry Van Nocker in the crowd?"

"He went home. His old lady's giving birth."

"Is Walter Moore here?"

"He's gone fishing."

"Is Jay Green here?"

"Where's Jay? Hey, Green! That's funny. He was just here a minute ago. He must've gone to the john or something."

The men jeer at Wolcott, asking how much he weighs and whether he can fix a ticket for a family member. Ignoring the taunts, the sheriff plods on through his court-ordered task, reading the injunction in a mumbling monotone. The strikers shout at him to speak up. When he does, they drown out his voice by singing "Solidarity." Finally Wolcott sets down his papers.

"Well, boys," he tells the strikers, "I read this to you and it means you got to get out. I'll give you half an hour to get out of here. If you don't come out peacefully, other means will be used to force you out."

Wolcott doesn't expect the strikers to heed his threat, but he's said what he has to say.

On his way out of the plant, Wolcott encounters a *Flint Journal* reporter waiting on the sidewalk. "I wanted them to understand how serious this thing was," the exasperated sheriff tells the newsman. "They wouldn't let me read it. They made a lot of noise, and I knew they didn't want to hear it. The last time they just said they didn't want to hear it."

Next, the sheriff visits the Pengelly Building, looking for the man whose name is listed at the top on the injunction, in capital letters—the ringleader himself, Homer Martin. Wolcott knows Martin is in Flint for a long-scheduled meeting of GM locals. When the sheriff asks to see Martin, he's told the meeting is open only to union members. In fact, even as Wolcott is trying to serve Martin with the injunction, the union president is at the podium in Pengelly Hall, vowing to defy it.

"Forty years ago," Martin tells the cheering delegates, "it was illegal even to call a strike. It was illegal to walk on a picket line. In my opinion, Mr. Sloan would make it illegal today if he could do so. This is certainly in keeping with the all-inclusive injunction which the General Motors Corporation just got from their judge here in Flint."

If the strikers have broken the law, Martin asserts, they have only done so to defend their rights against a company that broke the law first, and broke it repeatedly.

"Legality?" Martin says sardonically. "It was General Motors that fired hundreds of men because of their union affiliations as violation of the law. It was General Motors that spent thousands of dollars for labor spies to spy upon union men and destroy labor unions. It was

General Motors that piled up all kinds of armaments for the purpose of warring against men who went on legitimate strike. We ask if General Motors is sincere. If so, we say, 'What about your gas and other weapons of war? Will you destroy them or keep them for strike breakers to use on the picket lines?'" Besides the money spent on Pinkerton spies, GM has also spent thousands of dollars on tear gas, which it has distributed to plants and local police departments to be employed in the event of labor trouble.

Finally, Wolcott is admitted to a side office, where he is able to serve the injunction on Adolph Germer, a CIO field representative. While he does so, Martin and the rest of the UAWA leaders climb down a fire escape, hustle into their cars, and drive back to Detroit. Undeterred, Wolcott drives to Detroit on Monday to serve union officials at UAWA headquarters.

Martin is not quite finished with Judge Black, however. The union has discovered that the eighty-three-year-old judge, like many members of Flint's establishment, is a General Motors stockholder—a major stockholder, owning 3,665 shares worth $219,000. So Martin writes a letter to the Speaker of the Michigan House of Representatives, demanding that Black be impeached and removed from the bench for violating a state law prohibiting a judge from ruling "in any cause or proceeding in which he is a party or in which he is interested."

Martin knows the state House won't impeach Judge Black, just as Judge Black must have known that a circuit court ruling won't evict the strikers from Fisher One. Both sides are appealing to audiences beyond Flint, even beyond Michigan, where Governor Murphy has declared himself neutral in the dispute. In Washington, DC, the secretary of labor, Frances Perkins, is aware of the sit-down strike. Perkins has already spoken to John L. Lewis and several GM executives and is trying to persuade President Roosevelt to intervene personally.

During their meeting in Flint, Martin and the local officers settled on a list of eight demands for ending the strike:

1. A national conference between the UAWA and GM
2. Abolition of all piecework systems of pay

3. Six-hour day and thirty-hour week; time and a half for work above these
4. Minimum wage commensurate with an American standard of living
5. Reinstatement of all employees unjustly discharged
6. Straight seniority
7. Speed of production to be mutually determined by each plant's management and shop committee
8. Recognition of the UAWA as the sole bargaining agent for General Motors employees

General Motors will have none of it. The next message comes not from Knudsen but from the company's president and chairman himself, Alfred P. Sloan Jr. It's an appeal to non-striking workers, especially those who have been idled by the sit-down. From his office in New York, Sloan issues an open letter, published as a full-page ad in the *Flint Journal*, spelling out the company's rejection of every union demand and its commitment to the open shop. "General Motors grew up on the principle that a worker's job and his promotion depend on his individual ability—not on the say-so of any labor union dictator. And on that principle, General Motors stands and will continue to stand," Sloan writes.

> General Motors workers are earning more than they ever have in the entire history of General Motors, and as much [as], if not more, than the workers of any other business. No one can honestly say otherwise.
>
> Yet under these conditions you are being forced out of your jobs by sit-down strikes, by widespread intimidation, and by shortage of materials produced by similar tactics in many allied industries.
>
> Your employment and wages and the welfare of your families are being endangered by actions beyond your control and that of the company.

The chairman concludes: "The real issue is perfectly clear, and here it is: Will a labor organization run the plants of General Motors or will the management continue to do so? On this issue depends the question as to whether you have to have a union card to hold a job, or whether your job will depend in the future, as it has in the past, upon your individual merit."

General Motors posts Sloan's letter on bulletin boards in every GM plant. The strikes are spreading throughout the company. At the Toledo Chevrolet plant, where 3,000 workers build transmissions, unionists walk out on orders from the international, joining strikes in Flint; Cleveland; Atlanta; Kansas City; Harrison, New Jersey; and Anderson, Indiana. In Anderson, 350 UAWA members are staging their own sit-down, occupying the Guide Lamp plant, which manufactures headlights. The General Motors universe is not a collection of self-contained factories, but an interdependent system in which assembly plants cannot operate without the contribution of body and transmission plants, which in turn cannot operate without the contributions of parts suppliers. Less than a week after the strikers in Fisher One sit down, General Motors production is cut by 75 percent. In Flint, the Chevrolet assembly line, which normally produces 30,000 cars a week, has been idled for lack of bodies. All across the nation's manufacturing belt, GM plants in Ohio, Pennsylvania, Illinois, and New York have either cut hours or shut down entirely. So has Buick, whose normal weekly output is 7,500 cars. By the end of the first week of January, it's possible that 335,000 GM employees—nearly the company's entire workforce—will be laid off, costing the company millions of dollars in lost production.

The union's strategy is working, but it will only keep working as long as it occupies Fisher One.

CHAPTER 4

THE SIEGE

"Well, diary, Fisher #2 gets pretty cold when the heat has been turned off," Francis O'Rourke writes in his strike diary on January 7. "I'm glad we have those blankets from home—they sure come in handy. Play pedro, sure helps pass these long days by. Never played much pedro in my life—I'll bid seven—just another day. Eat, no thank you, I'm not hungry. You don't have much appetite when all you do is walk back and forth—one end of the shop and back again—always thinking of what tonight will bring. Here it is evening again—be on your guard at all times Men. Are the guards on each door? Watch the back of the shop. They could come across the railroad bridge and sneak up on us from the rear—be on your guard at all times, men!"

The men who remain in the shops have the task of making temporary homes out of workplaces. Not only that, they have to live every day with the anxiety of sudden eviction. General Motors, which owns these buildings, wants them out. The court wants them out. The sheriff wants them out. The law, unlike a landlord, is empowered to enforce its demands with violence.

Inside the plants the assembly lines are frozen at the moment the strike began: half-built bodies parked on the conveyor belt, the motion for which they were designed indefinitely delayed. Some are missing doors, others door handles. Above them, on hooks at the end of chains, dangle car seats that have been waiting a week to be lowered through open roofs. The completed bodies are now bunk beds where men sleep on spacious bench seats, marking their accommodations by chalking on the doors "Hotel Astor," "Mills Hotel," or just the name of the temporary tenant.

To organize life inside Fisher One, Simons sets up seventeen committees, each chaired by a steward. There's an athletics committee whose members lead the men in calisthenics every morning. The police committee assigns strikers to guard the entrances and makes regular thirty-five-minute rounds of the plant, looking for spies and saboteurs. To defend themselves from an anticipated police attack, men fashion blackjacks out of braided leather and solder. A "kangaroo court" punishes violators of strike rules—three offenses and you're out of the plant. The health and sanitation committee ensures that men unbound by connubial influence wash up every morning and pick up after themselves during the daily 3 p.m. cleanup of their quarters. Some men stop shaving and grow strike beards but their flat caps and round spectacles make the facial hair look more bohemian than Civil War.

Most important is the food committee. During the early days of the strike, the men consume baloney sandwiches slapped together by their wives in the Pengelly Building. But they have to eat better than that, both for their health and for their morale. (One worker later complains, "I ate so much damn bologna when I was striking!") So the union sets up a canteen in an old restaurant across the street from Fisher One. It's operated by Max Gazan, a former chef at the Detroit Athletic Club who was fired for trying to organize the kitchen staff. After asking the union to provide him with two new ranges and a collection of stockpots and roasting pans, Gazan and his thirty volunteers prepare daily meals using five hundred pounds of meat, half a ton of potatoes, a hundred pounds of coffee, three hundred loaves of bread, two hundred pounds of sugar, and thirty gallons of milk. Breakfast is scrambled eggs, fruit, cornmeal mush, fried cakes, and coffee. For lunch the canteen serves pot roast, boiled potatoes, and green beans; for supper, chili, sandwiches, cookies, and tapioca pudding cooked in forty-gallon pots. The meals are hoisted through the windows in ten-gallon milk cans and brass kettles. Not all the food is popular. One ten-gallon can of chili produces an outbreak of the runs so severe that some men go to the hospital to have their stomachs pumped.

Where do men who aren't working and belong to a union with a five-figure treasury get all that food? Some they buy. After trying to cook the "beef kidney, meat scraps, dog bones and wormy oatmeal" from neighborhood grocers, Gazan demands that the union pay for "the best cuts of meat" from wholesale butchers. In addition, a lot of the food is donated by sympathetic farmers and grocers who depend on the shop trade when the lines are running. For example, the food committee approaches the Hamady cousins, Lebanese immigrants who operate a chain of supermarkets in the Flint area.

"Why do you figure we should donate food and stuff for you guys?" Mike Hamady asks the striker Elmer "Red" MacAlpine.

"Look at it this way, Mike," MacAlpine puts it to the skeptical merchant. "My folks have bought food from your store from the time you started business in Flint, when you just had one store. My folks and lots of people are buyin' from Hamady Brothers. Now, you still want our trade? We can go just the opposite. Not that I'm tryin' to threaten you or anything like that. But look at it this way: we helped you become a big business. Now we're askin' for some help. You want to give it to us?"

Finally, Hamady grins.

"You got it," he says. "I'll have truckloads delivered wherever you want."

Red tells Hamady to deliver the food to the Pengelly Building. And to throw in a few cartons of cigarettes. Smoking helps the men kill time.

Although Francis O'Rourke plays the card game pedro, low-stakes poker is the most popular pastime in the plants. There's also music. The "Hillbilly Orchestra," made up of strikers on guitar, harmonica, banjo, and violin, plays popular folk tunes as well as songs composed for the sit-down. "The Fisher Strike," sung to the tune of "The

Martins and the Coys," is a ballad about the Fisher One takeover—folk music as journalism, practically.

Gather round me and I'll tell you all a story,
Of the Fisher Body Factory Number One,
When the dies starting moving,
The Union Men they had a meeting
To decide right then and there what must be done.

CHORUS
These 4000 Union Boys,
Oh, they sure made lots of noise,
They decided then and there to shut down tight,
In the office they get snooty,
So we started picket duty,
Now the Fisher Body Shop is on a strike.

Now the strike it started the bright Wednesday evening
When they loaded up a boxcar full of dies.
When the union boys they stopped them,
And the Railroad Workers backed them
The officials in the office were surprised.

The lyrics are printed in the *Flint Auto Worker*, a strike newspaper edited by Henry Kraus, a pamphleteer and graduate of the University of Chicago. In the winter of 1937, Kraus has insinuated himself into the UAWA's leadership and is fighting the proletariat's battle in Flint. His paper is intended as a counterpoint to the company's *I.M.A. News*, whose January 7 headline is "Little Group Perils 40,000 Jobs," above a cartoon depicting an angry group of men labeled "Minority Strikers" blocking the gate of "Flint Industries" while thousands of locked-out workers look on.

As the strike wears on into its second week, more and more men find reasons to leave Fisher One. With the gates sealed shut or barricaded, they go in and out through a window, stepping onto a plank balanced atop four trash cans, then climbing down a ladder. Anyone who wants to go home is supposed to ask the strike committee for a pass. Not everyone does. At times, the population inside the plant drops below a hundred—too few to guard every gate. Some men temporarily desert for conjugal visits. Josiah Jordan sneaks out to see his newborn baby. When Jordan's wife is taken to the maternity ward, a neighbor carries a bologna sandwich with a note wrapped inside to the plant. Standing under a window, the neighbor calls out "Joe! Joe! Come here. I've got lunch for you."

When Jordan appears, the neighbor tells him, "Joe, your wife is at St. Joseph Hospital, having the baby."

During lunch, when no one is looking, Jordan jumps out a window, then hitchhikes to the hospital to visit his wife, who has just given birth to a daughter. The union doesn't hold it against him. When he returns to the plant, he's given fifty dollars to pay the doctor bill.

Bud Simons appreciates the pressure the men are under from home. Rumors circulate that prostitutes visit the plants to service the strikers. Angry wives show up at the gates shouting, "I'm not lettin' my husband in here where you're importin' whores for them to work on. Now you come on and go home and get out of there." Plenty of families support the strike, though. Wives and children picket outside the plants, carrying placards declaring "Our Dads Will Win!" "My Daddy Is a Union Man," and "My Daddy Strikes for Us Little Tykes: On to Victory."

A husband and a father himself, Simons understands the lure of family life. One lure he will not tolerate, though, is the urge to drink. Liquor is strictly prohibited inside the union-held plants. It can't look like a party in there. When the police committee catches a striker with a whiskey bottle, he's told, "Pour it in the sewer, buddy." The next time the committee catches the man tippling, he's banned from the plant.

The strikers allow the journalist Mary Heaton Vorse inside Fisher One to research an article for the *New Republic*. Before Vorse climbs up to the window, a picket asks to see her credentials, then frisks her for liquor. "It was discomforting, very, but no different from the procedure of entering an armed camp in a war zone," Vorse later writes in her report. "This was a war zone."

Exploring the stilled first floor, Vorse finds men listening to a radio, men sitting on auto seats reading newspapers, and an overhead sign declaring the ordinarily rackety shop floor a "Quiet Zone." On the second floor she finds the stock room, with "piles of seats, parts of seats. I never knew so much wood went into the making of a body." Vorse next visits the much busier, much livelier Pengelly Building, where "activity . . . never stopped. Each moment saw a steady flow of people climbing and descending the narrow wooden stairways."

On the ground floor of the Pengelly, the strike's Ladies' Auxiliary maintains a first-aid station. In the second-floor offices is a room where picket captains organize the defense of Fisher One and Fisher Two. In the publicity room, Kraus and students from the University of Michigan lay out the *Flint Auto Worker* and mimeograph strike bulletins. In the reader room, strikers collect meal tickets, and sympathizers who have volunteered their vehicles to the cause receive gas and oil tickets. A welfare room handles relief applications. In the winter of 1937, the number of relief cases in Genesee County is five times what it was in the summer and fall because the sit-down strike interrupted work and wages. From 2,027 in December, the number of cases increases to 6,840 in January; to 10,835 in February; and to 11,027 in March. Defying pressure from anti-labor organizations, Governor Murphy makes relief funds available to strikers' families.

Pengelly Hall, where mass meetings are held, resembles "thousands of union halls, with its dirty windows, missing panes of glass, its old piano and loudspeaker," Vorse writes. For an evening rally the hall is standing room only.

> All of striking Flint was there: the strikers, their wives, fathers, daughters. Eyes turned to the green and white berets of Emergency Brigade women from Detroit and Toledo and they were given a cheer. Cheers greeted the names of Homer Martin and John L. Lewis. By ten-thirty the speaking was over.

> Young hands folded and stacked the chairs. Pengelly Hall became a self-service night club. Dancing, entertainment, singing never stopped. In the first light of morning, the broom brigade arrived to sweep away the day's collection of dust and cigarette butts, the dancers stepping in and out among the dirt piles.

In order to succeed, in order to gain credibility as a citywide, industrywide movement, the union has to expand its membership beyond the Fisher Body plants. Harried Chevrolet workers are more promising recruits than workers who build the luxury Buick. So the strikers set up a loudspeaker outside the Beer Vault, one of the many diners and taverns whose neon marquees and "Drink Coca-Cola" signs lure in workers from Chevy Nine, on the other side of Kearsley Street. Because the Beer Vault is so close to the plants, the union has rented space there to set up a temporary headquarters. During the afternoon shift change on Thursday, January 7, the unionists set up an amplifier and encourage the workers streaming in and out of the gates to stand up to General Motors. It turns out to be the last shift change at Chevrolet. GM shuts down the plant at 11 p.m. that night due to lack of auto bodies, bringing the number of idled workers in Flint to 26,775. The union also announces a mass meeting scheduled for that evening in Pengelly Hall. While union representatives are speaking, a foreman and a superintendent emerge from the plant, carrying hammers. The foremen and the supe smash the amplifier. The company men brawl with the strikers until the police arrive. The cops arrest two men, Ray Slee, a UAWA organizer from Toledo, and Harold Hubbard, a Fisher One employee. The cops also shut down the Beer Vault as a warning to other pro-strike shopkeepers. They then escort the foreman and the supe back inside the plant.

As word of the arrests circulates, 350 strike sympathizers pack Pengelly Hall for the evening meeting. Roy Reuther encourages the crowd to march on police headquarters, surround the building, and demand the prisoners' release.

"This afternoon," Reuther declares, "the police rushed in and shouldered the foreman and his assistant aside and took away the trouble-makers, under their protection, but they came back and got two of our men who also were wounded, took them down to the station, and under orders from GM, they refused to let anyone see them until tomorrow . . . tomorrow!"

With cries of "Let's do it!," a troop two hundred strong marches through a cold drizzle from Pengelly Hall to the Flint Police Department. When the marchers arrive, six men are allowed into the chief's office, where a lieutenant bluntly informs them that Slee and Hubbard will not be released to the mob outside. After complaining of "discrimination" because GM's men were not arrested for smashing their loudspeaker, the delegation returns to the street, where a sound car is parked. From inside the car, Roy Reuther announces that he has sent a telegram to Governor Murphy demanding that "unless the two men who have been arrested in Flint today are released immediately, now, in accordance with their democratic rights, we ask you to remove Police Chief James V. Willis and City Manager John M. Barringer, from whom the police chief takes his orders."

The men on the sidewalk pick up the thread of Reuther's harangue, assailing Flint's law enforcement establishment.

"Are there any decent judges in Flint at all?" one man shouts.

"If the chief of police wants to keep his job, he'd better listen to what the workers say," cries another.

"Police are using strike breaking tactics when they arrest innocent bystanders!"

"Since when have they got the right to lock people up without proof?"

From their offices on the second floor, Chief Willis and Sheriff Wolcott can hear the speeches and the responding cheers. After two hours, Flint's top law enforcement officers decide this demonstration has gone on long enough. They emerge onto the steps.

"The chief and I have talked this thing over," the sheriff tells the crowd, "and have decided that you are in violation of the disturbance of the peace ordinance. We will give you exactly five minutes."

Unlike his hapless attempt to enforce the injunction at Fisher One, this time Wolcott is defending his own turf. The strikers taunt him with "Hello, Tommy" and "Come on, Tommy," but as soon as Wolcott finishes speaking, eight police officers appear behind him, carrying gas cartridges and wearing World War gas masks. The threat of a gassing breaks up the crowd, which straggles back to the Pengelly Building in small clusters. When the strikers again fill the hall, Victor Reuther, Roy's younger brother and a fellow organizer, tells them that General Motors ordered the police to use tear gas. Only a desperate company, a company that knows it's losing, would try to attack its own employees, he says.

"If General Motors tells them to give you tear gas, they come out and give you tear gas," Victor asserts. "General Motors has a finger in everything here. Everything in the city of Flint. Everything but your mind and my mind is run by General Motors. But I say General Motors is on the run. United labor is stronger than ever. Hundreds of thousands of workers from one end of the country to the other will rise up and stand by us!"

That Friday morning, at 11 a.m., Slee and Hubbard are arraigned in municipal court on charges of breach of the peace. The union pays their two-hundred-dollar bonds. After they're released, with a trial date of February 17, they follow a crowd of strikers back to the Pengelly Building.

The protestors don't just take out their ire on cops, the judges, and the company. They direct their deepest anger toward a man named George Boysen, a former Buick paymaster who briefly served as mayor of Flint. Boysen is the founder and chairman of the Flint Alliance, an anti-strike organization that claims to speak for the silent majority of Flint residents, including Flint autoworkers. The Alliance's core membership consists of 200 Flint businessmen. On January 6, its first day of operation, the organization receives 5,000 membership applications at its downtown office. It also collects 11,300 signatures on a petition circulated among Chevrolet workers just before the plants shut down. That's 91 percent of the workforce, but the men are asked to sign in the plants, in the presence of their foremen. The petition states, "We the undersigned employees of the Chevrolet Motor Company of Flint, wish to go on record that we are not in sympathy with the present organizing movement and its attendant shut downs."

A GM employee, Leo Schwesinger, writes to the Labor Department, "Most of the men who sign do so under pressure. They fear that the company will check petitions with payrolls. Why not take a secret ballot to determine if the men want the union or not? GM knows if a secret ballot is taken, that eighty-five percent of men would vote in favor of union."

After a Flint Alliance meeting at the Durant Hotel, attended mostly by bankers, realtors, and shopkeepers, Boysen composes a brief manifesto for his new group, which he wires to both Governor Murphy and President Roosevelt:

> The purpose of the Flint Alliance is to give the great majority of workers in Flint plants and other citizens a medium through which to express their sentiments on the present labor difficulties. The Flint Alliance is convinced that differences between employer and employee can be solved in a legal and orderly manner.
>
> The Flint Alliance objects strongly to the methods which have been used in this community and which have resulted in unemployment for thousands of men and women who want to work and have expressed themselves by petition and otherwise.

The strikers call Boysen a rat and the Flint Alliance "a vigilante rat scab outfit." They parade an effigy labeled "Boysen the Rat" outside the gate of Fisher One.

Despite the Alliance's respectable leadership, there is some truth to the union's claim that it's a vigilante organization. At one point Flint's city manager, John M. Barringer, calls on the group to provide twenty armed men to augment the police department. Barringer has heard a rumor that several busloads of strike sympathizers are headed to Flint from Toledo, and he doesn't think his men can handle all that trouble. In a private conference at the Durant Hotel, Boysen tells two members of the Alliance's leadership that a group of "hammer men" from Buick are going to march on Fisher One and "clean out those people who are barricaded in there." The march is scheduled for eight o'clock that night. The hammer men are just waiting for Boysen's OK. (Among the anti-union autoworkers are members of the Black Legion. The legion is a Midwestern offshoot of the Ku Klux Klan that considers the labor movement a Communist front and that has previously murdered and terrorized union organizers in Michigan.)

"Violence begets violence," Boysen's fellow businessmen warn him. They've promised Governor Murphy that the strike will be settled peacefully.

"I'm going to do it anyway," Boysen says defiantly.

The men lock the hotel-room door.

"You got to fight both of us," one tells Boysen, "but you are not going to get out of this room at eight o'clock."

The hammer men never receive an order to march. Instead, the Alliance decides to hold a mass meeting at the IMA Auditorium on the afternoon of Monday, January 11.

In the *Chevy Auto Worker*, a penny tabloid, the union publishes its official rebuke to "Mr. Boysen, who has appointed himself (with G.M.'s approval!) Flint's scab handler. No one says that he represents the people of Flint. He says we are only a 'small minority' who even need protection against the 'anger' of Flint's autoworkers, and therefore he is organizing the so-called 'Flint Alliance' to give us that protection!

"We are not afraid of Mr. Boysen and his 'Alliance.' We know the Flint autoworkers are too smart for his tricks and too solid with the splendid boys of the Fisher plants. A few screwballs and a large number of company foremen and stools will probably join the 'Alliance.' Maybe some honest but deluded workers will join him. But the vast majority of men will remain true to their fighting brothers!"

In fact, there are plenty of autoworkers on both sides of the issue, pro- and anti-strike, and they're writing letters to public officials, especially President Roosevelt and Secretary of Labor Perkins. A Buick employee writes to FDR, "I wish to call your attention to the terroristic activities of the union agitators here. These agitators are mostly outsiders with no stake in Flint and have been desperately trying to scare us workers into joining their so called union. I, for one, wish to say that I do not wish to join their moreless [*sic*] racketeering organization." A sympathetic worker writes Perkins, "If the union won't win, we will get killed on the job. Abraham Lincoln freed the colored people from slaves and now we are slaves. . . . Please help to keep the white people from slavery."

The man most caught in the middle of these competing sentiments is the man who represents every autoworker and every auto executive in Michigan: the newly inaugurated governor, Frank Murphy. The sit-down strike is the first test of Murphy's leadership. If anyone can bring the company and the union together, it ought to be him.

Yet Murphy's first attempt at negotiation and conciliation is a failure. After long telephone conversations with both Knudsen and Martin, he invites both men to a conference at his office in the state capitol in Lansing. Knudsen agrees to attend if the union evacuates its plants. The union agrees to evacuate GM's plants if the company recognizes the UAWA as its workers' bargaining agent, and refrains from restarting the lines or moving equipment until a national agreement is reached. No deal, Knudsen tells Murphy. The strikers must surrender Fisher One and Fisher Two unconditionally before he'll sit down with the union.

"Unfortunately, the union officials were unwilling to start negotiations on this basis and insisted on further restrictions of the Corporation's freedom of action," Knudsen tells the press.

Murphy is still hopeful that he can get GM and the UAWA to talk it out.

"I do not consider that our efforts at conciliation are ended," he writes hopefully.

In spite of Murphy's hopes, it will take an outbreak of violence to bring both sides into the governor's office.

CHAPTER 5

THE BATTLE OF THE RUNNING BULLS

ON JANUARY 11, the heat inside Fisher Two goes off at noon, around the same time the Flint Alliance is gathering at the IMA Auditorium.

In the middle of January, in Michigan, the air is so cold that a man's nostrils flop shut when he draws a deep breath. Every exhalation manifests itself as a cloud of steam. Hands become chapped and reddened. That day, the temperature tops out at sixteen degrees. As the early winter chill begins seeping through the brick walls of Fisher Two, the hundred or so men inside realize that the company means to freeze them out.

Fisher Two is situated on a rise just north of the Flint River. When the plant is running, a thousand workers produce four hundred and fifty bodies a day, which are shipped to the assembly line at Chevy in the Hole via a viaduct that crosses Chevrolet Avenue.

Since the beginning of the sit-down, the strikers inside Fisher Two have spent most of their time playing cards, singing union broadsides, and keeping fit with daily rooftop calisthenics. But some have been preparing for the confrontation General Motors now seems about to incite. Fred Ahearn, who installs trunk boards, fashions a blackjack by loading a leather pouch with lead. Men unload car-door hinges from storage kegs, lining them up on window sills to employ as missiles against a potential assault by the "bulls"—the plant guards and police. To prevent a rearguard attack, they weld steel plates to the back doors and the doors leading to the overpass, then roll auto body dollies against the vulnerable entrances.

For the first two weeks of the strike, General Motors has provided heat to the strikers occupying the second floor of Fisher Two and has allowed their wives to pass homemade hams, stews, bread, and pies through the windows. Gus's Café, a Greek diner with a big shop trade, donates meals. The plant guards inspect the care packages to ensure they contain no alcohol, then allow them past the gate.

Every evening at six o'clock, a union delegation delivers supper from the strike mess. The eleventh of January is different. That evening, the usual contingent of eight company guards, led by Pete Peterson, has been reinforced by a twenty-two-man detachment armed with clubs and led by the chief of the Fisher Body plant police. Around the same time, a contingent of Flint police is gathering a few blocks south of the plant, blocking traffic on Chevrolet Avenue. First, the guards carry off a twenty-four-foot ladder the strikers have been using to clamber in and out of a second-story window. Then, when the food arrives, the guards bar the door. Not only is GM planning to freeze the strikers out, it's planning to starve them out, too. The company has been told by a Pinkerton spy who was part of the original occupation that there are only a hundred men inside Fisher Two. It seems like an easier target than Fisher One, whose striker population is two or three times greater.

One of the sit-downers, Roscoe Rich, is standing at the front gate, a set of metal-reinforced glass doors, when the food delivery is blocked. He runs upstairs to report the blockade to strike leader Red Mundale, who is working in one of the administrative offices.

"Red, they stopped the food from comin' in," Rich reports.

"Who the hell stopped the food from comin' in?" Mundale asks.

"Well, Pete Peterson, he locked the door," says Rich.

"Well, you go and tell Pete Peterson you want the keys to that door. Either he opens it or gives you the keys. If he don't give you the keys, Roscoe, you take your flying squad, and you bust that damn door in. That's all there is to it. Just go down there and tell him you want the keys." The flying squads are paramilitary units ready to rush to trouble spots.

Word of the blockade reaches strike headquarters at the Pengelly Building shortly after six o'clock. Genora Johnson is rehearsing a play there with her husband, Kermit, her sister, and two friends. Hearing that the strikers are being denied food and heat, they all drive over to Fisher Two. Outside the plant, pickets singing "Solidarity Forever" march in circles on the sidewalk, pausing to warm themselves at kerosene-fueled salamander heaters. From a second-story window a man shouts, "We are having a meeting and electing a committee to see about getting our meals through!" The committee decides that the method least likely to provoke a scrap with the guards is to pile food into picnic baskets and hoist it through the windows on ropes.

At 8:15, Victor Reuther arrives from the Pengelly Building in a sound car, accompanied by his brother Roy and a United Rubber Workers organizer from Akron. By then the police have barricaded Chevrolet Avenue both north and south of the plant, but Victor is able to slip through the blockade via a side street.

"Well, so they turned the heat off on you," Victor broadcasts through his loudspeaker. "So they shut off your food! They have talked of avoiding violence. Now they have taken the first step." Victor has brought along a phonograph. He asks the men if they want to hear some music.

"No," shouts a club-wielding striker leaning through the windows. "We want action!"

"Send a committee to the gate and tell those guards to open it up and turn on the heat!" Reuther shouts back.

With instructions from Red Mundale inside the plant and Victor Reuther outside, Roscoe Rich returns to the main gate with a fifteen-man flying squad, including Pete Pavelich, a brawler nicknamed Black Pete. They will break through the gate with brute force if the guards refuse to open it. Black Pete has prepared for this showdown by wrapping stick solder around his hands. Rich confronts Peterson, who is standing inside the locked main entrance to the plant. From the street, Victor Reuther issues a decisive command: "Take the gates!"

"Now either you open that door, Pete, or I'm gonna open it," Rich demands.

"I lost the keys," Peterson retorts.

"I'll give you three minutes," Rich replies.

Rich begins counting down. When he reaches zero, the flying squad surges past the unresisting guards and busts the locks on the doors. The strikers rush outside and mingle with the pickets on the sidewalk, while the overwhelmed plant police seek shelter in a women's restroom. From there, they radio the Flint Police Department to report they have been "captured" by the strikers.

Minutes after the strikers break through the doors, two columns of Flint police officers begin crossing the bridge from their position on the south bank of the river. They're armed with tear gas and wrapped in bulletproof vests. Their faces hidden inside World War tear-gas masks, with goggle eyes and rubber snouts, the officers look like a platoon of bipedal insects.

"Here they come!" the pickets cry.

Striker William Connolly is standing just inside the door. Gripping both ends of a blackjack he has threaded through the door handles, he braces his feet against the center post. Captain Edwin Hughes of the Flint police commands the strikers to open the gates. He gets no response. Above the front door is a window reinforced with chicken wire. A police officer smashes the glass with the butt of his tear-gas gun. Connolly thinks the weapon looks like a pistol, but he also thinks, "He ain't got guts enough to shoot a harmless worker." The cop does have guts, firing a tear-gas shell into the crowded lobby, the room where, on ordinary work days, employees punch in for their shifts. The flame from the discharge singes Connolly's cheeks and temporarily blinds him. He drops to the floor and begins crawling backward on his knees, seeking the safety of the shop floor.

Meanwhile, a team of strikers has hooked up fire hoses. They kick open the door and direct the nozzles at the police, who are still firing tear gas through the broken window.

"By God," thinks Mundale, "we haven't got a lot to protect ourselves with, but if we can get those water hoses down, we will just wash them the hell out of here."

Gas seeps in, water gushes out. The spray knocks several officers to the ground. Mundale notices a canister still discharging gas. He orders the men with the hose to sweep it out the door: "Jesus, hit it with that water hose! Hit it with a water hose!"

From the open windows on the second floor, strikers pelt police with door hinges stockpiled for this moment. The tide of battle turns in the strikers' favor. The wind is blowing out of the north, wafting the tear gas back toward the police, who cannot advance into the cold, stinging spray from the hoses. Emboldened strikers surge out the front door and chase the retreating police toward the bridge, hurling any projectile they can lay their hands on: hinges, bricks, nuts, bolts, milk bottles, shards of curb stone, even snowballs. "The Stars and Stripes Forever" blares from the sound car, a surreal patriotic soundtrack to the melee. The pickets join in the rout, smashing police car windows and overturning a Genesee County Sheriff's Department cruiser, which contains Sheriff Wolcott himself.

"It was bad enough they turned my car over," Wolcott later remarks. "But they did it with me in it."

When he emerges from his upside-down vehicle, Wolcott is struck in the head by a flying missile. He's one of nine law enforcement officers injured that night. Others are set upon and roughed up by pickets and strikers. Fred Ahearn tears an ashtray out of a police car and uses it to crown a cop who is beating a fellow striker with a nightstick.

Halfway through their retreat toward the bridge, the police turn and open fire into the pursuing mob. "Goddamn, I got hit," Mundale hears a man cry. He turns to see blood running down Hans Larson's leg—struck by buckshot from a police rifle.

Police gunfire wounds fourteen strikers and two pickets. Striker Robert Mamero is shot in the leg and the hip; Gig Moe takes a bullet to the shins. A young strike supporter who works for the streetcar company is hit twice in the belly.

Nearly three thousand spectators have gathered outside the plant, most of them sympathetic to the union. Reuther asks anyone with a car to park it on Chevrolet Avenue, to block the police from resuming their attack. "Go home and get your guns," Reuther beseeches through the sound car megaphone. "Don't give up. Keep on fighting. We have reinforcements on the way from Toledo and Akron to help you fight these guys." (Despite this call to arms, there are never guns inside the plants. Travis doesn't want to give the cops another excuse to use violence.)

The wounded men are taken to a restaurant, then driven to Hurley Hospital in ambulances and private cars. Inside the plants, women press wet towels against the faces of tear-gassed men.

"The corporation has charged the sitdowners with disregard for property," bellows Reuther, who has become both field lieutenant and Greek chorus for the conflict. "But it is General Motors who tonight through the city police have destroyed property. All during these days the Fisher Body workers have been sitting down peacefully, protecting their jobs; yes, and religiously guarding the machines at which they earn their livelihood. Not a scratch has marred a single object in the plant until tonight when the police shot their gas and bullets into it in a cowardly attack upon these unarmed and peaceful men. What could they do but defend themselves as best they could? They must now fight not only for their jobs but their very lives. Let General Motors be warned, however, the patience of these men is not inexhaustible. If there is further bloodshed here tonight, we will not be responsible for what the workers do in their rage! There are costly machines in that plant. Let the corporation and their thugs remember that."

Genora Johnson, who has rushed over from the Pengelly Building after hearing the strikers were being denied food, asks Reuther if she, too, can address the crowd from the sound car. He hands her the microphone. "Those men had no firearms!" Johnson shouts. "They were defenseless in the face of firearms. I ask all the women here tonight to come down and stand with your husbands and brothers. If the police are cowards enough to shoot down defenseless men, they're cowards enough to shoot down women. Women of the city of Flint, break through these police lines, and come down here and stand with your husbands and your brothers, your sons and your sweethearts."

In response to Johnson's exhortation, women surge toward the plant. As they pass through the police lines, one has her overcoat torn off by a cop, but the police don't stop the women, nor do they fire again once there's a danger of hitting one. Having been repulsed once, and facing a hostile crowd, the police hold their position on the bridge, only occasionally, to save face, lobbing a gas bomb that illuminates the sky above the plant. The Flint police run out of gas shells at midnight; they appeal to Detroit for more but are told that none can be spared. Sheriff Wolcott himself halts an attempt to distribute rifles for a second attack.

"There's going to be no shooting here," he tells Chief Wills. "I'm the leading law enforcement officer in the county during any troubles and those are my orders."

Elsie Larson, the wife of the wounded Hans Larson, is at home listening to reports of the skirmish on the radio when two men from the union knock on her door. Earlier that night, Elsie and her son tried to bring food to Hans but were told by the police, "Take the kid and go home, there's going to be trouble tonight."

Now, the visitors tell Elsie, "Hans has been shot. Shot in the leg."

At first, Elsie thinks they said "Shot in the head."

"Where is he?" she asks, panicked.

"They're taking him to Hurley."

Elsie jumps into the strangers' car and races to the hospital. She finds her husband in the emergency room, where, to her relief, doctors are dressing his leg. Elsie wants to bring Hans home with her; instead he is taken to the Genesee County Jail by two police detectives, who will not even allow her to ride the elevator downstairs with her husband. So the union men drive Elsie to the lockup, where she confronts Sheriff Wolcott, who has recovered from being overturned with his car to supervise the jailing of wounded strikers.

"You can't go in," Wolcott tells Mrs. Larson.

"I just want to take him some cigarettes and underwear."

"You come back another time . . . alone," the sheriff orders.

Back at Fisher Two, after the police have retreated and run out of tear gas, Francis O'Rourke sits down to write in his strike diary: "We got them on the run again. Don't stop now. Heavenly Father stop this outrage. Now all is silent again. Is that all of this? Peace on Earth, Good Will Toward Men. What kind of peace if this, I ask you? Now stories of the attack. Tears running down cheeks, tears caused by tear gas bombs. Swollen faces, bloody clothes. What a mess. No one can sleep after this. But I'll say my prayers."

Fifty miles to the southwest, in his office beneath the slender eggshell dome of the state capitol, Governor Murphy is receiving reports of the unrest from Flint City Manager John M. Barringer. At midnight, he leaves Lansing for Flint, accompanied by State Police commissioner Oscar Olander and Adjutant General John S. Bersey, commander of the Michigan National Guard. Arriving at the Durant Hotel an hour later, Murphy meets with Mayor Harold Bradshaw, who presents him with a formal request for troops on the grounds that "riot and bloodshed have occurred and all our law enforcement agencies have attempted to maintain law and order and have proven inadequate and unable to cope with the situation because of the great number of persons involved."

When Victor Reuther gets word that the pro-union governor is in Flint, he taunts police with the news. "You'd better go home before Governor Murphy gets after you!" He then calls the cops "murderers" before blaring more music through his loudspeaker. The conference at the Durant is later joined by several labor leaders, including Adolph Germer of the CIO and Bob Travis, who had been speaking to twenty members of the Flint Federation of Teachers at the YWCA when the violence broke out. General Motors keeps its distance, issuing only a statement the company "deplored" the violence, and is awaiting "accurate information."

The next day, to protest the "brutality" of the battle, Walter Reuther calls a sit-down strike at GM's Fleetwood plant in Detroit, which manufactures bodies for Cadillacs. Although Flint is the focus of the UAWA's strategy, the union is trying to expand the strike to as many GM plants as possible: in the weeks following the Flint sit-down, unionists in Detroit, Toledo, St. Louis, Oakland, and Janesville, Wisconsin, will either sit down in their plants or walk off the job. They join the strikers in Flint, Cleveland, Atlanta, Kansas City, Harrison, New Jersey, and Anderson, Indiana, until, in the union's estimation, twenty GM facilities have been shut down by strikes.

As governor, Murphy would be within his rights in declaring the occupation of GM's plants in Flint illegal and ordering the better-armed, more numerous National Guard to finish the job the Flint police have started. During a meeting of President Roosevelt's cabinet that month, Vice President John Nance Garner, a conservative Texas landowner, suggests that Secretary Perkins order Murphy to do just that.

"What is it these fellows are doing out there anyhow, Mr. President?" Garner asks Roosevelt. "This is terrible. This sit-down strike is just terrible. What's the state of it?"

Roosevelt yields the floor to Perkins.

"You sum it up," he tells her.

Perkins explains to the vice president that the men are occupying the factories in hopes that GM will listen to their grievances on wages, line speed, and job security, but the company is refusing to meet with them.

You don't think the employers should meet them while they're in the factories, do you?" Garner asks, his round face reddening in outrage.

"Yes, I see no reason why they shouldn't," replies Perkins, a Yankee reformer who has devoted her career to fighting for shorter workweeks, worker safety, and the abolition of child labor. "What good is it going to do to stick it out? It just makes the thing worse. If people are mad, they get madder. If they've made a mistake, they'll make the mistake harder if they get angry. The employers could solve this right now by meeting a committee, I think. If it goes on much longer, they may not be able to solve it by just meeting a committee. They may have to do more than that. But I'm sure that if they would agree to meet a committee, and meet it under the auspices of Governor Murphy, or of our department—it doesn't matter, but preferably under the auspices of Governor Murphy—I believe that this thing could be settled in a very short time and we would have a cease to this particular kind of action."

"These men are reprehensible," Garner grumbles. "Why isn't Murphy doing something? Why doesn't he get out the troops? What does he have a state guard for? What's the militia for if it isn't to run these fellows out? They've seized the property of private citizens."

"They have not in any way attempted to assert ownership and no court of law would hold that they have seized it, because they have not done anything with it," Perkins replies calmly. "It's still there. It's unharmed and it's there. They haven't seized it. They are staying in it."

Ignoring the labor secretary, either because he's hard of hearing or because he's angry, Garner turns to the president and bursts into a tirade against the labor movement.

"I think this is terrible," the vice president rants. "I think this is awful, Mr. President. I just don't think this kind of thing ought to happen in this country. These labor men have been too much coddled. They've been too flattered. Too much attention has been paid to them. Hugh Johnson [former administrator of the National Recovery Administration] had these same automobile workers right here in the White House a couple of years ago. They were laying down the law as to what they would have. Hugh Johnson encouraged them. The Secretary of Labor here deals with them when they come in. Now she says they're not going to be pushed out of these factories."

"I didn't say they're not going to be pushed out," Perkins interjects. "If Governor Murphy wants to push them out, he can push them out. It's up to him to do it."

"Well, why doesn't he do it?" Garner challenges Perkins. "Why don't you tell him to do it?"

Roosevelt finally intercedes to end the argument.

"Well, Jack," he tells Garner, "we haven't yet gotten to the point where the president of the United States tells the governors of sovereign states what they're able to do. If Murphy says that he needs help from the federal government, you can be sure we'll give it to him. But Murphy's got his duty to perform. He's the governor of the state. He's got to use his own best judgment."

Roosevelt is conflicted about the strike. Although he personally believes the occupation of the plants is "reprehensible," Roosevelt has no desire to dispatch federal troops to expel the strikers from GM's property. He doesn't understand why the two sides can't settle their differences under the New Deal labor laws he signed during his first term in office.

"These workingmen," the president says to Perkins during a later meeting, "are doing something quite wrong and hazardous and they ought not to do it in a country like this where, although their employers have been difficult to deal with, the men now have certain rights under the law, and eventually the government will get around to seeing that those rights are recognized and that the employers deal with them in collective bargaining."

The patrician president from Hyde Park has more faith than the autoworkers of Flint that his signature on the Wagner Act will convince General Motors to recognize a union's right to bargain collectively. Significantly, though, Roosevelt believes that although the occupation of the plants is wrong, removing the men by force would be an even greater evil.

"Well, it is illegal," he tells Perkins, "but what law are they breaking? The law of trespass, and that is about the only law that could be invoked. And what do you do when a man trespasses on your property? Sure you order him off. You get the sheriff to order him off if he tries to pitch a tent in your field without your permission. If he comes on to your place to steal, why, you have him for theft, of course. But shooting it out and killing a lot of people because they have violated the law of trespass somehow offends me. I just don't see that as the answer. The punishment doesn't fit the crime. There must be another way. Why can't these fellows in General Motors meet with the committee of workers? Talk it all out. They would get a settlement. It wouldn't be so terrible."

This is a more enlightened view of the rights of labor versus the rights of property than previous presidents have held. It is certainly a view shared by Murphy, a political soul mate of Roosevelt's. It is even shared by some auto executives. Lawrence Fisher, one of Fisher Body's founding brothers, has warned Murphy against expelling the strikers by violent means. His company's reputation, he believes, is more important than ending a temporary trespass on its property.

"If the Fisher Brothers never make another nickel, we don't want bloodshed in that plant," Fisher tells the governor. "We don't want blood on our hands."

After an all-night conference in the Durant, Murphy issues a statement at five thirty on the morning of January 12—with the strikers inside Fisher Two still asleep after the exhausting battle.

"Whatever may happen, there is going to be law and order in Michigan," Murphy declares. "The public interest and public safety are paramount. The public authority in Michigan is stronger than either of the parties in the present controversy.

"Neither of them by recourse to force and violence will be permitted to add public terror to existing economic demoralization. A serious riot has occurred. Local police are evidently inadequate to handle the situation and preserve order.

"Without wishing to countenance unlawful seizure of property, the state had heretofore refrained from taking strong measures in hope that an amicable settlement might be reached. It is apparent, however, that the situation in Flint has gotten beyond the control of local authority, and leaders of the two factions having been so advised, and requested by local officials, it has become the duty of the state (and it is prepared) to act in the present emergency for maintenance of public order and the protection of the rights of private property in the city of Flint.

"I am accordingly ordering the state police and units of the national guard to be in readiness."

Murphy is attempting to portray himself as a neutral arbiter in the dispute, interested only in preventing more violence in Flint, but his decision to dispatch the Michigan National Guard on a peacemaking mission is a victory for the strikers, since it will create a militarized buffer between the workers and the better-armed police. Furthermore, when Murphy returns to Lansing after his wee-hours negotiating session, he calls officials at General Motors, and asks them to turn the heat back on in Fisher Two and allow food to pass through the gates. A continuing campaign to freeze and starve the strikers will cause a public health crisis and will "only befuddle the already complicated situation." The company complies.

That day, Michigan National Guardsmen begin converging on Flint by truck and train, arriving at the Grand Trunk Western Railroad station on East Fourteenth Street. Among the first to reach Flint are sixty-five men of a howitzer company from Monroe, led by Captain Brice C. W. Custer, grand-nephew of the ill-starred general killed at the Little Bighorn. By the morning of the thirteenth, nearly two thousand guardsmen are in Flint, outfitted in doughboy uniforms left over from the World War: tin helmets, khaki field coats, and puttees wrapped around their legs to the knees. Each soldier is armed with a .38-caliber rifle, tipped with a seventeen-inch bayonet. Some tote pup tents, in case they are required to camp in the bitter cold, but the city opens a disused junior high school to shelter the guardsmen, who are transported there from the station in trucks. The soldiers so overwhelm the school's sanitary capacity that they have to dig trench latrines in the playground. The YMCA offers the winter soldiers its showers. Soon, Flint is alive with the smells, sights, and sounds of a military encampment: A field mess outside the school prepares ham and eggs for the troops. The 126th Infantry Company from Detroit drills on the school grounds. A regimental band parades up and down Third Street.

To keep the police and strikers apart, the troops set up carriage-mounted machine guns and howitzers outside the occupied factories. An artillery officer from Kalamazoo, a World War veteran, tells a strike captain, "You better behave yourself, or I'll have that mortar company drop one down the chimney."

It's the first time the Michigan National Guard has been called to intervene in a labor dispute since 1913, when Governor Woodbridge Ferris sent guardsmen to the Upper Peninsula during a violent nine-month strike against the Calumet and Hecla Mining Company. (The strikers lost that struggle when the troops were withdrawn, and violence between strikers, sheriff's deputies, and scab miners resumed.)

When word circulates through the plant that the National Guard is in Flint, the strikers are thrilled. "We men are pleased. The Governor is in town," Francis O'Rourke writes in his diary. "We are glad the State Troopers and the National Guard are here. We have faith in them, maybe we can trust them. We thought the same of the City Police and look. . . . We want no violence and will not seek any. Maybe the State Troops and National Guard will act as our protectors from another attack. Tonight maybe we can sleep."

With the National Guard in the streets, the men inside the plants no longer fear for their lives. They trust the governor. Guardsmen from local units are personal friends of the strikers. Some guardsmen are unionists from other Michigan auto plants. They display their sympathy for the strikers by swapping cigarettes for union buttons. The UAWA leaders try to emphasize the common bond between laborer and foot soldier by addressing the guardsmen from the sound truck and distributing the *Flint Auto Worker* among the troops. A lieutenant from Holland, a village on the shore of Lake Michigan, on the conservative western side of the state, gets a copy of the paper, finds it "one-sided," and passes it on to the Guard's commander in Flint, Colonel Joseph H. Lewis, a veteran of both the Calumet mining strike and the World War. Lewis orders the lieutenant to burn it, then calls Travis and tells him to stop propagandizing the troops. In a bulletin to his men Colonel Lewis writes, "We must not take sides. We must lean backwards so as to avoid the semblance of seeming to take sides. Our troops include men of all walks of life and many of us are naturally sympathetic to one side or another. However, as long as we are in uniform, our personal leanings must be made secondary."

Travis doesn't want to cross a military force his men consider an ally. Instead, he continues his campaign to sway public opinion in the press, issuing a statement assigning "full responsibility" for the attack on Fisher Two to "the General Motors corporation and its agents, the police of Flint." The plan, he charges, was hatched at the Flint Alliance meeting. A double-stacked headline in the *Flint Auto Worker* declares "Heroism Defeats Police Brutality" and lists the names of the fourteen wounded strikers, calling them "Heroic Victims of Police Brutality."

General Motors says only that the violence is "very much to be deplored," but the *Flint Journal*, which retails the company line, praises the police department for using restraint against the provocations of out-of-town agitators; instead of unleashing a massacre, they only shot a dozen strikers in the legs.

"Standing out starkly in the utterly tragic and unnecessary turmoil of Monday night are the courage and self-control shown by the greatly outnumbered city and county officers and the conclusive evidence of out-of-town leadership and participation," the *Journal* writes in a front-page editorial. "In the face of the weapons and missiles with which they were assailed it must have been difficult for the police and sheriff's staff to refrain from repulse with general gunfire. It is to their credit that they remained frustrated rather than open an attack from which the toll would have included many misguided followers of inflammatory incitation."

In union lore, the victory over the Flint police becomes known as the Battle of the Running Bulls—"because we made 'the bulls' run," as William Connolly, the striker temporarily blinded by the tear gas shell, puts it. The battle even inspires a ballad, which joins the repertoires of the picket line and the Hillbilly Orchestra. Sung to the tune of "There'll Be a Hot Time in the Old Town Tonight," it includes a pointed reference to Evan J. Parker, the unpopular manager of Fisher Two:

Cheer boys cheer
For we are full of fun,
Cheer boys cheer
Old Parker's on the run;
We had a fight last night

And I tell you boys we won
We had a hot time in the old town last night

Tear gas bombs
Were flying thick and fast
The lousy police
They knew they couldn't last
Because in all their lives they never ran so fast
As that hot time in this old town last night

The police are sick
Their bodies they are sure
I'll bet they'll never fight no anymore
Because they learned last night
That they had quite a chore
We had a hot time in the old town last night

Now this scrap is o'er
The boys are sticking fast
We'll hold our ground and fight here to the last
And when this strike is o'er
We'll have our contract fast
We'll have a hot time in the old town tonight

The men hope the battle will speed the signing of a union contract. On the morning after, a fed-up governor sends letters to both Knudsen and Martin, inviting them to a conference in Lansing on Thursday the fourteenth, "so that we may together discuss the problem and endeavor to reach a prompt solution, tentative or otherwise, that will permit peaceful resumption of normal business activities and at least bring to an immediate and peaceful termination of the present anomalous situation, which is incompatible with American principles of law and order and ought not to be countenanced."

This time, Knudsen agrees to attend.

CHAPTER 6

THE WOMEN'S EMERGENCY BRIGADE

Genora Johnson's husband, Kermit, works on the line at Chevy. He's part of the strike leadership's inner circle, along with Travis, Mortimer, and the Reuther brothers—the only GM worker in that cabal. So when the sit-down begins, Genora considers herself a striker too. She goes down to the Pengelly Building to volunteer—and is told she can work in the kitchen.

Genora Johnson is no ordinary factory wife. At least, she doesn't consider herself one, not like those farm girls, or the migrants from Missouri. Born and raised in Flint, the daughter of a middle-class businessman, she almost graduated from high school but dropped out during senior year to marry Kermit. They have two sons, a two-year-old and a six-year-old. What really makes Genora different is the depth of her participation in the labor movement, which long predates the sit-down strike. Several years before, she helped found the Flint Socialist Party, under the influence of her father-in-law, a college-educated "intellectual worker" who belonged to Chevrolet's AFL union. Her grandfather was a Civil War veteran who campaigned for Flint's socialist mayor in 1911. Together, Genora and her father-in-law read the *American Guardian*, a socialist newspaper;

How the Other Half Lives, Jacob Riis's photographic documentary of the New York City slums; and the works of Jane Addams. When, after the aborted 1934 strike, Roy Reuther teaches labor history classes in Flint, Genora attends. Flint's Socialist Party founds a chapter of the League for Industrial Democracy, a socialist chautauqua that brings in speakers such as Norman Thomas, a six-time Socialist Party of America presidential candidate. Genora invites Walter Reuther to the Masonic Temple on Saginaw Street to speak about his experiences as an autoworker in the Soviet Union. She sells two hundred and fifty tickets at twenty-five cents apiece. So once the sit-down begins, she considers herself an experienced labor organizer, and tells the men at the Pengelly Building that organizing is what she intends to do.

"Look," she lectures the strike official who tries to assign her to kitchen duty, "you've got a lot of little skinny, thin men that aren't capable of going out and standing, marching around the picket lines, and they can peel potatoes as well as we can."

Along with the other women who belong to the Socialist Party, Genora organizes a wives' and children's picket line outside Fisher One. She paints the signs at the Pengelly Building, with slogans she makes up herself. The *Flint Journal* photographs her two-year-old boy, wearing a snowsuit and holding a placard reading "My Daddy Strikes for Us Little Tykes." The photo goes out over the national wires. Mother is proud, not just of her son but also of the publicity he's gained for the strike.

As the women picket, though, Genora sees that not all wives support their striking husbands. On New Year's Eve, women show up at Fisher One and call through the windows, "If you don't take me out tonight, I'm going to divorce you!" Fearing for their marriages, some men slink through the windows and over the fence, to the jeers of their fellow strikers.

Even though women have been expelled from the plants, to avoid any suspicion of sexual mingling, GM knows that marital relations are a weak spot for the strikers, so company representatives visit wives at home, spreading rumors that striptease dancers and even prostitutes are keeping their men company.

"Something has got to be done," Genora tells her fellow picketers. "We have got to call a meeting of the wives now. We have got to try to organize the wives because this is going to break up this whole union development. If we don't do something, this is going to be the Achilles' heel of the whole union movement here in Flint."

Building moral support among strikers' families inspires for the creation of the Ladies' Auxiliary of the UAWA. On New Year's Eve, eighty women gather at the Pengelly Building to listen to speeches from Roy Reuther, Bob Travis, and Wyndham Mortimer.

"General Motors has abused your husbands for years," Reuther tells the women. "They come too tired to relax and they come home with no kind of security whatsoever. They don't know from one day to the next whether they are gonna work. Some of them have been coerced into buying homes through General Motors and then when they get so far, why, the company will find some reason to let them go and sometimes they'll lose the home."

At the meeting is twenty-year-old Nellie Besson, who until recently worked a punch press for AC Spark Plug, earning only half as much money as the men for work that was just as dangerous. One night, when Besson arrives for her shift, she has the gruesome experience of finding two severed fingers from the hand of the day girl inside her press. The sight radicalizes her. So does the sight of women quitting metal-filing jobs after just thirty days because their lungs fill with shavings. When Wyndham Mortimer begins signing up GM employees for the new United Auto Workers of America union, Nellie attends a few secret meetings—held in a basement, in the backroom of a restaurant, in a coal shed—and finally signs a union card. When GM discovers—possibly from a stool pigeon—that she's joined the union, Nellie finds a pink slip in her pay envelope.

Losing the job is a hard blow. Christmas is coming up, and her father, a union carpenter, isn't working, leaving Nellie as the sole support of her four younger siblings. AC wasn't a great job—she had to ride two buses to work and put up with horny-handed foremen patting her bottom. Of course, she didn't get paid for the hours when the machines were broken down, and the workers had to kill time in the cafeteria. But her paycheck covered the rent and fed the family, and that was better than a lot of people were doing during the Depression.

"That's all right, honey," Nellie's father consoles her, after she shows him the pink slip. "Tomorrow, I'll take you to the Pengelly Building, and we'll have a talk with them."

At union headquarters, Nellie meets Roy Reuther and tells him the story of her dismissal. "Nellie," he says, "we are not near strong enough to do anything for you yet, but you can help us. Do you have any experience in public speaking, or know any parliamentary procedure? We need someone to talk to the women at AC and sell them on the union."

With plenty of time on her hands, and a grievance against General Motors, Nellie begins spending her days and nights at the Pengelly Building, sleeping on chairs, sleeping on the floor, subsisting on bologna sandwiches and black coffee, going home only to change clothes and bathe.

At the New Year's Eve meeting, Genora Johnson is elected president of the Ladies' Auxiliary. She calls for a mass meeting at the Pengelly Building, a few days after the New Year. In the meantime, the Ladies' Auxiliary prints up a leaflet to be distributed to the homes of strike widows; its text is published in the *Flint Auto Worker*:

> Womenfolk of Automobile Workers
>
> You had learn how to stretch your husband's pay—
>
> And do with less food for the family—
>
> Do without a new dress or coat this winter—
>
> Do without a new stove—you've waited so long.
>
> Now would you like to know how to help increase that pay?
>
> Your menfolk are trying to increase that pay by joining the Union. Their success depends to a large extent upon you womenfolk of Automobile Workers.
>
> We must understand the problems of our men in the shop, because their problems are our problems, too.
>
> Low wages mean less food, clothes and educational opportunities for our families.

> Speed-up means an exhausted, grouchy husband, father or brother. Loved ones who grow old and worn out long before their years.
>
> Bad working conditions mean industrial diseases, for which there is no compensation. Lead poisoning, chromium poisoning; silicosis, the dread disease caused by metal dust settling in the lungs, which can never be cured, and countless others too numerous to mention.
>
> A strong Union can raise your husband's pay. It can reduce the terrific speed-up. It can force the Company to install adequate ventilation systems and furnish all the necessary measures to reduce the health hazard to a minimum.
>
> You can help your menfolk get things for themselves, you and your families, by joining the Ladies' Auxiliary of the United Automobile Workers, which is the Union of Womenfolk.

Accompanying this manifesto is a document titled "Program of the Ladies' Auxiliary," whose eight points are both social and political. They include "to set up educational activities for the women and children such as tap dancing, drama, sewing classes, libraries, classes in home problems, marketing condition, consumers' problems, etc.," and "to take an active part in promoting legislation in regards to Child Labor Laws, Minimum Wage laws for Women, and all other progressive legislation for the welfare of the worker and his family."

Before she addresses the first mass meeting of the Ladies' Auxiliary at Pengelly Hall, Genora is escorted through Fisher One to make an inspection, so she can reassure suspicious wives that "there is nothing in there except that they have got pads made up to sleep on, and the guys are sitting around playing cards, and they have the metal up at that window with the hose pointed through it for protection, but that is the only reason those windows are bolted up."

In the first two weeks of January, five hundred women sign up for the Auxiliary. Plenty end up working in the kitchen, but they also set up a first-aid station in the Pengelly Building, and a nursery, furnished with donated playpens and pillows, to care for the children of picketing women. Women even walk the railroad tracks, gathering coal that has spilled out of railcars and delivering it to strikers' families hard pressed to heat their homes. One of the volunteers is a mother of thirteen whose husband and son are both sitting in. This woman is so devoted to the strike that she walks to the Pengelly Building every snowy day in a pair of canvas shoes. Finally a nurse orders her to wrap newspapers around the canvas sneakers and gives her rubber bands to secure the improvised insulation. The Auxiliary cranks out union leaflets on the mimeograph machine, leads labor history and public speaking classes, organizes fundraising dances, puts on plays, and screens movies, including Charlie Chaplin's *Modern Times*, a dark satire of industrial life. With its famous scene of Chaplin trapped in a set of gears, *Modern Times* portrays the factory worker as a component of his machine—just another interchangeable, replaceable, disposable part. It's a movie that resonates with the families of men who have gone on strike because their bodies cannot keep up with the inhuman pace of the assembly line.

As a woman taking part in a dispute between men, Genora has to ensure she is not regarded as either too feminine or too masculine. If she looks too feminine, she will be seen as being "on the make"—possibly out to steal a striker from his wife. So she doesn't wear makeup or curl her hair and tells off men who make advances. On the other hand, if she comes across as too masculine, she is usurping a man's role in the strike and, maybe eventually, on the job.

A social worker visits Genora's apartment, which is on the top floor of her mother's house, while Genora is at the Pengelly Building. "Why aren't you in school?" the social worker asks Genora's six-year-old, who is in his grandmother's care.

"I'm on strike duty, watching my little brother until my grandmother comes upstairs," the boy says.

"What do you mean, you are on strike duty?"

"Well, our fathers and our whole family is out on strike and we have got to win this strike and this is my strike duty."

And so the word goes around that Ladies' Auxiliary members neglect their children and encourage their truancy. But in an interview with the *Flint Journal* for an article titled "Women Give Their Views of

GM executives William Knudsen, Alfred P. Sloan, C. S. Mott, and Charles Barth, Flint, 1927.

AFL president William Green, labor secretary Frances Perkins, and United Mine Workers president John L. Lewis outside the White House, 1935.

Strike organizer Bud Simons leans out a window to shake hands with UAWA vice president Wyndham Mortimer.

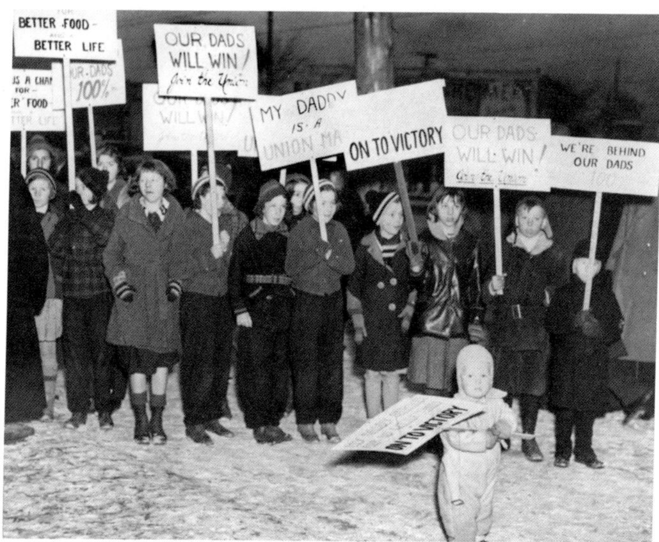

Strikers' children on the picket line.

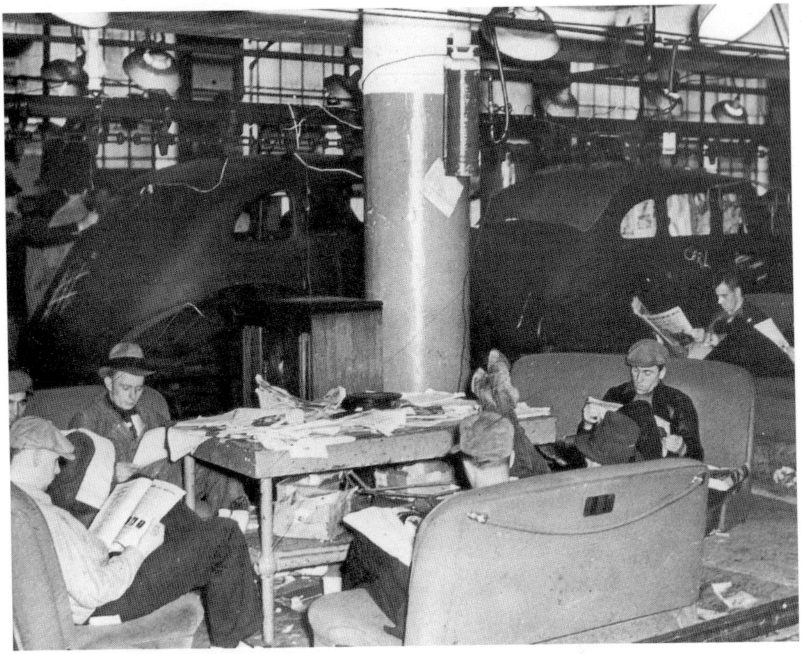

Sit-downers pass the time in Fisher One by reading newspapers.

Organizer Bud Simons (right) and other strikers hang an effigy of a "scab" out a plant window.

A crowd of strike supporters pickets Fisher One.

Michigan National Guardsmen patrol the streets of Flint.

Guardsmen pose with a machine gun outside a General Motors plant.

The "Hillbilly Orchestra," which entertained strikers with ballads about the conflict.

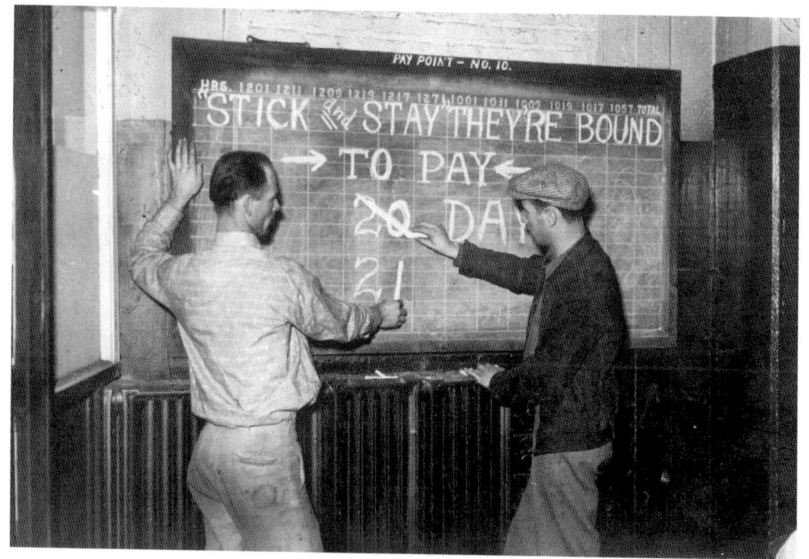

Sit-downers mark the midway point of the strike.

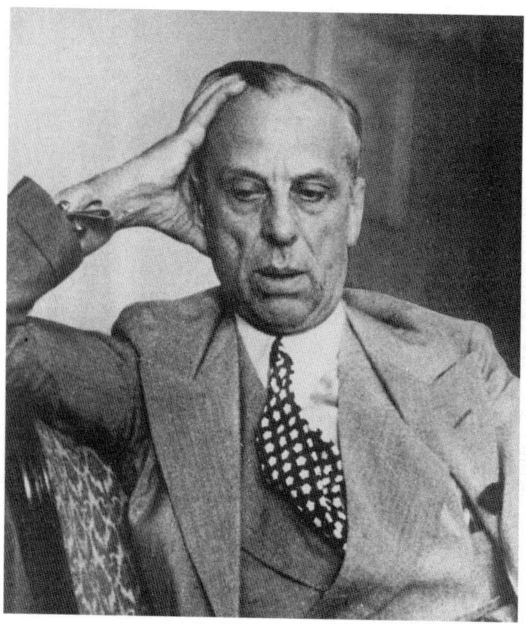

Alfred P. Sloan, around the time of the sit-down strike.

The Women's Emergency Brigade, after smashing windows in Chevy Nine to allow tear gas to escape.

Michigan governor Frank Murphy (center), flanked by the UAWA's Wyndham Mortimer (left) and GM's William Knudsen (right), oversees the signing of an agreement ending the sit-down strike.

Sit-downers celebrate the end of the strike.

Striker Roscoe Van Zandt holds an American flag as he leads victorious sit-downers out of Chevy Four.

Strike Controversy," Genora presents herself as a defender of marriage and the home. General Motors is destroying families by driving men so hard they are too exhausted to participate in family life, she says.

"My husband is a young man grown old from the speed-up of the assembly line," Genora tells the newspaper. "He has done his part and it ruined him. I have seen him come home at night when the new models were just starting, so tired he couldn't even eat. He has gone to bed and awakened the next morning with his hands so swollen he couldn't hold a fork."

The Battle of the Running Bulls transforms the Ladies' Auxiliary from a homemakers' sodality to a quasi-military force. After the women break through the police lines outside Fisher Two, they realize they are just as courageous as the men, and just as capable of standing up to the police—maybe more so, because the "flatfeet," as they call the cops, won't attack women. After the battle, the triumphant women warm themselves at the salamander heaters until after dawn, prepared to repulse another police attack. They sing labor songs, including their own anthem, "The Women's Song of Freedom," to the tune of "Marching Through Georgia."

The men are in the factories sitting in a strike we know,
Holding down production so that we can get more dough.
The Union's organizing, and we'll see that it is so,
Shouting the Union forever!

Hurrah, Hurrah, the Union makes us free
Hurrah, Hurrah, it's all for you and me
Organize your brothers and we'll win the fight you'll see
Shouting the union forever!

The women get together and they formed a mighty throng
Every worker's wife and mom and sister will belong
They will fight beside the men to help the cause along
Shouting the union forever!

"We have got to organize the women," Genora Johnson declares that night. "We have got to have a military formation of the women. If the cops start firing into the men, the women can take the front line ranks. Let them dare to shoot women!"

The next day, fifty mothers, daughters, wives, and sisters gather at the Pengelly Building, in answer to Genora's call for women willing to place their bodies between police and strikers. "It can't be somebody who's weak of heart!" Genora announces. "You can't get hysterical if your sister beside you drops down on a pool of blood. We can't be bothered with having to take care of two people, if one is injured and another is going to go hysterical. Do not sign up for the Women's Brigade, take your role in the strike kitchen, take your role in the first aid station in the Ladies' Auxiliary."

The first to stand is a woman in her seventies.

"This is going to be difficult for you," Genora cautions.

"You can't keep me out," the old woman insists. "My sons work in that factory. My husband worked in that factory before he died, and I have grandsons there."

The women applaud as the grandmother steps forward and signs her name to the register. Next to sign is a teenaged girl.

"My father works in that factory," she says. "My brothers work in that factory. I've got a right to join, too."

Of the thousand women who belong to the Ladies' Auxiliary, four hundred join the Women's Emergency Brigade, as Genora names the paramilitary wing. Every member is issued a red beret and red armband with the white letters "E. B." Genora appoints herself captain, the highest military rank she can think of. Tall, with raw-boned features, a deep background in socialist rhetoric, and an authoritative manner, Genora is a natural commander. She's on a first-name basis with strike leaders most Brigade members have only read about in newspapers. This makes the other women look up to her. Her five lieutenants each command a squadron ready to gather outside a factory at the summons of a phone call.

One of Genora's lieutenants is Nellie Besson. Besson considers the captain "a born leader," with drive and direction, and is flattered by the appointment. She wears her red beret and her armband everywhere, even though she considers the choice of color unfortunate, because of its association with communism. She adopts a military-style costume of jodhpurs, a waist-length jacket, and knee-high boots. And she arms herself. Nellie's father suggests she carry a bar of soap inside a bobby sock, because the police can't claim that's a concealed weapon, but Nellie decides she needs something that can do a little more damage. From the men inside Fisher One she acquires a blackjack, attaching it to a wristlet concealed inside her sleeve so she can flick it out at the first sign of trouble. All the women in the Brigade carry billy clubs, whose handles have been whittled down to fit a female grip. Although they are not allowed to sit down inside the plant, the militarized women believe they're just as important as the men to the strike's success.

"The red beret became a symbol of a new type of woman who was ready to sacrifice her life as the men felt they were gaining the victories that we won from the world's largest corporation," Genora tells the documentary filmmaker Lorraine Gray decades later.

If the National Guard somehow fails to keep the peace, Flint's Spartan women are ready for battle.

CHAPTER 7

"GENERAL MOTORS HAS DOUBLE-CROSSED US!"

FRANK MURPHY THINKS he has a deal to end the sit-down strike. The industrial dispute in Flint has consumed every moment of his fortnight-old governorship. At two-fifty on the morning of Friday, January 15, the doors open in the executive suite on the second floor of the state capitol, where the governor has been sequestered for the past fifteen hours with representatives of General Motors and the United Auto Workers of America. In the room for GM are Knudsen, general counsel John Thomas Smith, and Donaldson Brown, a member of the company's executive committee. Representing the UAWA are Homer Martin, Wyndham Mortimer, and John Brophy, national director of the CIO. Murphy has also invited Frank Dewey, a federal labor conciliator. As the bright chandelier hanging from the conference room's ornate ceiling burns through the wee hours, the union and the company finally reach an agreement. The strikers will evacuate the plants by Sunday. In return, GM agrees not to move any machinery out of the plants and to begin negotiating with the union for fifteen days, beginning on Monday, on the issues detailed in Martin's January 4 letter: wages, seniority, line speed, and the UAWA's status as the exclusive representative of all GM workers in collective bargaining.

Murphy steps into the capitol rotunda, where newsmen have been gathered since Thursday morning. To preserve the confidentiality of the negotiations, when he skips out for lunch and supper he locks the doors to the governor's office and refuses to comment to journalists on what's happening inside. Murphy does, however, express annoyance when reporters inform him that Secretary of Labor Perkins has announced that "progress is being made" in the strike. Murphy never authorized such a statement. He wants to demonstrate that he can solve his own state's problems without federal help. Since dispatching the National Guard to Flint, the governor has received three thousand telegrams from all over the country praising his handling of the disorder. Some have compared it to Calvin Coolidge's settlement of the Boston Police Strike in 1919, when he was governor of Massachusetts. Coolidge's actions earned him a vice presidential nomination. The newspapers are calling Murphy a "great figure," a candidate for the cabinet or the presidency. At a dinner of Michigan Democrats in Washington, DC, Representative John Dingell of Detroit declares that Murphy's election as president is "a certainty" if he settles the strike.

In a 4:00 a.m. hallway news conference, Murphy gives the capitol press corps the terms of what he calls a "truce," then announces that he plans to withdraw the National Guard from Flint. "In my opinion, there is little to be concerned about now," Murphy says. "The National Guard will be demobilized when I am absolutely certain there will be no violence or any repetition of what occurred Monday night, and I am confident there will be no more."

"What about the warrants that have been issued in connection with the riot?" a reporter asks.

"Those matters rest with the responsible authorities," the governor responds.

"Which authorities?"

"The authorities of Flint."

At that moment eleven strikers are being held in the Genesee County Jail, and five more are under arrest at Hurley Hospital, where they are recuperating from gunshot wounds. Fearing that the strikers' union brothers will try to free them—especially after learning of the arrival of a thousand strike sympathizers from Kentucky, Indiana, and Ohio—Sheriff Wolcott is refusing the prisoners any visitors. A special squad of deputies armed with tear gas, shotguns, and pistols guards the jail round the clock. Wolcott has asked hardware stores to stop selling guns and has installed floodlights on streets surrounding the jail, to discourage attackers.

"What about the injunction proceedings?" asks another reporter, referring to the court order to evacuate the plants, which is seemingly rendered moot by Murphy's truce.

"That is a matter I do not care to discuss," Murphy replies.

In contrast to the tense, tired governor, Homer Martin is in a good mood. All day and night, the UAWA president has been wisecracking with reporters during recesses.

Once the truce is announced, the *Flint Auto Worker* rushes to print with a "Strike Extra." "Victory Is Ours," its headline declares in seventy-two-point type. The lead story begins: "The road to victory for the auto workers was cleared today of its chief obstacle with the announcement that General Motors has signed a truce agreement with the United Automobile Workers of America after a lengthy conference Thursday in the Governor's office in Lansing."

Indeed, the agreement appears to be a victory for the union. General Motors is getting back something it has always had: its auto plants. The UAWA is getting something it has never had: the opportunity to negotiate a company-wide deal with GM, as the representative of all its members in every plant.

The sit-down has driven General Motors to accept this position. Half the company's plants are closed, either because they're occupied by strikers or because they lack parts produced by occupied plants. If the strike lasts another week, every plant will close, throwing 135,000 employees out of work. The new hard-top models have created so much demand among dealers that GM planned to step up production in January to 24,000 cars and trucks per month. Now, the company will produce a third of that. Unless the strike is settled, GM will have to stop deliveries to dealers by the end of the month. A letter to Murphy, signed by the GM negotiators, and released to the public, can hardly be seen as anything other than a capitulation, since it commits the company to a course it flatly rejected just eleven days earlier:

"It having been agreed that all the plants now occupied by sit-down strikers including Fisher plants No. 1 and 2 at Flint, Guide Lamp plant at Anderson, [Indiana], Cadillac and Fleetwood plants at Detroit, will be immediately evacuated, General Motors corporation representatives will meet on Monday, January 18 at 11 a.m. at its Detroit office with the representatives of the International Union, United Automobile Workers of America, for the purpose of bargaining collectively on the proposals contained in the letter from the international union dated Jan. 4, 1937. Negotiations will be conducted frankly and without prejudice to anyone. The corporation reiterates its policy that in respect of its continuing operations, there will be no discrimination against any employees because of union affiliation."

Many peace treaties, especially those that end civil conflicts, include an amnesty for the combatants. The winners refrain from punishing the losers, so both sides can live together without bitterness afterwards. In its letter, GM has pledged not to fire union members. Murphy tries to prevent local law enforcement, which the union sees as an ally of GM, from prosecuting strikers involved in the Battle of the Running Bulls. On Friday afternoon, after recovering from his all-night meeting, the governor summons the Genesee County prosecutor, Joseph R. Joseph, and Sheriff Wolcott to his office. The union has already sought to prevent Joseph from prosecuting strikers, because he owns sixty shares of GM stock.

At least don't put those guys in the hospital on trial, Murphy implores Joseph. Don't add incrimination to injury. We're so close to getting this settled, and I'd hate for you to do anything that might throw a wrench into these negotiations next week. The entire country is counting on a settlement, everyone from the president on down. Getting the world's largest corporation up and running again doesn't just affect Michigan's well-being, it affects the entire country.

Murphy tells the prosecutor and the sheriff that the strike is Michigan's problem to solve. The president believes the state authorities are handling this just as well as the federal authorities could.

Roosevelt won't get involved until Murphy has exhausted every effort. Every official, both state and local, has to do his part.

Joseph agrees to drop the charges against the injured men. He explains to the *Flint Journal* that Murphy has convinced him that the actions of his little countywide office now have national consequences: "I do not want to be in the position of interfering in any matter which affects the lives and savings of thousands of workers, and if my granting the governor this request will help, I am glad to comply," the prosecutor says.

Also at Murphy's insistence, Wolcott agrees not to serve three hundred warrants for criminal syndicalism, malicious destruction of property while rioting, kidnapping (for trapping the plant police in the ladies' bathroom), and felonious assault. The warrants issued for "John Doe" cover every striker inside Fisher Two during the battle.

However, Joseph insists on prosecuting four union officials he considers "outside agitators": Victor Reuther, Roy Reuther, Bob Travis, and Henry Kraus. He believes the union leaders are radicals who turned a peaceful strike violent by preying on the psyches of frustrated men: "I realize that the sit-down strikers were undergoing mental and physical hardships, and those persons were on edge, but they were maintaining a passive resistance to obtain their objective in the strike and I have every reason to believe that this passive and peaceful resistance would have been maintained had it not been for the frenzied appeals of these men," Joseph tells the press. "In their mental condition, it took the propaganda of these defendants to incite them to riot which but for the Grace of God, would have resulted in more terrible bloodshed."

On the afternoon of Joseph's meeting with Murphy, the four are arraigned on charges of unlawful assembly and malicious destruction of property. They each post a five-hundred-dollar bond and are ordered to return for a hearing the following week.

In the interest of settling the strike, Murphy has done Joseph a political favor: he can refrain from prosecuting any of his own constituents, while at the same time appearing to stand up for law and order by blaming the Battle of the Running Bulls on out-of-town Reds. A local politician can't ask for anything more.

The UAWA's number-one goal is to be recognized as the sole bargaining agent for every GM employee, in every GM plant. To the union's way of thinking, collective bargaining is meaningless unless it lifts the fortunes of every worker. This is not a condition of the truce, however. At a press conference in Washington, John L. Lewis declares that the CIO will insist on the UAWA as the "exclusive bargaining agency" in the upcoming negotiations. But Alfred P. Sloan has previously declared that the company will not allow "labor dictators" to run its plants and "will not recognize any union as the sole bargaining agency for its workers."

The issue of the union becoming the exclusive bargaining agent "was discussed but it is not part of our agreement with Governor Murphy," Knudsen tells reporters. "We have not granted that power to the U.A.W.A. We don't believe in that. Our idea is that there should be non-exclusive collective bargaining. Mr. Lewis is reported to have said that he must have the exclusive bargaining power. That is not my idea of how to proceed and it would be a poor way to bargain."

On this point Murphy's truce falls apart: the Flint Alliance wants to participate in the negotiations too. At the same time Murphy is conducting his parley in Lansing, the Flint Alliance holds a meeting at the IMA Auditorium with four thousand autoworkers in attendance—ten times the number of strikers inside the occupied plants. Because of those numbers, the Alliance considers itself the true voice of Flint's autoworkers. In his speech, George Boysen, the Alliance's chairman, says that 95 percent of the people of Flint condemn the tactics of the sit-down strikers. If Flint really supported the strike, the UAWA would not have had to import pickets from all over the Middle West.

"There are a great many men—agitators—in Flint," Boysen says. "I don't think they have the right by any law to keep you out of your jobs. It is unheard of for a small group to put over forty thousand men out of work. It's not America's way of doing things."

A UAWA member, a Buick employee, tries to mount the stage to plead the union's case. He is told that the gathering is not an occasion for debate. Alliance members surround the man and hoot him down with catcalls of "Throw him out!"

Finally, a Buick sheet-metal worker and part-time pastor who is loyal to GM takes the podium. "We appeal to God Almighty to put the wheels back in motion so that we can go back to work," he shouts. "Let us settle this strike over the arbitration table and not over the workingman's dinner pail. That's the American Way. Now, I want everyone who wants to go back to work to stand right now."

The crowded bleachers squeak as the entire mass of merchants and workmen rise to endorse this appeal to God, patriotism, and the right to work. Convinced by this demonstration that the Alliance has the support of as many or more workers as the union, Boysen fires off a telegram to Knudsen asking GM to include the Alliance in the upcoming negotiations.

"By far the greatest majority of General Motors employees in Flint will not be represented at the conference with United Auto Workers union officials starting Monday," he writes. "These employees do not want to be represented by spokesmen of the United Auto Workers union. . . . The great majority of workers are requesting an assurance from you that their position will not be overlooked in your dealings with this small group."

Knudsen wires back that "the rights of every man working for General Motors is respected" and that "every effort will be made to get the men back to work as soon as possible."

That corporate boilerplate does not include the promise of a meeting, so the UAWA goes ahead with its preparations to evacuate the plants on Sunday. The workers at the Fleetwood plant in Detroit leave on Saturday, accompanied by a marching band from Cleveland; the band heads next to Flint to herald the evacuations of Fisher One and Fisher Two. In Anderson, Indiana, workers ending their sit-down are met outside the gates by 150 police officers, accompanied by supervisors and plant guards, who smash their wooden picket headquarters and tell them no further strikes will be tolerated. (The workers at Fisher Cleveland, who started all this, evacuated the plant on New Year's Eve, because of the difficulty of feeding sit-downers, but continue their strike with nonstop picketing.)

Inside Fisher Two, Francis O'Rourke is thrilled to be going home after nearly three weeks of sleeping on car seats and bathing in a sink.

"Extra! Extra! Men are to evacuate plants," he writes in his diary. "There will be a celebration . . . and Sunday evening, we will all be in our homes and are the boys pleased? I wonder how the furniture looks and the children's toys. I'll be so glad to be with them again. Boy, I'm even anxious to see Mike (Mike is the cat)."

On the Sunday morning of the evacuation, the men scrub their faces, shave their strike beards, shine their shoes, and pull on neckties. They pack their belongings into bundles and set about cleaning up the plants so that when work resumes, the shop floors will look exactly as they did at the moment the assembly lines halted. The morning is drizzly and gray, but hundreds of union members and their families gather outside the gates of Fisher One, which will be the first plant to empty out. They're attracted by the band, by the chance to march out with the strikers, and by a celebratory roast chicken dinner the strike kitchen has prepared for this historic moment. By eleven o'clock, the hour the strikers have agreed to leave, nearly five thousand people are mobbing Saginaw Street's sidewalks.

But the strikers don't leave the plants.

Shortly before the deadline, Bill Lawrence, a reporter for the United Press, approaches Henry Kraus in the vestibule of the Pengelly Building. Lawrencc has just been in the offices of the Flint Alliance on Saginaw Street, where he's seen a press release from Boysen announcing that Knudsen will meet with the group on Tuesday. A GM PR man tells him he can take a copy, as long as he doesn't publish it until after the evacuation. That doesn't mean he can't show it to Travis, though.

"Where's Bob?" Lawrence asks Kraus.

"Can't you ever give a guy some peace?" Kraus snaps back. He is feeling deflated about the end of the strike, and with it, the end of his crusading newspaper, the *Flint Auto Worker*.

"But I've got something," Lawrence insists.

Persuaded by Lawrence's urgency, Kraus leads him to Travis. The reporter hands the labor leader the press release and asks him for a comment. Immediately grasping the significance of a meeting between GM and the Flint Alliance, Travis excuses himself and steps into the mimeograph room. There, he places a long-distance call to Homer Martin, who is attending a victory celebration at Cass Technical High School in Detroit.

"Homer, I just got hold of something important," Travis tells his union's president. "It's a publicity release that Boysen's giving out tonight. Knudsen's agreed to meet with the Flint Alliance on Tuesday."

Martin doesn't seem bothered. He has already told the press that he expects to negotiate with GM only on behalf of UAWA members. Travis is bothered, though. If GM is recognizing the Flint Alliance, which isn't even a worker's organization, how can the UAWA negotiate for exclusive representation? The issue will be off the table before the talks even begin.

"I don't think that means anything," Martin tells Travis. "What's the difference if they have their meeting? It can't have any real effect. I think you ought to go ahead with your plans."

"Like hell I will!" Travis shouts. He bangs down the receiver and places another call to the same number. This time, he asks for CIO director John Brophy. Travis reads Boysen's message to Knudsen:

"We earnestly request an appointment with you at nine o'clock Tuesday morning, if possible, for a committee of twelve members of the Flint Alliance on which will be representatives of the vast majority of workmen of each of our Flint plants. The purpose of this meeting will be to discuss collective bargaining as it affects the great majority of your employees."

Then, he reads Knudsen's response: "We shall notify you as soon as possible as to a time and place for a meeting."

Brophy agrees that this is a double-cross, a violation of the settlement brokered by the governor, in which both sides agreed to negotiate for fifteen days. Hanging up the phone, he pushes his way to the podium in the Cass Tech auditorium, where he tells Martin, "We've got to see the governor right away; this changes everything."

In Flint, Travis dispatches a "runner" from the Pengelly Building to Fisher One with a note for Wyndham Mortimer, who is overseeing the evacuation. Mort calls a meeting of the strikers inside the plant, explains the "double-cross," and suggests calling off the evacuation. The men cheer.

"Yeah, man, that's the stuff!" one shouts. "We stuck it out this long, let's stick till we win!"

Ten minutes after the evacuation is scheduled to begin, Mort steps outside into the rain and tells the crowd of five thousand, which includes all the strikers' wives and children, that the men will be staying inside the plant. The White Motor Band from Cleveland, which had been prepared to play a buoyant march as it led the strikers through the gates, instead strikes up "The Star-Spangled Banner." While the band plays, the strikers hang an American flag out a window. Then they appear with dummies labeled "GM Stoolpigeon," and "Boysen Stoolpigeon." They beat the stuffing out of both with hammers, finally beheading the Boysen effigy, so its body drops to the ground.

"We've been double-crossed," Mort announces from a sound car parked on Saginaw Street. "Word has come to us that General Motors is receiving overtures from the Flint Alliance to bargain with others. The men inside this plant have just voted unanimously to remain inside until General Motors agrees to bargain collectively with our union only."

When Mort announces another meeting at Fisher Two, the crowd disperses, rushing to their cars to make the three-and-a-half-mile drive between the factories. When they arrive, they hear Victor Reuther shouting from a union sound car.

"General Motors has double-crossed us again!" Reuther hollers. "They and our representatives entered into an agreement in Governor Murphy's office on which to carry out negotiations. They took their solemn oath to abide by that agreement. Now, they have broken it by accepting Boysen and his Flint Alliance into the negotiations. We are going to stay in the plants until General Motors comes across!"

After christening the square outside the plant 'Bulls Run,' "for it was here that we put the bulls on the run," Reuther hands the microphone to Nelson Wooley, a striker who was shot in the battle.

"Tell us how it feels to get shot," Reuther asks Wooley.

"You don't feel anything for twenty-four hours, and then it begins to get sore," Wooley says.

Inside Fisher Two, Francis O'Rourke feels "discouraged" and "heart-sick" at the news that he won't be going home to his wife and children that night, but he doesn't blame the union. "General Motors would not keep an honest agreement. Boysen and his Flint Alliance. This thing would have been settled long ago and we would have been back at our jobs if not for them."

The rest of the men inside Fisher Two feel the same way. They hang a Boysen from the windows, after adding another straw man labeled "Papa Sloan."

After a meeting with the UAWA strategy committee, Homer Martin also adopts the line that the Flint Alliance is to blame for the truce's collapse. That night, he addresses a packed meeting at the Pengelly Building attended by men and their families who have quickly gotten over any disappointment over the strike's continuing and now feel a determination to win, however long that will take.

"It is impossible to have more than one collective bargaining agency determining wages and working conditions of employees in the same group," Martin tells the crowd. "One part of an assembly line cannot be on a six-hour day while an adjoining part of the line or a scattering of workers along the line is on an eight-hour day. There is no feasible method of collective bargaining other than through unified representation. That being true, to say the corporation will not recognize any union to be the sole bargaining agency is in fact to say, 'We refuse to bargain with our employees altogether.'"

The following morning, Monday, January 18, Martin is back in Detroit, where he appears at General Motors headquarters, accompanied by Brophy and Mortimer, at eleven, the time scheduled for the truce conference. The meeting lasts five minutes. It consists of Knudsen and two associates handing the union representatives a formal statement, then leaving the conference room as soon as the UAWA men finish reading it. Each side blames the other for breaking Murphy's agreement: the union charges that the company's agreement to meet with the Flint Alliance is a violation; the company won't negotiate until the strikers leave its plants.

"With reference to the Flint Alliance, all communications received and answers sent have been published," GM's statement reads. "No commitment has been made for a meeting at a definite time and place, but we have not, at Lansing or anywhere else, made a guarantee that we would not talk to anyone other than the United Automobile Workers of America.

"Suffice to say that the agreement made by the union with the governor at Lansing last Thursday to evacuate the plant by Monday as a conditioning of bargaining has not been kept as the strikers have not left the plants in Flint."

So that's that. Three days after Murphy thinks he's settled the strike, the Lansing Truce is null and void. Martin leaves GM headquarters, telling reporters, "The conference is over."

Murphy, who is at home in Detroit, cancels plans to travel to Washington for President Roosevelt's inauguration. The governor also cancels the National Guard's demobilization, even as guardsmen are packing up and preparing to return home. The already miserable men—forty-four are in the hospital with the flu—are instead ordered out of their lodgings for further drill. After speaking with Frances Perkins on the telephone, Murphy plans another trip to Washington, not for the inauguration, where he had hoped to receive Roosevelt's congratulations for settling the strike, but to the Labor Department, for a meeting with Frances Perkins and John L. Lewis. He plans to be on his way back to Michigan before the president is sworn in for a second term at noon Wednesday.

"These difficulties in the days of mass production are no longer private affairs," Murphy tells the press before boarding the Pennsylvania Railroad's 6:21 p.m. *Red Arrow* train in Detroit's Michigan Central Station, bound for Washington. "The government must play a helpful part. Disorder, lawlessness and widespread suffering that will follow the government simply cannot tolerate."

That means the federal government. A strike that has immobilized the nation's most important company has turned out to be too big for a rookie governor to handle on his own.

CHAPTER 8

MISS PERKINS AND MR. SLOAN

Frances perkins is a distinctive figure. The first woman ever to serve in a presidential cabinet, the secretary of labor is seen always wearing a black dress, pearls, and her trademark black tricorne. Early in her career, she concluded that, at least for her, a matronly appearance wins the confidence of the men in whose world she operates.

Industrial unionism is certainly a man's world, but the sit-downers could have no better ally in Washington than Perkins. A well-educated daughter of the New England gentry, Perkins is cut from the same cloth as Eleanor Roosevelt, and even speaks with the same transatlantic accent, pronouncing her job as "secretary of lay-buh." The newspapers refer to the secretary as "Miss Perkins." Although she is married and has an adult daughter, Perkins still uses her maiden name professionally, which detractors see as further evidence of her radicalism.

After graduating from Mount Holyoke College, near her hometown of Worcester, Massachusetts, Perkins moves to Lake Forest, Illinois, to teach science at a women's college. But as a volunteer at Jane Addams's Hull House in nearby Chicago, Perkins learns that her passion is social work, not teaching. At Hull House, Perkins meets the muckraking novelist Upton Sinclair, author of *The Jungle*, and the labor leader Sidney Hillman, future leader of the International Ladies Garment Workers Union. She encounters a settlement house founder's son, who tells her that the only solution to urban poverty is "the organization of working people into trade unions," because unions negotiate wages that enable laborers to live without resorting to charity or government aid. In Chicago, Perkins also learns the trick of shaming employers into paying immigrant workers by threatening to tell the employers' landlords that they're deadbeats.

Embarking on a career as a social worker, Perkins next goes to Philadelphia to rescue girls from prostitution, then to New York, where she earns a degree from Columbia University and takes a job with the National Consumers League, an organization which exposes companies that employ child labor and force women to work long hours for low wages. During this period of political awakening, Perkins joins the Socialist Party. (Later, she, like the sit-down strike's organizers, will attempt to conceal this affiliation.)

On the afternoon of March 25, 1911, Perkins is drinking tea with a wealthy patron on Washington Square, when her hostess's butler informs the women that the screams and fire bells they're hearing from the street are responses to a fire at a nearby clothing manufacturer, the Triangle Shirtwaist Factory. Rushing outside, Perkins witnesses dozens of young women jumping from the high windows—the only way to escape the fire, since the doors have been locked to prevent the employees from leaving the factory floor.

In the aftermath of the fire, which claims 146 lives, Perkins is appointed executive director of a Committee on Safety, formed by New York State to advocate for labor and workplace safety laws. The young reformer is recommended for the post by former president Theodore Roosevelt. In alliance with Tammany Hall Democrats, some of whose constituents have been killed in the disaster, Perkins successfully lobbies the legislature to pass a host of labor laws: limiting women's workweeks to fifty-four hours, banning labor for children under fourteen, and requiring sprinklers, fire escapes, fire drills, and occupancy limits in factories. Perkins understands that employers hold the power in the workplace and believes that relations between capital and labor can only be brought into balance through unionization and government activism. As she writes to the *New York Times* in support of a wagon drivers' strike: "That any group of men should be obliged to strike for an eleven-hour work day in this enlightened age, when the eight-hour day is already established as the attainable standard, seems to us to indicate that in the cause of social progress the fair-minded members of the community should see to it that the demand of the striking expressmen for a shorter working day is granted."

As politicians seek to bring newly enfranchised women into government, Governor Al Smith appoints Perkins to the New York State Industrial Commission, which oversees the workman's compensation program, in 1919. In 1929, Smith's successor, Franklin D. Roosevelt, names her to run the Industrial Board, where she supervises factory inspectors. When Roosevelt is elected president, in 1932, he invites Perkins to join his cabinet. Before accepting she asks Roosevelt to include a platform of progressive labor legislation in his New Deal: ending child labor, an eight-hour day to spread work more widely, a minimum wage, and nationwide systems of workmen's compensation, unemployment insurance, and Social Security. Roosevelt agrees, although he worries that a minimum wage is unconstitutional.

The labor movement Perkins has been appointed to oversee is at its lowest ebb in decades. The American Federation of Labor, which had four million members in 1919, has been reduced to half that number during the Depression. Believing that unions are a "natural and good" institution in an industrial economy, Perkins convenes a conference of seventy-five labor leaders during her first year in office, and regularly attends AFL meetings.

In one of Perkins's first crises as secretary, she faces a situation similar to what Murphy is facing in Flint. During a violent longshoreman's strike in San Francisco in the summer of 1934, police kill unionists who are trying to prevent strikebreakers from moving goods out of the port. In response, workers all over the city walk off the job. San Francisco grinds to halt. Roosevelt is in the Pacific, touring the Third Fleet. Secretary of State Cordell Hull, running the government in the president's absence, wants to deploy federal troops stationed at the Presidio. Fearing bloodshed, which would embitter the workers even further, Perkins cables FDR, suggesting arbitration instead. Roosevelt agrees. Arbitration wins the longshoremen a hiring hall and better wages from the steamship companies. Perkins settles the strike with negotiation rather than force, the same strategy Murphy is trying to follow for resolving the sit-down.

"For years, labor never had a chance," Perkins tells the *New York Times* in 1934. "Then in March a year ago, a vast change came about. In the midst of the catastrophe to our economic life the New Deal was inaugurated. A different point of view was established. Labor and capital were put on an equal footing and a new technique was worked out to settle the differences which might arise between the two great classes which make up industry."

As pro-labor New Deal Democrats, Perkins and Murphy have plenty in common, especially a desire to end the sit-down in Flint without force. They talk about the strike on the phone every night between eleven-thirty and midnight. But the negotiations that Perkins convenes in Washington accomplish no more than Murphy's talks in Lansing, because of the intransigence and egotism of the principals on each side: the captain of labor, John L. Lewis, and the captain of industry, Alfred P. Sloan.

Murphy steps off the train in Washington on January 18, two days before the inauguration, and heads immediately to Perkins's office at the Labor Department's brand-new headquarters on Fourteenth Street, built in the Classical Revival style. Lewis is waiting there for him. Murphy's goal is to persuade the CIO president to evacuate Fisher One and Fisher Two, since that's the company's bottom-line condition for negotiating. He tries two gambits. First, the governor offers to maintain a National Guard buffer around the plants, so that they cannot produce automobiles during the negotiations. Lewis turns this down. Lewis also turns down a proposal to hold a union representation election, under the auspices of the National Labor Relations Board. Possession of the plants is the union's greatest tactical advantage. Lewis, who is adamant that the UAWA should become the sole bargaining agent of GM's autoworkers, is not going to give up his occupied territory to risk a vote that might reveal the UAWA actually represents only a minority of workers.

Perkins thinks she can broker a settlement if she can just get Sloan and Lewis in the same room. But Sloan refuses, sticking to the company line of not negotiating with the union as long as it occupies his factories. So Perkins invites the chairman to Washington for a private meeting, on Inauguration Day.

"We can't do that," Sloan protests over a long-distance call from GM headquarters in New York. "We can't come to Washington. It'll be known that we're there. The men will get hold of it and they'll think we're giving in to the government. We've got to ride this out. We've just got to be firm. If this crazy government we've got here will just send some troops and put them out of the shops, it'll be all right. The local police aren't powerful enough to do it. If they just put them out of the shops, we can handle it all right. It'll be all right if they just leave the shops. That we can't tolerate. And we can't operate under those conditions. But once they're out, then we can settle things."

"You don't mean you're going to recognize the union?" Perkins asks.

"Well no, not settle it like that, but we'll talk things over with some of the men, or with the government. But we're not going to talk to anyone about anything now. We've said so. We won't even look at the situation until they go home. Then we'll see what we'll do next. That's all that's necessary. If they hear we've gone to Washington, it will stir up hopes in their minds."

"Well," Perkins proposes, shifting into the maternal language that reassures powerful men, "you come down here and nobody will know you're here, Mr. Sloan. I'll guarantee you that. I'll see that nobody knows about it. Come on Inauguration Day. The newspapermen will have their attentions all focused on the White House, on the Capitol, on the parade. They won't be looking around at what's happening in the Secretary of Labor's office. They won't know you're here. They won't know anything about it. I certainly won't tell. You can rest assured of that." Sloan agrees to come incognito.

In an effort to keep the meeting secret, Perkins dispatches her chauffeur to Union Station in a private car to pick up the GM delegation, which consists of Sloan, Knudsen, and Donaldson Brown, the vice chairman of the GM board of directors. Meanwhile, she rides in the inaugural procession and appears on the reviewing stand with the president.

"I'll tell you a secret," Perkins whispers to Roosevelt, as they watch the parade. "I hope I can trust you not to repeat it. Keep it to yourself."

Roosevelt loves gossip. He laughs to indicate he wants to hear more.

"I have some of the people from General Motors coming to see me today, and I'm going to slip right away now out the back door of the White House and am going to meet them privately. Nobody is to know it. I have promised that no one will know they're here. I can keep that promise. It's very important that we should. I'm hoping we can make some headway toward the settlement of this strike."

"Good, all right," Roosevelt says approvingly. "I won't say a word."

Perkins and Murphy meet the General Motors executives at an office on G Street, where she spends the next two hours trying to extract some concession, any concession, that might persuade the men to leave the plant.

"Labor costs in an automobile is only fourteen percent of the costs of an automobile," she lectures, trying to convince the men that accepting a union would not put GM at a competitive disadvantage. "You could raise the price of labor without affecting that fourteen percent more than a fraction. That's not true in all industries. In coal, the labor cost is seventy-seven percent."

Knudsen is a car guy. He tells Perkins, "I've got to go back to Detroit and make automobiles. I can make automobiles under any labor policy. I don't care what it is. Just let the other people make the labor policy. I'll make the automobiles."

(Knudsen will later become famous as the "dollar-a-year man" who oversees war production during World War II, transforming American industry into the "Arsenal of Democracy.")

Sloan, on the other hand, is a finance guy, the other half of an eternal dichotomy in the auto industry's boardrooms. He started his automotive career as president of a company that produced wheel bearings for Ford and GM automobiles. After its merger with GM, he created the General Motors Acceptance Corporation, the company's credit bureau: enabling customers to buy cars on the installment plan helped GM surpass Ford as the nation's most popular automaker.

Sloan is immovable. "My recognition of the union, or any dealing with the union, will almost immediately, within a very short time, raise our labor costs to the point that we won't be able to compete in the general market, not only with other cars, but with other things that would satisfy the American people, other than a car," he insists.

Sloan is amiable enough, but Perkins finds him stiff-necked and inflexible on the point of meeting with the UAWA. No, Sloan says, GM won't accept the union as the exclusive bargaining unit. GM *might* recognize the union's right to represent its own members. But the company won't even discuss that until it gets its plants back.

Perkins feels she has accomplished nothing that afternoon, except perhaps breaking the ice with GM's leadership and providing a basis for future discussions. To make matters worse, the press has discovered that Sloan is in Washington. The chairman has blown his cover by traveling to the capital in a fancy private rail car. During the meeting, Perkins is called away to take a phone call from her government chauffeur.

"Private, Miss Perkins?" the chauffeur tells her. "Did they say this had to be private? Do you know how these fellows came down here? They came down in a great big private car, all trimmed with brass trimmings with a little piazzo [*sic*] on the back of it. It's out there in the Pennsylvania Railroad Station drawn right up close on one of the sidings. Anybody can see it. Everybody in the railroad station knows that's the General Motors car. It'll be all over town by night. What did they do that for if they wanted it to be so private?"

The capital press corps is hunting all over Washington for the GM delegation, badgering officials at Labor Department headquarters.

The next day's newspapers report on the meeting. While they don't offer any details, Sloan is unhappy that he's been found out. The chairman is even less happy when his nemesis, John L. Lewis, gives a press conference in which he bombastically condemns both GM and the government. Speaking at the United Mine Workers headquarters at Washington's Fifteenth and Eye Streets to as many reporters as ordinarily cover the president, Lewis declares, "This strike is going to be fought to a successful conclusion. There will not be any half-baked compromises, either in the automobile industry now, or in the steel industry later on. General Motors might as well settle now as later on. The workers I represent are the people Mr. Roosevelt talked about in his inaugural speech yesterday." Lewis is alluding to Roosevelt's now-famous phrase, "I see millions of families trying to live on incomes so meager that the pall of family disaster hangs over them day by day. . . . I see one-third of a nation ill-housed, ill-clad, ill-nourished." Lewis then publicly reminds Roosevelt that labor supported him in his reelection campaign against the same forces of corporate greed—the president's "economic royalists"—that the sit-down strikers are resisting. He demands the president's support in return.

"We have advised the administration through the secretary of labor that for six months the economic royalists represented in General Motors used money and influence to drive the president from the White House," Lewis continues. "The administration asked labor to repel this attack, and labor responded. These same economic royalists now have their fangs in labor. Labor now expects the administration to support it in every legal way in the fight against this rapacious enemy. Labor is on the march for those better things promised by the president. Our council, like Mr. Roosevelt, stands for the proposition of more Americans participating in the bounties of industry. This is no time for neutrality and no time for pussyfooting."

"Are you implying that the Roosevelt administration is pussyfooting?" a reporter asks Lewis.

"That means just what it says," Lewis fires back. "We have made no request to the White House, but labor intervened when the president needed help. We expect this administration to stand with the workers when they are right."

"Has the administration provided any aid?"

"I have not been able to apprise the value of the intervention of Secretary Perkins," Lewis deadpans.

Even more union negotiators are on their way to Washington, where they will remain until General Motors agrees to meet with them, Lewis declares. What Lewis says next, though, ensures that no such meeting will take place. "Both sides will remain armed until there is a settlement," he says. "We will keep the strikers in the plants and General Motors can keep its detectives, guards, strikebreakers, clubs and tear gas."

Lewis knows how to get Sloan's goat. In fact, he loves to impersonate the straight-laced Sloan for reporters, after hours and off the record. He knows Sloan is uptight about having to negotiate with the workingmen who are occupying his company's plants. As Sloan sees it, he has the law on his side, and the government's duty is to enforce the law, so he shouldn't have to be truckling with radical New Dealers just to get his property back. Sloan has never negotiated with the government before, and he's never conducted business with a woman, either. Lewis makes sure that, despite Sloan's desire for secrecy, the press knows he has just done both. Now that his visit to Washington is out in the open, and now that he's been disparaged by Lewis, Sloan feels he has no choice but to hold a press conference of his own.

"We came to Washington at the invitation of Secretary Perkins," Sloan tells the newsmen. "After seeing a transcript of the Lewis press conference, we knew it was useless to discuss further any plans we may have had. It was plain from his statement that it was impossible to get the men out of the plants voluntarily."

Sloan is asked whether he will return to Washington if President Roosevelt requests him to do so. He will. An invitation from the president of the United States is a command. "I do not think at the moment that we can accomplish anything in Washington," Sloan adds. "We must find a solution and we will work day and night to do so." Then Sloan and his men pile into their private rail car for the trip back to

New York. Lewis cracks that Sloan has left Washington because "he feels his intellectual inferiority to me."

If either man hopes to win Roosevelt's public support, he will be disappointed. The president does not like to personally involve himself in labor disputes. He has a labor secretary for that. In this particular dispute, which has captured the nation's attention since the Battle of the Running Bulls, he does not want to be seen as taking sides. Roosevelt can, however, chide both principals for placing their personal pride above the nation's economic interest.

"I think that, in the interests of peace, there come moments when statements, conversations, and headlines are not in order," the president says after Lewis's press conference.

But then Perkins again asks Lewis and Sloan to meet with her in Washington. Lewis says yes. Sloan says no. This time, Roosevelt chastises the chairman. "I was not only disappointed in the refusal of Mr. Sloan to come down here, but I regarded it as a very unfortunate decision on his part," he says.

"Unfortunate for whom, Mr. Sloan?" a reporter asks, eliciting a laugh from the president.

Only the most powerful man in America can scold two men as powerful as Sloan and Lewis, but Roosevelt's admonishments do nothing to restart the negotiations. Sloan takes out another full-page newspaper ad decrying the "widespread" intimidation and "ruthless tactics" that have imperiled the livelihoods of thousands of workers. Despite the efforts of "labor dictators, . . . General Motors will not recognize any union as the sole bargaining agency for its workers . . . [and] General Motors will continue to keep its plants going just as long as we are able to obtain the essential materials from other plants on which we are dependent in order to build our various products."

After that, the chairman is silent.

The strikers are getting no support from Flint's congressman, either. Democrat Andrew Jackson Transue has a "plague on both your houses" attitude toward the strike. He tells Perkins that the strikers represent a minority of GM workers, and he tells Murphy that there is no congressional backing for the strike, save from a progressive member from Wisconsin who makes daily speeches in favor of the sit-down. Indeed, when Lewis visits the office of Speaker of the House William Bankhead, a Democrat from Alabama, to demand his support, Bankhead turns him down, despite having voted for pro-labor legislation, including the Wagner Act.

"Extra! Extra! Sloan walks out of the conferences," Francis O'Rourke writes inside Fisher Two. "I wonder what scheme he intends to use to get us out? I pray for no violence. Each time a conference is broken I have a funny, sick feeling in my stomach. . . . The boys seem to take these broken conferences on the chin and standing up. We have a loud speaker installed now and some of the boys are getting good at the microphone. We have a string quartet who are planning on a minstrel show. We have a ping pong table in the shop now and it is in use continuously. The boys sure get along well for being cooped up here so long. No arguments, no fights, only a bunch of brothers united in the same cause."

As their fate is debated in the White House, in the Capitol, in the Labor Department, in the newspapers, and on the radio, the handful of men who have created this national crisis are trying to maintain their morale. It's been nearly a month, and the confinement and isolation are beginning to wear on the strikers. They're young men, most of them. In fact, Perkins believes GM may have brought the strike on itself by refusing to employ workers over forty, hiring instead "a large group of people at the peak of their physical powers and at the peak of the recklessness." They run on the roofs of the plants, invigorating themselves with cold air and exercise. The security committees make endless rounds of the exits, on guard for the next attack by the bulls. Nonetheless, men are deserting, either slipping out of the plants to visit their wives or going home altogether. Life is becoming even more pinched and penurious for the sit-downers' families. The union pays strikers twenty-five dollars a week, but that's far from enough to meet a family's household expenses, even with food donations. The strikers' families are among nearly ten thousand families on relief in Genesee County, with one hundred and sixty new applications a day, forcing the county to hire three new workers to handle all the cases.

So many strikers defect from Fisher One that at one point, only forty-four men are garrisoning the plant—hardly enough to resist a police attack, although that's unlikely with the National Guard outside. One fed-up striker slips out the window without a required pass, giving the story that he's going to the union hall. In fact, he's defecting to the Flint Alliance's cause. At first, he's roughed up by workers loyal to GM who see him leaving the plant, but when he tells them he's quitting the strike, they let him go.

"Guys would slip out and never come back" striker Ellis Carver later recalls. "And there was nobody seemed to want to replace 'em. . . . Generally, when a guy wanted to get out of there, wanted to slip out, why he didn't want anyone else to know. Because he didn't want nobody to know he was reneging on the other guys. So he kept it kind of quiet, as quiet as he could. But sometimes there'd be two or three of them make a plan to get out of there themselves. They were goin' after lunch or goin' over to bring somethin' over for the guys to eat or somethin,' and cigarettes or somethin' like that, you know."

Sensing the city's strike weariness, General Motors announces plans to reopen its unoccupied plants at least two days a week, so non-strikers can start working and earning money again. It's the company's bid to win its employees' sympathies: the union is preventing you from working, but we're putting you back on the job. The Chevrolet assembly plants will go back to work on Wednesday, January 27. They won't be able to produce cars, but they'll be able to build up parts for the moment the strike ends. That's expected to provide work for 25,000 employees who are off the job because of the strike. Companywide, GM thinks it can bring back 40 percent of its 125,413 idled workers in twenty-five cities, at least on a part-time basis.

"We are trying to do as much as we can for the workmen and their families," Knudsen says. "We are trying to get as many of our people some income as we can."

At a mass meeting outside Fisher Two, Roy Reuther responds by threatening sit-down strikes in the reopened plants.

GM's second ploy to break the deadlock is another injunction to evict the strikers. Knudsen has promised, "We have no intention of exercising our property rights except in a legal way. We are not going to do anything that might taste of ruthlessness or violence or anything of that sort."

At the end of January, GM's lawyers return to Genesee County Circuit Court to file a complaint that the strikers "have threatened personal violence . . . and used vile and abusive language to intimidate fellow employees." Furthermore, "they are damaging and soiling the upholstery in auto bodies by using the seats as beds" and are creating an "unsanitary condition . . . because of the fact that there are not sufficient sanitary facilities to take care of the said employees remaining inside continuously for long periods of time." In fact, the strikers say their numbers have grown so thin that each man has his own private toilet, and they have access to mounds of bathroom tissue left behind in the plant. GM does not just ask that the strikers be evicted; it asks that they be prohibited from picketing. The company's attorneys are requesting an injunction more binding than Judge Black's, one that will specify a deadline for the strikers to leave the plant and a punishment if they don't and that will require the sheriff to clear the plants.

The Flint Alliance does not share the company's commitment to nonviolence. The Alliance holds another rally at the IMA Auditorium, this one attended by eight thousand workers. With a unanimous cry of "Aye," the workers appoint a four-man delegation to go to Lansing and request that Governor Murphy use the National Guard to protect employees who want to go back to work in the occupied plants.

"Will you guarantee all workers full protection in going to and coming from the plants?" Sanford Rasbach, a Buick employee, asks the governor when the delegation meets him in the capitol.

Murphy refuses their request. "I can't give you a direct answer," he says. "It's my intention to avoid bloodshed or violence in connection with the strikes."

One reason Murphy is unwilling to help the Flint Alliance is that he blames the group for destroying the truce he worked out between GM and the UAWA. If the Alliance hadn't tried to participate in the labor negotiations, the strikers would have evacuated the plants.

"You know I helped negotiate peaceful negotiations between General Motors and the strikers," Murphy reminds the delegation. "Unfortunately, those negotiations were disturbed in part by the Flint Alliance. If that had not happened, you might all have been at work now. It is your duty to use forbearance and care."

"I demand a direct answer for the eight thousand workers who sent us here!" Rasbach says bluntly.

"You'll go away without one."

"We want bread and butter and the right to work guaranteed by the state."

"Since the arrival of the militia, there has been no rioting or bloodshed in Flint," Murphy points out. "The president, the secretary of labor and the state government are working for peaceful conciliation. I would advise you not to attempt to inflame your members when you return to Flint. Do you want the state to intervene so workers can go into plants occupied by sit-down strikers?"

Rasbach does not answer, so Murphy continues, "That could not be done without the use of force. The effects of force might be nationwide. There must be no inflammatory action at this time. We first must exhaust every avenue of peace. I am confident a solution along peaceful lines will be reached soon."

"There are two sit-down strikes in Flint: one by the National Guard, and one by the strikers occupying General Motors plants," Rasbach argues, suggesting that both the union and the governor are violating the court injunction and the trespass law. "I want a definitive answer as to whether workers will be protected to the gates of *all* plants."

"Nothing is going to get me to desert my position of working this thing out peacefully," the governor says, trying to remain politic in spite of the peevishness Rasbach has worked up in him by accusing him of breaking the law and acting as a union stooge. "There is not enough power in General Motors, the Flint Alliance or the CIO to force me to leave my position. I know of plans recently in Flint to manufacture riots to get the militia involved. I consider such plans unworthy. You go back and tell your people I sympathize with them. I am anxious that the state maintain an intelligent policy. Men on strike are sincere whether they represent a majority or minority. The Flint Alliance entered the controversy unfortunately. Had it stayed out you might all be working now."

Murphy believes that a chief executive's most important responsibility is maintaining law and order. However, he also believes that enforcing laws to the letter is not always the best way to achieve that goal. The strikers have legitimate grievances. So does the company. So does the sheriff's office. And the Flint Alliance. It is in the interest of peace to prevent the contending sides from attacking each other and instead bring them together to settle their differences at the negotiating table. Another Battle of the Running Bulls could lead to more violence, not just in Michigan but across the nation, now that the strike is being reported on by columnists such as Walter Lippmann—he calls it "a little industrial war"—and debated within Congress and the Roosevelt administration.

The Flint Alliance isn't buying that, not when it believes it has the law, and most GM workers, on its side.

"That was a nice speech but an awfully poor answer," Rasbach tells Murphy.

"May I say you asked an awfully poor question," Murphy retorts. "No agreement was made in the Lansing conference for exclusive bargaining by the UAW. I hope you'll go back to Flint and counsel your members to cooperate with the state and the federal government to permit negotiations toward a peaceful settlement of the strike."

"I can't go back without an answer," Rasbach says.

"You will have to go back."

"Yes, we have to go back. Can I go back and tell ten thousand people that their governor refuses protection?"

"The governor is going to keep this all peaceful."

"All we are asking is that we are protected in accordance with the laws of the state."

"You are going to be."

"But we haven't been," Rasbach finishes.

Frustrated by their inability to persuade the governor to break the strike, the Flint Alliance decides to embark on its own sit-down on the second floor of the capitol's rotunda, outside the governor's office.

"When government does not or will not function for political or other reasons, it may be necessary, to protect the civil rights guaranteed by law, to return to the methods used in the Old West in 1849," says Alliance member George Gilbert.

Murphy tells them to go ahead. He's going home to Detroit for the weekend anyway. If he won't evict the sit-downers from private property, he's certainly not going to evict the Flint Alliance from public property. Before leaving Lansing, though, the governor gives an angry press conference at which he suggests that General Motors is using the Flint Alliance to pressure him into using violence to break the strike.

"I plan to start an investigation to determine whether General Motors is behind a sinister, vicious and skillful plot to compel me to use force in the strike situation," he says. "A committee representing the Flint Alliance has called on me for no good."

As he departs the capitol, Murphy offers a final rebuke to the delegation camped outside his office are "You ought to be ashamed to play with a situation of this kind."

In Washington, Perkins makes yet another attempt to bring Sloan and Lewis together, inviting them to a conference at the Labor Department. Again Lewis says yes, while Sloan says no. Disappointed and frustrated, Perkins announces that she plans to ask Congress for legislation allowing her to subpoena the disputants in labor strikes. "Now I believe that an episode like this must make it clear to the American people that the workers here lost confidence in General Motors," Perkins says.

Perkins has composed a letter to Sloan appealing to his moral sense and his duty to the American people to negotiate an end to the strike; she asks him to follow Christ's Golden Rule of doing unto others as he would have done unto him. But she has not yet posted the letter.

"I think there is a moral challenge involved in this situation," Perkins tells reporters after Sloan's latest rebuff. "Here is the situation: a large number of employees want to meet with their employer. General Motors will not confer while they remain in the plants, calling this a legalistic principle. This is as though I said I would not talk with a man who had parked his car on my property until he took it off, no matter what his reasons for parking it were." General Motors, Perkins says, "has made a great mistake—one of the greatest in their lives by failing to see the moral issue. The people don't expect them to sulk within their tent because someone is conducting a sit-down strike whose legal phases have not been realized. No pattern can be forced upon them to solve the problem. There is no power of subpoena in this department at this time."

When reporters aks Perkins whether President Roosevelt knows she is giving General Motors hell, the secretary demurs. "I'm not giving them hell. Please don't think I gave them hell. However much I think General Motors have failed in their public duty I am still willing to talk to them and explain the situation."

Although they are both, in their own way, members of the Northeastern upper class, Frances Perkins and Alfred P. Sloan Jr. are never going to understand each other. More than any other executive, even Henry Ford, Sloan has transformed automaking from an industry run by tinkerers, inventors, and dreamers to a corporate, technocratic operation. Sloan is from Brooklyn and all his life speaks in a Dead End Kids street accent quite incongruous with his later achievements and lifestyle. Other than that, though, he escapes his origins as quickly as possible, graduating from the Massachusetts Institute of Technology with an engineering degree in only three years. He begins his business career with the Hyatt Roller Bearing Company of Harrison, New Jersey, which sells wheel bearings to Ford and to Weston-Mott, a Flint manufacturer that produces axles for Buick, Oldsmobile, and Cadillac. Sloan sells the company to General Motors for $13.5 million, which not only makes him a wealthy man but brings him into the ranks of GM executives. His rise to the chairmanship begins in 1920, when GM's exuberant founder, Billy Durant, is fired after his final bout of overexpansion and financial adventurism nearly bankrupts the company.

Under Sloan's leadership, General Motors surpasses Ford as the world's leading auto manufacturer. While Ford persistently produces his black Model T, the vehicle that dominated the twentieth century's early agrarian decades, GM rolls out a variety of automobiles that appeal to the new urban middle classes: the "car for every purse" brand ladder that will come to define the company's offerings, from the plebian Chevrolet to the aristocratic Cadillac. One of Sloan's early contributions to GM, titled "Organization Study," details how each of the company's multifarious divisions can operate independently, but nonetheless in an integrated fashion, under the GM umbrella. Never before has anyone assembled a concern so large, with so many factories, so many employees, and so much output.

Sloan is, by his own admission, a "narrow man" with no interests whatsoever outside the business world. A newspaper comparison of Sloan and Ford claims that the GM executive "works every hour," "has no hobbies," "never reads," is "too busy for friends," "never drinks," "doesn't smoke," and "never tells stories." Sloan might be the original organization man, but he dresses nattily in high, starched collars, colorful ties, hand-tooled spats, and tailored suits that flatter his tall, gaunt frame. Perhaps he is so thin because he takes no time for business luncheons, always bringing to work a sandwich wrapped in wax paper, which he eats hurriedly at his desk.

The colorless man who sits atop General Motors turns out to be perfectly attuned to the tastes and attitudes of the prosperous 1920s, the decade that F. Scott Fitzgerald, one of its most popular and flamboyant authors, has nicknamed the Jazz Age. In the 1930s, though, Sloan bitterly resists the changes in politics, business, and labor relations brought about by the Great Depression. He is suspicious of Franklin D. Roosevelt, donating lavishly to Herbert Hoover's reelection campaign, and then joins the Liberty league, the group of anti–New Deal businessmen Roosevelt will denounces the so-called economic royalists. That epithet could not be more different than the nation's attitude toward industrialists in the 1920s, when they were seen as heroic individualists providing Americans with the Good Life. Unsurprisingly, Sloan particularly objects to the New Deal's empowerment of the labor movement. In the eighty-nine branches of the corporate tree in his "Organization Study," none is labeled "United Auto Workers of America." Sloan particularly objects to the Wagner Act, seeing it as the creation of a pandering politician who doesn't understand that businesses operate best when sensible businessmen are given the freedom to make decisions that balance the needs of customers, shareholders, and employees.

"I like Senator Wagner—he is a fine fellow—but, after all, he is only a politician and is in no sense of the word a statesman and, naturally, he has his ear to the ground from the political standpoint," Sloan writes to Pierre du Pont, a former GM president and board member. "I do not blame him for that. . . . He recognizes the number of votes labor has."

Defeated politically on the labor issue, Sloan spends the New Deal years attempting to control his workforce through internal measures. He appoints a director of industrial relations to deal with labor. Under his chairmanship, GM spends nearly $1 million on Pinkerton detectives who infiltrate the plants and report on organizing efforts. Sloan's undercover operations are a deliberate contrast to the labor relations of Henry Ford, who employs an armed goon named Harry Bennett to intimidate union organizers. Public relations is a new profession, but Sloan understands it well enough to see that labor violence would be bad for GM's brand. Working out of GM's New York headquarters, though, Sloan has little contact with, or understanding of, the corporation's Midwestern workforce.

The sit-down strike takes Sloan by surprise, but once the strikers shut down his plants, he becomes the voice of resistance to the union, signing his name to the somewhat paternalistic manifestos that appear in the *Flint Journal* and other regional newspapers. In the most recent, published the day after he rejects Secretary Perkins's latest invitation to meet with Lewis, he declares:

"Efforts have been made to make you believe that General Motors is responsible for the breakdown of negotiations; that we refuse to meet with representatives of our own employees; that we are shirking our moral responsibility; that we have no respect for the public interest. You know this is not true. So, why all these charges? Simply because we refuse to negotiate with a group that holds our plants for ransom without regard to law or justice, thus depriving over 100,000 of our peaceful and law-abiding employees of their inherent right to work. That is the reason and the only reason."

Perkins isn't giving up on Sloan, though. She knows his cooperation is the key to cracking this impasse. So she tries a new tactic. Before confronting Sloan again, she consults with his fellow industrialists to find out what they would consider an acceptable settlement. Myron Taylor, the chairman of US Steel, is currently involved in negotiations with the CIO regarding a proposal that allows unions bargain for their members in the plants while at the same time not requiring any employee to belong to a union—exactly what GM had offered in the Lansing Truce (eventually this arrangement becomes known as the Myron Taylor Labor Formula). During her next weekend trip home to New York, Perkins takes this proposal to Walter Chrysler, meeting the auto executive in his lavish, Circassian walnut–paneled office inside the Chrysler Building. Chrysler seems amenable to the concept.

"Why don't you call up Alfred Sloan and see if he'll agree to it?" Chrysler suggests to Perkins. "But don't let Alfred know where you are. If Alfred thought you were in my office he wouldn't have anything to do with it."

"Why, Mr. Chrysler, I thought you and Mr. Sloan were friends!" says Perkins, surprised.

"Oh, yes, we're good friends, but I don't let him know what I'm doing, and he doesn't let me know what he's doing," Chrysler says. "Alfred's that kind of fellow. If he thinks it's your idea, he'll beat you down on it. I think this would be practical for him."

Using Chrysler's private office line, Perkins telephones Sloan at home. The butler answers. He tells Perkins that Mr. Sloan is not taking phone calls, but she manages to convince Sloan's manservent that it's important for his boss to speak with the secretary of labor. Finally

Sloan comes on the line. Perkins is not surprised by the wait. Sloan has ways of avoiding people he doesn't want to talk to. One is pretending to be even harder of hearing than he actually is.

"I'm sorry that you had trouble getting me," Sloan apologizes, "but I have to keep people off me. The fresh people on the newspapers call me all the time. They'll do anything to get through to my telephone. Even some of these fresh fools from the union call me up. I just have to keep a strict watch around here. I won't even speak to my good friend Walter Chrysler. He tried to call me up the other day."

"You wouldn't speak to Mr. Chrysler?"

Perkins winks at Chrysler. From behind his desk, Chrysler winks back.

"Finally he came over here," Sloan grumbles. "I was very much upset. I thought it was somebody impersonating him. They'll do anything to get a talk with me, get me to commit myself, to say something."

"Well, Mr. Sloan, all I wanted to suggest to you was this. I have been thinking about this a great deal. I have wondered if there was any possible loophole which would make it possible for you to deal with the union in at least a limited way."

"What do you mean, 'limited way'?" Sloan asks edgily.

"Well, with some limitation on their degree of representation."

"Well, I don't see how that would work," Sloan protests. "I would never agree to anything that makes a man join a union. They can work for me any time they want to and they don't have to join a union. I don't think it's fair. I don't think it's American. They don't want to belong to a union. None of them want to."

"Well, now, Mr. Sloan, some of them do," Perkins argues. "We do know that so many thousands of them have joined the union and paid their dues. They had a convention. There were an awful lot of people in it. I don't know how many of the employees of General Motors belong to the union and I won't for one moment say that I believe the figure given by the union itself is necessarily the correct figure. But we know that a great many people do belong to the union. What about them? Haven't they got a right to? The law says they have a right to join unions of their own choice. Where are you going to draw the line?"

"Well, I wouldn't deal with any union unless the men absolutely, bona fide, belonged to it and work for me," Sloan says. "If they work for somebody else, I won't have anything to do with it. I won't deal with anybody who doesn't work for me."

"Well, the officers of the union probably don't work for the General Motors Company. They may work somewhere else."

"That doesn't matter. They've got to work for the General Motors Company. I'm not dealing with people who don't work for General Motors."

Sensing a relaxation in Sloan's "no unions, no matter what attitude," Perkins writes down his proposal to negotiate with UAWA men who work for GM. She doubts the union will accept it, though. As she tells Sloan, the entire point of a union is that officers who specialize in bargaining can negotiate with a company more "courageously" than its own employees. But she'll put it to the union, nonetheless.

"I don't want you to think that I'm going to walk into anything like that," Sloan hedges. "After all, what we do in General Motors will tend to commit the whole automobile industry. It isn't right for me to commit the whole industry. They'll try and press all the others."

"Oh, well, now, Mr. Sloan, you've got to accept something, you know," Perkins wheedles. "I'm not sure the men will accept this, but I want to propose it to them as a possibility, as a basis for the beginning of talks with your company and your people."

"I don't think so. I don't want to do anything."

"Mr. Sloan, I think I'm at liberty to tell you this. I believe that Big Steel is going to deal with them on something along those lines."

Sloan is surprised to hear this, since US Steel has not experienced any labor trouble. So Perkins suggests he call Myron Taylor himself. After he does so, he can reach her at the Cosmopolitan Club, a private women's club on the Upper East Side of Manhattan. Perkins hurries the mile and a half between the Chrysler Building and the club, where she awaits Sloan's call. Her "Ma Perkins" act has not persuaded the curmudgeonly executive to meet with the union, but perhaps he will heed the advice of a fellow industrialist. In fact, Taylor is the first to call Perkins at her club.

"I thought I would like to tell you that a most extraordinary thing has happened," Taylor begins. "Mr. Sloan called me up earlier this afternoon. He, of course, had a great deal to say about the strike they've got on. He asked my opinion of a formula of allowing the union to bargain for their members who worked for the company, but not a general representation."

"That is very interesting, Mr. Taylor. What did you say to him?"

"I said to him about what I said to you, that it was tolerable. Sloan asked my advice as to whether I thought that General Motors could safely proceed in that way. I told him I thought that they could—that some of this was safe for us, but at least it was fair. Why don't you call up Sloan now?"

Perkins calls Sloan back from the Cosmopolitan Club. Just as she hoped, he defers to Taylor, whom he considers to be more experienced in labor relations than he is.

"I should think that if they can endure it, we can endure it," Sloan says. "I think that might be a good thing."

Elated, Perkins heads to Penn Station to catch the Royal Blue to Washington, feeling she has finally engineered a breakthrough in the sit-down strike. She pitches the proposal to Sidney Hillman, the garment workers' union leader who helped found the CIO and serves as its vice president. Hillman thinks the CIO can negotiate along those lines, as long as it's made clear that the idea for limited representation originates with the Labor Department. When the press visits her office, a confident Perkins tells them, "You can print, if you want, that the Secretary of Labor thinks the situation is better, and that it is not unlikely that a formula can be found which will end the strike and make possible some kind of negotiations, looking toward a settlement of the dispute."

But then Sloan backs out. The chairman calls the secretary at the Labor Department and tells her, "I've been talking to somebody about that matter we talked about yesterday. I can't do that. That's all off. I'm not going to do anything of that kind."

Perkins is shocked.

"But Mr. Sloan, you can't do that!" she objects. "You told me I could go ahead and make that proposal, without saying that you've agreed to it. I haven't said that you would agree to anything, but I have made the proposal and I have discovered that it would probably be acceptable. You can't back out now. It's too late."

"I'm not going through with it," Sloan says firmly. "That's all there is to it."

Sloan hangs up the phone. A deflated Perkins leaves her office, to find the anteroom filled with reporters who now want details of her plan for a strike settlement.

"What is it that's going to be done that you feel so hopeful about?" a newsman inquires.

"All right, I lost my hope?"

"What do you mean?" The newsmen are flipping open their notebooks, gripping their pens and pencils. They have come to report on Perkins's success, but her failure is a story, too.

"Well, Mr. Sloan ran out on me, that's all. Mr. Sloan ran out on me. But we'll think of something else. There'll be some other way."

Despite his abrupt termination of their previous negotiation, Perkins manages to lure Sloan back to Washington for a final confidential conference. Again, he travels to the capital in GM's private rail car, and again, he and his assistents meet with Perkins for two hours in her office. Sloan wants to know what the terms of a settlement will be: How much will GM have to pay in wages and piece rates? What hours will the men work? Which holidays will they take off? Perkins tells him that she can't negotiate for the company or the union. Her job is to get them talking. If General Motors will agree to sit down with representatives of the UAWA in Detroit—just sit down and talk, not even agree to a settlement—then the union might be able to persuade the strikers to vacate the plants.

There are two versions of how the meeting concludes. According to Perkins, the GM delegation gives her permission to tell Sidney Hillman and John L. Lewis that the company will meet them but will not negotiate contract terms until the men leave the plants. According to Sloan, he promises to give Perkins an answer by ten o'clock the next morning, January 30, after he has consulted with his company's general counsel, John Thomas Smith, who has also made the trip to Washington. At 4:45 p.m., Sloan telephones Perkins from Union Station to tell her that he has spoken with Smith, and will have an answer for her once he returns to New York.

Sloan's answer is no. That evening, as Perkins is dining with her daughter and a friend in her DC apartment, the telephone rings. The maid answers and interrupts the family dinner.

"Miss Perkins, a gentleman wants to speak to you. He says it's very important."

"Did he say who he is?"

"He says his name is Mr. Sloan from New York."

Perkins takes the call. She is enraged by what Sloan tells her.

"I don't think these men are in good faith," he says of the union's leadership. "I think they've got a crook in the organization. I'm not going to do anything of the sort with the men."

"Mr. Sloan, you gave your word. You gave your word in front of witnesses."

Her bile rising, Perkins begins shouting insults that are entirely out of character for a well-bred, well-educated New England woman. Only once before in her life has she been so angry.

"You are a scoundrel and a skunk, Mr. Sloan! You can't do that kind of thing. That is a rotter. That's a quitter. You have deceived people. You've misled people."

Perkins's daughter, Susanna, has never heard her mother speak to *anyone* with such invective. The secretary continues tearing into Sloan.

"You don't deserve to be counted among decent men," she roars. "Decent people don't do such things. You'll go to hell when you die if you do things like that. You have let down people. You have betrayed your government. You have betrayed the men who work for you, betrayed your stockholders. Are you a grown man, Mr. Sloan, or are you a neurotic adolescent? If you're a grown man, stand up and be a man for once!"

Perkins would be out of line speaking to any US citizen this way, much less one of the principals in a strike she is trying to settle. Sloan is justifiably outraged by her tirade, but his wounded dignity produces a response that doesn't make him look much better than his antagonist.

"You can't talk to me like that," he shouts back when he is finally able to edge a few words into Perkins's raving. "You can't talk to me like that. I'm Alfred Sloan. I've got seventy million and I made it all myself! You can't talk to me like that."

"Haven't you ever read what happens to the rich man?" Perkins scolds. "It's like the camel trying to go through the eye of the needle. If you've got seventy million dollars, it's going to drown you, Mr. Sloan. It's going to sink you. For God's sake, don't say those words to me again. It makes you a worse rotter than I thought you were."

This time, Perkins hangs up on Sloan. The story of their disagreement gets into the newspapers (although not their angry words to each other—Perkins even conceals those from FDR and Frank Murphy, because she does not wish to embarrass Sloan). Once those papers get inside Fisher One and Fisher Two, the men despair even more of a settlement.

"Mr. Sloan breaks his promise—now what?" Francis O'Rourke writes in his strike diary. "Were those promises made? It does not seem possible that a man in his position would do that, or have they thought of another scheme to try?"

The next day, a Sunday, O'Rourke imagines he is taking his daughters, Patsy and Sunny, to church—combing their hair, placing their prayer books in their hands. Once the hour of Mass has passed, his mind takes him home, where he shares Sunday dinner with his family and helps his wife, Sweet, put away the dishes.

"Monday and a new month," O'Rourke writes on February 1. "Who would have thought this would go on so long?' How much longer will it go?"

Across Chevrolet Avenue, in the Chevy complex, the union is carrying out a plot it hopes will make the answer "Not much longer."

CHAPTER 9

CHEVY FOUR

Bob travis drives his Willys-Overland puddle jumper—an early version of the Jeep—along Bluff Street. He idles the motor outside Chevrolet Plant Number Four, part of the vast industrial village along the Flint River. Chevy Four is now the most important facility in the GM universe: it employs 3,800 workers over two shifts and produces a million engines a year. The company managed to reopen the plant during the strike, but if the union can shut it down, why, then, capturing Chevy Four will show GM that the union is still on the offensive—and that the plant won't be covered by the new injunction the company is seeking, which only applies to Fisher One and Two. That stiff-necked Sloan will have to negotiate.

As Travis cases the engine plant, he begins to think like a military tactician. The men who work at Chevy Four have told him that since the plant began running again, its manager, Arnold Lenz, has fired three unionists: one for wearing a UAWA button, one for soliciting memberships and one for "protection" against anti-union workers angered by his organizing efforts. The place has been lousy with company guards, some carrying clubs, some carrying guns, some carrying both. Taking it over will require a diversion to draw away plant security.

That night Travis invites three of his most-trusted men inside Chevy Four—Ed Cronk, Howard Foster, and Kermit Johnson—to his room at the Dresden Hotel. Examining a map of the Chevy complex, they see that Chevy Four forms a triangle with Chevy Six and Chevy Nine, each separated by a few hundred yards. If the union can trick GM into believing it's instigating a sit-down strike in Chevy Nine, a ball-bearing plant, and coax the company guards into running over there, then Chevy Four will be left undefended.

"If we can put this across," Travis crows, "we can crack the backbone of GM's right-to-work movement, and the strike is ours!"

Here's the rub, though: only a few men can know the plan. If it gets out to the entire membership, some Pinkerton stoolie will spill the beans to management.

On the afternoon of January 31, Travis addresses fifteen hundred Chevrolet workers in the auditorium of Pengelly Hall. He tells them something big is about to happen, and he tells them their jobs will be at stake if it fails, but he doesn't tell them exactly what. Just be ready for action, he says.

"Men," Travis begins, "when the unstruck plants re-opened last week, we gave our pledge that we wouldn't interfere. We saw no reason to. We know that you boys could use the money. Then, too, we didn't want to antagonize the fence-sitters by a dog-in-the-manger attitude. However, it seems that Arnold Lenz took this as a sign of weakness. He's fired several men already and intimidated hundreds of others. If this continues, every union man in the shop can kiss his job goodbye!"

Bundled in mackinaws, peering at the dais from beneath billed woolen caps, the men sweat and shout in the crowded, steaming room. They'd joined the union to stop shop-floor tyrants like Lenz from firing any worker who got on his bad side.

"Amen!" one cries.

"That's right!" exclaims another.

"I've called Mr. Lenz and asked him for a conference," Travis continues. "Now, I haven't asked you yet what you want me to tell him, but I'll tell you what I *think* you want me to tell him. You want me to say, 'Mr. Lenz, these three boys who were fired have got to be taken back—or else!'"

Fifteen hundred throats roar agreement. Travis is on the ball!

"The organizers have worked out some plans that we're going to discuss with the stewards," he tells the men. "You know why we can't just merely talk about them in the open, though we'd like to do that. All I'm going to say is, 'Keep your eyes and ears open.' When it comes time for you to act, you won't be able to mistake what you're going to do."

Travis loves drama. He loves mystery. He loves skullduggery. After the meeting, 150 stewards and organizers remain in the hall. They are asked to walk, one by one, into an adjoining room, where Travis, Roy Reuther, and Henry Kraus stare each man in the eyes, as a test of trustworthiness. The thirty who pass the test are handed a signed slip of paper and told to present it at Fisher One at midnight. The rest get slips that read only, "Follow the man who takes the lead," or "Follow the American flag."

"If you get a slip with the information on it, be sure that nobody sees it," Travis orders. "You tell nobody. Don't tell your wife. Don't tell anybody."

After the men leave, Reuther tells Travis, "You know, I think two of those guys you picked are stool pigeons." Travis knows they're stoolies. He wants stoolies.

When the chosen men crawl through the windows of Fisher One at midnight, Travis leads them down a dark hallway to an office so small they have to sit on the floor.

"We're going to take Plant Nine," Travis tells them.

"What the hell's Plant Nine?" Reuther objects. "GM can get bearings from Muncie."

"Don't worry about that," Travis says. "They can't get the same size and same kind of bearing. It'll take 'em six months to make new dies for the bearings."

That's not true. Travis knows it isn't true. But he wants all the men in this office to believe that his plan is to capture Chevy Nine during the 3:20 p.m. shift change the next day. If they all believe it, then Travis's hand-picked stoolies will feed Lenz the false information. Lenz will think it's the real McCoy, rush his goons over to Chevy Nine, and fall right into Travis's trap.

In the wee hours of February 1 Travis holds a second meeting, in Kermit Johnson's apartment. Also in attendance are Ed Cronk, Bill Roy and Carl Bibber, a trio of Chevy workers loyal to the union.

"Now, look here," Travis tells his confederates, "this Plant Nine that we just decided we're going to take, that's not the plant we want. We want Plant Four. And you guys are the ones that are gonna have to take it. If we're sufficiently able to dramatize this thing to the extent that we can fool General Motors, we can draw every goddamned guy from Lenz on down into Plant Nine, see? And we can draw all the Flint law enforcement agencies to Plant Nine. They'll all be there. We can take it if you can make it over there. Do you think you can do it?"

"Yeah," Cronk assures Travis, "we can do it. I got the guys in Plant Six. We can get over to Four and do it."

Travis gives Cronk his orders: First, kick the supervisors out of Chevy Four. Then, kick out the anti-union workers. Then, weld the doors shut to prevent company goons from counter-attacking once they figure out what's going on.

"Now this is it," Travis tells his men before the meeting breaks up. "You must not tell one soul, not even your wife, or your kid, or anybody. It's to be in your head, and your head only. If the secret gets out, nobody is to blame but you, you four guys. You can bet that I'll never tell. Now, you four guys . . . or else we can't do it."

When Travis returns to the Dresden Hotel for a brief night's sleep, only five men and one woman—Genora Johnson, Kermit's wife and captain of the Women's Emergency Brigade—know the plan that will determine the fortunes of thousands of autoworkers.

The next afternoon at two-thirty, an hour before shift change in the Chevy plants, Travis convenes a meeting in the Pengelly Building, ostensibly to organize a march on the county courthouse, where Genesee County Circuit Court Judge Paul Gadola is holding a hearing on GM's request for a second injunction to force the sit-downers to vacate Fisher One and Fisher Two. As Travis speaks, a pair of UAWA sound cars troll the streets, urging union members to come hear the speech at the Pengelly. But the cars' rounds take them closer and closer to the Chevy complex. A little after three o'clock, one car parks on Bluff Street, near the Chevy Six gate. The other comes to a halt on Kearsley, in front of Chevy Nine. Its passengers are pickets, some of them imported from Detroit at Travis's request.

At ten past three, Dorothy Kraus hands Travis a blank sheet of paper. Pretending to read it, he tells his audience, more than half of them members of the Women's Emergency Brigade, "Brothers and sisters, I don't want to get you excited, but I've just gotten word that there's trouble at Chevy Nine. The guards are beating up our fellows inside the plant! There are some pickets down there already, but they can use some reinforcements. I suggest that we break up this meeting and go right down there."

The crowd races out of the Pengelly Building. When they arrive at Chevy Nine, newspapermen are standing on the sidewalk in front of the plant and movie trucks from Paramount and Pathé have set up film cameras for their newsreels. As part of Travis's ruse, the press has been tipped off that an action will take place at Chevy Nine. The Women's Emergency Brigade also finds the trouble Travis promised. Like everyone else in Flint, the Brigade has heard the rumors of a takeover at Nine, so most of its members are carrying twenty-inch-long wooden clubs concealed beneath their overcoats.

Inside Chevy Nine, just as the day shift is about to finish work, a cadre of twenty-five or thirty night-shift workers emerges from the cafeteria. Marching three abreast down the assembly lines, they chant "Strike! Strike!" A few workers shut off their machines to join the march. A few more continue working. The unionists boo and jeer the workers loyal to the company, who silently keep working until they see the strikers gathering gear blanks and door hinges, obviously to employ as missiles. To the loyal workers this is a provocation. Abandoning their machines, they gang up on the strikers. Fistfights break out on the shop floor.

The factory doors burst open. Into the melee rush company guards wielding hickory sticks, led by the foreman, Arnold Lenz.

"Reds!" the guards shout as they chase the strikers through the plant. "Communists!"

"You bastard!" a striker curses Lenz. "We ought to tear you apart!"

The guards beat the strikers with clubs and blackjacks, pummeling two men into unconsciousness. The strikers fight back by hurling blanks, pulleys, and hinges. Guards are blocking the doors, tripping workers trying to flee the fray. Brawls between guards and strikers break out in the aisles between the machines, with the strikers fighting off their antagonists just long enough to carry wounded men back to the cafeteria.

When the three-thirty whistle blows, signaling the beginning of the night shift, the guards retreat to the rear of the plant, but only to employ another weapon, tear gas. From their redoubt the guards fire cylinders of tear gas at the strikers. As the close air of the shop floor fills with the stinging fumes, a striker manages to break a window. Pushing his bloodied face through the hole in the glass, he shouts to the women on the sidewalk, "They are gassing us! They are gassing us!"

"Smash the windows!" orders a voice from the sound car.

Dressed for battle in red berets and "EB" armbands, parading with an American flag at the head of their column, thirty women of the Women's Emergency Brigade pull their clubs out from under their long winter coats and swing them at the bank of windows.

"They're gassing our husbands!" one Women's Emergency Brigade member yells. "Give them air!"

With the butts of their clubs the women shatter every pane they can reach, littering the shop floor with tinkling shards of glass, allowing the gas to flow out through the jagged holes. When the Flint police attempt to arrest a club-wielding Brigade member, she wriggles in their grasp, shrieking "Get your hands off me!"

The next day's *New York Times* reports their action under the headline "Women's Brigade Uses Heavy Clubs." The *Flint Journal* writes, "These women smashed scores of windows in the plant in a hysterical frenzy, seemingly with an urge to destroy, for officials could find no other reason for smashing glass in window after window."

Meanwhile, inside Chevy Four, Kermit Johnson has sneaked in during the shift change but has managed to persuade only a few union members to stay behind for a takeover attempt. The plotters conceal themselves in the balcony bathroom until the night shift is up and running. Then they burst onto the factory floor, shouting, "Shut 'er down! Shut 'er down!" The cries of a small group of men trying to incite a sit-down are overwhelmed by the racket of drills, presses, and punches. Thwarted, Johnson retreats to the northeast gate, at the rear of the plant.

Ed Cronk is supposed to arrive there with reinforcement from Chevy Six, where the union is stronger. Cronk, who works nights in Six, has indeed managed to attract a crowd of followers. At shift change, he fires up his press, then shuts it down, picks up a lead pipe, pulls an American flag from his pocket, and runs through the plant shouting "Shut 'er off and follow me!" With his left hand, Cronk waves the flag, hoping the men will remember Travis's order to "watch for the American flag." With his right, he bangs on auto parts to gain attention. Leaping over conveyor belts and supply stacks, Cronk brandishes his pipe at a group of foremen trying to stop him.

Cronk leads thirty-five men over to Chevy Four. That's not enough, Johnson tells him. But the good news is that the plant is undefended. Over in the decoy plant, Chevy Nine, not only the company guards are battling it out but so are Chevy Four's anti-union workers, who have been enlisted by management to join the fight.

"Well," Cronk tells Johnson, "let's go back and get more men. I would have waited for more, but I thought you'd just about be shut down here by this time."

Back inside Chevy Six, a hundred loading-dock workers are marching through the plant, urging the guys on the line to shut down their machines. Cronk's band joins them, and soon the shop floor is silent. Waving the flag over his head, Cronk gives an order to all workers who have answered the call to shut down the line.

"All right, boys," he cries. "Everybody over to Chevy Four now!"

The idled workers surge across the snowy factory grounds. Cronk returns to the target plant with seventy-five men who march up and down the line, shutting off machines.

Gib Rose, a crankshaft grinder who has been organizing the plant for the UAWA, sees the commotion and starts flipping conveyor switches in the department, shutting down the assembly line. "Dremon, get the master panels," Rose calls to Leo Dremon, a mechanic who also belongs to the union.

"Where are they?" Rose asks. "You know where they are?" Dremon opens a door to reveal a panel of half-inch-thick copper bus bars—conductors that control the distribution of current to the entire plant. Rose picks up a crow bar and flings it at the panel. The iron missile clangs against the bus bars. Sizzling orange sparks cascade to the floor. Flames melt the bus bars until they sag.

Rose's foreman, Mr. Emory, sees him shutting down machines and destroying company property. The foreman steps into an aisle to block Rose's way.

"If you don't get back to work, I'll fire you," the foreman threatens.

An old man in a clean white shirt is confronting a young man holding a crowbar. Beyond Rose's obvious physical advantage over the foreman, Rose sees that the momentum is with the strikers. All over the plant, foremen are telling workers to return to the assembly line or lose their jobs. And all over the plant, workers are defying them and demanding that their line mates do the same.

"Mr. Emory," Rose tells his foreman, "I always liked you and I don't want to see you get hurt. I always respected you. Now, do me a favor: get out of the way, 'cause you won't get hurt."

The old foreman is hard of hearing, so he jabs a finger at Rose, then at the grinding machine he expects his subordinate to operate. As gently as possible, Rose turns Mr. Emory around, grabs ahold of his belt and collar, marches him to the loading dock, and pushes him off. Fortunately for both men, Mr. Emory lands on his feet.

"Now, go before you get hurt!" Rose commands. "I'm your friend, dammit! Run!"

Mr. Emory runs as fast as his creaky legs will propel him, coatless into the winter afternoon.

Elsewhere in the plant, a worker holding a wrench heavy enough to crack bones growls at a man still tending his machine, "Get off your job, you dirty scab."

The threatened workers either join the victory parade or take shelter in the balcony.

Chevy Four's cylinder-head department shuts down. Then the piston department. Once all the machines have been stilled, the victorious strikers tell the supervisors they have fifteen minutes to leave the premises. Management makes one last attempt to regain control by appealing to the workers hiding in the balcony. They're not union men, but they don't want a fight, either. One by one, they don their coats and head for the gate. As they walk out, the strikers implore them to leave behind their dinner pails. The plant may soon be isolated, cut off from meal deliveries. If the occupiers can't feed themselves they will be obliged to surrender from starvation. As a favor to their line mates, four or five hundred men drop their lunches, on the promise that they can retrieve the buckets once the strike is over.

After failing to rally the neutral workers, the foremen lock themselves inside the plant superintendent's office. From there they try to call the personnel office, to ask for reinforcements. It's not a long phone call. Cronk and a few fellow strikers kick in the door, rip the phone out of the wall, and issue one final order from labor to management: "You've got five minutes to leave!"

The supervisors retreat to the shipping department, a small building outside the factory. Chevy Four belongs to the strikers now.

Of the four thousand men on the night shift, more than half have decided to go home. The remainder, around twelve hundred, begin barricading the exits. The plant guards doing battle in Chevy Nine have finally caught on to the union's game, but when they try to storm Chevy Four's northeast gate, the strikers fight them off by hurling pistons, connecting rods, and rocker arm rods and spraying them with fire hoses.

Outside, on the sidewalk running along Bluff Street, strikers have erected a shack and ignited salamander heaters. A sound car is parked in the street. Hundreds of pickets crowd the walk, including women from the Emergency Brigade, who lock arms in front of the gate. A striker named Joe Sayen scales its metal mesh to deliver a speech.

"We want the world to understand what we are fighting for," Sayen shouts hoarsely into the cold Northern dusk. "We are fighting for freedom and life and liberty! This is our one great opportunity. What if we should be defeated? What if we should be killed? We have only one life. That's all we can lose, and we might as well die like heroes than live like slaves."

When the Flint police arrive, a teenage girl who has joined the Emergency Brigade's human barricade tells them, "You can't get into this plant. Nobody can get in except our men. We are only protecting our husbands. Your wives would protect you just the same if they had to. We are peaceful and law-abiding citizens, but we are not going to let you into the plant."

"What kind of cowards hide behind women?" a cop bellows back, loudly enough so the men inside can hear.

Genora Johnson takes this taunt personally. Her Brigade members consider themselves combatants equal to their husbands, brothers, and fathers, with just as much at stake in this strike. Climbing into the sound car, Johnson grabs the microphone to denounce the company's "hired thugs." Her firm voice ricochets off the factory's façade.

"We don't want any violence," Johnson says. "We don't want any trouble. My husband is one of the Sit Down Strikers. We are going to fight to protect our men."

Stymied by the feminine wall they're facing, the police mill around on the sidewalk, their aimlessness pointing up the stalemate between the company and the union.

From city hall and the county jail, Mayor Bradshaw and Sheriff Wolcott are placing desperate phone calls and composing desperate telegrams to Governor Murphy at the Book-Cadillac Hotel in Detroit. Wolcott cables: "I respectfully request the use of the National Guard to take care of the strike situation in the city of Flint[.] The city police force and the sheriffs force combined is wholly inadequate to take care of the serious situation existing today[.]"

It's the first Murphy has heard of the Chevy Four takeover, and he is furious with the strikers. By occupying even more of General

Motors' property, they're fudging up his efforts to restart negotiations between GM and the UAWA. The strikers, of course, see things otherwise: they think occupying Chevy Four is the *only* way to bring the company back to the bargaining table. The governor is also getting reports that unionists have been imported from Detroit to intimidate the police and assist in the plant takeover, a tactic he later tells Secretary Perkins he finds "morally repulsive." Murphy calls Colonel Lewis, the National Guard commander, instructing him to blockade the streets around Chevy Four with twelve hundred guardsmen. By midnight, the men are in place, forming a perimeter with fixed bayonets, eight machine guns, and a 37-millimeter artillery piece. They have orders not to allow anyone into the plant. If the strikers want food, they'll have to exit the plant and get it themselves.

At one-thirty in the morning, General Motors shuts off the lights and the heat inside Chevy Four. The company tried the same tactic at Fisher Two, before the Battle of the Running Bulls. If it's not their plant anymore, why should they provide utilities? The strikers light matches to find their way through the sudden darkness. They pace the floor to keep warm. Around four o'clock, outside the plant, Walter Reuther crawls under a boxcar beside the loading dock to sneak past the National Guard blockade. He manages to get inside. After making a tour of the plant, he tells Colonel Lewis what he's seen.

"The lights have been shut down and the men are making torches out of old waste," Reuther reports. "They're planning to build open fires to keep warm. If that plant goes up in flames, the company itself will be to blame."

The lights and the heat go back on, but the food blockade remains in effect. Even after consuming the left-behind lunches, the strikers refuse to raid the commissary for peanuts, candy bars or sandwiches, lest they be accused of theft.

Shortly after dawn on the second CIO director, John Brophy arrives in Flint from Detroit. Brophy places a call to the governor, begging him to allow the men to eat. "The good people of Michigan did not expect the governor to condemn to starvation thousands of workers [who] are fighting for their elementary rights," he shouts into the phone, working himself into a red-faced lather. "I'm sure you will be able to win the strike for General Motors that way."

Murphy calmly tells Brophy that the previous day's "riot," as the newspapers are calling it, was a double-cross of his efforts to resume negotiations.

"Well, I don't see how taking the Chevrolet plant breaks faith with you," Brophy replies. "After all, those workers are fighting a vicious, unscrupulous corporation, and it's asking too much to expect them to accept violence and attacks with meek submission."

Murphy points out that the strikers themselves employed violence, to which Brophy responds, "I don't say that two wrongs make a right, governor, but the cases aren't at all similar. General Motors broke its word, and the workers merely took steps to defend themselves."

At the National Guard Armory, a turreted brick bastille-like structure downriver from the Chevy complex, a union delegation—Brophy, Travis, Roy Reuther, Kermit Johnson, and the pamphleteer Henry Kraus—meets with Colonel Lewis, who tells them that both he and the governor object to reports that there are "outsiders" occupying Chevy Four. "You see, gentlemen," Lewis tells the union men, "the governor has been receiving information all night from certain sources that the entire new strike was executed by out-of-towners, who just went in and seized the plant. We understand now that isn't entirely correct."

"I should say it isn't," Kraus says. "I've just come from the plant after spending the night there. There were a few outsiders, but we asked them all to leave this morning. Outside of two organizers, every last man in there now is a Chevrolet worker."

"I'm glad to hear that," says Lewis, who nonetheless will require proof before relaying this information to Murphy. "Otherwise, you understand, it would be putting the governor in an impossible situation."

"We're willing to go in there with you and inspect all occupants," Brophy offers. "Any man who can't show a Chevrolet badge will be asked to leave."

"That wouldn't be necessary. If you will do that yourselves, I will take your word for it."

"And then the men will get food?" Brophy asks.

"I see no reason why not, once that point is clarified."

Lewis issues five passes to enter the plant, and four to exit—Johnson, a Chevrolet employee, plans to rejoin the occupation. Overnight, he climbed the fence to argue with the guardsmen and was kicked out of the perimeter. But before the delegation leaves the Armory, Reuther asks one last question.

"If that's the only reason for the governor's action, why couldn't he have let us know hours earlier, so that we could have satisfied him on that score?"

"Gentlemen," the colonel tells his audience, grinning faintly, "let's not embarrass the governor."

When the five men tour the plant, they find a few organizers inside, including Walter Reuther, who agrees to leave so the men can be fed. While climbing over the fence they see Arnold Lenz approaching, accompanied by two guardsmen.

"I'm the superintendent of the plant, and I intend to inspect it," Lenz huffs. "I'm representing the governor."

"You're not going in," Brophy shoots back. "I am the governor's representative. I have inspected the plant, and everything's all right. There are a lot of people in there who don't like you, so stay out here where you're safe."

As Lenz storms off, the men behind the fence cheer. Brophy drives the delegation back to the Pengelly Building in the sound car, blasting out "Solidarity Forever."

While the men inside Chevy Four are wondering where their next meal is coming from, Judge Gadola issues his decision on GM's request for an injunction to force the strikers in Fisher One and Fisher Two to end their occupation. His five-thousand-word decision is a complete victory for the company. Calling the actions of the UAWA "an unlawful conspiracy" and accusing the union of using "threats and intimidation" to prevent non-union employees from working, he gives the sit-downers twenty-four hours to evacuate the plants. The deadline is 3 p.m. on February 3. If they don't leave, they'll face a fifteen-million-dollar fine. Furthermore, he prohibits the union from picketing or "in any manner interfering with the free access of non-striking employees to the plaintiff's premises."

Judge Gadola instructs Sheriff Wolcott to read the injunction to the strikers, just as the sheriff did after the takeover of Fisher One, to no avail. If the strikers again defy the courts, the judge tells reporters after the hearing, he can order the National Guard to enforce his ruling. In actuality, only one man can order the National Guard to enforce a judge's ruling. At five o'clock, Governor Murphy hears from Colonel Lewis that all the men remaining in Chevy Four are Chevrolet employees.

"In that case," the governor says, "you may allow food through the lines."

That's one victory for the strikers. If they defy Judge Gadola, though, will the man in charge of enforcing Michigan's laws take their side, or will he use his troops to carry out the court's order?

CHAPTER 10

MURPHY'S LAW

Franklin delano roosevelt has a cold. In the damp, bleak Washington midwinter, the president is feeling weak, but he nonetheless agrees to pick up the phone and call William Knudsen. Perhaps it's a face-saving measure for Knudsen, or perhaps an acknowledgment of General Motors' place in the American hierarchy, but the company has made it clear it will sit down to negotiate with the union only if ordered to do so by the president of the United States himself.

John L. Lewis is already on his way to Detroit aboard a Pennsylvania Railroad liner, hoping to meet with company officials on the morning of Wednesday, February 3. "Let there be no moaning of the bar when I put out to sea," Lewis tells reporters as he boards the train. He never lets pass an opportunity to lend a colorful quote to the dailies. Shortly after Lewis leaves Union Station, Murphy meets with Knudsen and the GM executive Lawrence Fisher at the Book-Cadillac Hotel in Detroit. The GM men show the governor a letter that states they will not meet with Lewis—unless Roosevelt asks them to.

"I don't think they ought to feel that way," Murphy grumbles to an aide, but half an hour later he is on the phone with Frances Perkins, who tells him she will recommend that Roosevelt make the phone call.

Perkins types up a brief memorandum for the president. When she delivers it to the Oval Office, she tells Roosevelt, "Don't discuss issues with Knudsen. Just tell him that you want them to agree to go into conference and that you have reason to believe that if they go into conference there will be an evacuation of the factory and that a reasonable settlement of the dispute will be reached."

The president, who would much rather be in bed, rubs his aching temples. Then he asks the White House operator to connect him with Knudsen.

"Is that you, Bill?" Roosevelt booms into the receiver when Knudsen comes on the line—that bright, blaring voice recognizable to every radio listener in America. "I know you have been through a lot, Bill, and I want to tell you that I feel sorry for you, but Miss Perkins has told me about the situation and what you are discussing and I have just called up to say I hope very much indeed that you go through with this and that your people will meet a committee."

Knudsen tells Roosevelt that yes, he will meet a committee.

"Fine, fine, Bill," Roosevelt concludes. "Thank you very much, Bill. That's good."

Roosevelt puts down the phone, sighing as he says to Perkins, "Well, I'm glad that's over."

But it's not over, not even for Roosevelt, who will continue to nudge both GM and the union as negotiations proceed.

The next morning at nine-thirty, Knudsen and Lewis sit down for a meeting with Murphy in the courtroom of the governor's brother, Judge George Murphy, at the Detroit Recorder's Court. Lewis is assisted by Wyndham Mortimer and Homer Martin; Knudsen, by Vice Chairman Donaldson Brown and GM counsel John Thomas Smith.

In the aftermath of his combative phone call with Perkins, Sloan has handed responsibility for strike negotiations back to Knudsen. That's good for GM, good for the UAWA, good for Roosevelt, and good for Sloan. No corporate philosopher, Knudsen is not as dogmatically anti-union as Sloan. He just wants to build cars, and as the strike passes its one-month mark, GM is barely building any. In the first week of February, the company has produced only 125 vehicles, less than half a percent of its normal production. GM has spent a month insisting it won't negotiate while the strikers occupy its plants, but after a month of occupation the company has no choice. The summit in Detroit is a vindication of the union's strategy, and of Lewis's refusal to recommend an evacuation. Holding the negotiations in Detroit rather than Washington also allows Roosevelt to keep to his policy of maintaining distance from labor disputes.

Beyond that, Knudsen works in Detroit, regularly visits the factories, and is more in touch with the men and women on the shop floor. Roosevelt has dismissed the starchy, remote Sloan as a "low-comedy figure." Walter Lippmann, the most widely syndicated political commentator of the day, suggests in his "Today and Tomorrow" column that Sloan's attitudes toward labor are incompatible with the political and demographic realities of the 1930s.

"The irreconcilable anti-unionism of many large employers has become definitely antiquated," Lippmann writes.

> There is no other free country in the world where this attitude still prevails. That it has lasted and worked for so long a time in the United States has been due to historical conditions that are rapidly being modified. The slippage of immigration is one of the great reasons why the employers' anti-unionism cannot last very much longer. There are no new supplies of ignorant and semi-servile labor, separated from the native workers by languages and culture. Very soon, if not now, all the workers will have passed through American schools and will feel themselves to be citizens by right of birth. Men of that sort cannot much longer be refused full representation in all matters affecting their wages and conditions of work.

The "slippage of immigration" to which Lippmann refers is a result of the Immigration Act of 1924, which restricted immigrants from southern and eastern Europe, previously sources of cheap labor and strikebreakers for industry. The Republican Congress that passed the act probably did not intend it as a boon to the labor movement.

Inside Fisher Two, the strikers don't intend to obey Judge Gadola's order to evacuate the plants by 3 p.m. on February 3, but they nonetheless find it alarming: a proclamation of Armageddon, a license—indeed, a "command"—for the Flint police and the Genesee County Sheriff to launch another violent attack on their redoubt. Fearing for their lives, they send a desperate telegram to Murphy, begging him for protection.

"Governor, we have decided to stay in the plant," the telegram reads. "We fully expect that if a violent effort is made to oust us, many of us will be killed, and we take this means to make it known that to our wives, to our children, to the people of the state of Michigan and of the country that if this result follows from the attempt to eject us you will be the one responsible for our deaths."

(There's one aspect of the injunction the strikers aren't taking seriously: "If the judge can get fifteen million bucks from us, he's welcome to it," a Fisher One sit-downer cracks.)

But from Fisher One, strike leader Bud Simons writes a reassuring note to his wife, Hazel, telling her that "everything is okeydoke here. Now don't worry for my opinion is there will be no fight. Knudsen & John L. Lewis had a chat this morning. We hardly expect any fight but if it comes I will be here to do my duty as a warrior."

Yet even as Knudsen and Lewis talk in Detroit, Flint appears to be approaching a state of bloody conflict as both strikers and law enforcement call in reinforcements for an expected battle over the occupied plants. Bob Travis puts out a call to unions all over the Midwest: send men to defend the strikers. In Travis's hometown of Toledo, nearly a thousand unionists cram into cars for the drive up US 23. Several Toledo auto plants close down for lack of labor. South of Flint, the state police are stopping cars with out-of-state license plates, taking down the names and addresses of the passengers. From Detroit, Toledo, Lansing, and Pontiac come hundreds of women wearing green berets to identify themselves as allies of the red-bereted Women's Emergency Brigade. The union is calling the day of Gadola's deadline "Women's

Day," to suggest it intends to resist nonviolently, but besides their usual clubs the women have armed themselves with stove pokers, iron bars, and pipes. The defense force begins gathering around Fisher One on the evening of February 2, firing up salamanders and singing "Mademoiselle from Armentieres" to ward off the cold. As the ordered evacuation deadline approaches, thousands of picketers form a protective cordon six bodies deep around Fisher One. The women carry signs reading "We Stand By Our Heroes in the Plants" and "Shorter Hours Mean Happier Homes." They shout a football-style cheer:

We're the wives,
We're the mothers,
Of our fighting union brothers.
We'll fight for our kith and kin.
And when we fight, we fight to win!
Rah! Rah! Rah!

As Roy Reuther welcomes Detroit unionists from the sound car, men inside the plant gather at the windows to dump auto parts that can be used as missiles against law enforcement: bars of steel, truck hinges, truck stakes, body work wrenches, spuds. The crowd eagerly gathers up the improvised ordnance. When Flint Police Chief Wills drives past the plant with his sons, picketers recognize him and chase after his car, brandishing clubs.

In response to the union's show of force, Wills mobilizes five hundred "reserve officers," civilians who will be issued firearms and invested with police powers "if the situation gets out of hand." To prevent hooliganism, the state liquor control commission issues an emergency ban on alcohol sales in Genesee County.

Sheriff Wolcott, who is charged with enforcing the evacuation order, is offered the assistance of 1,300 deputies from around the state by the Michigan Sheriff's Association. He believes, though, that only the National Guard is powerful enough to carry out an evacuation and plans to ask Murphy for its assistance. Roy Brownell, GM's attorney in the case, tells the press he hopes that won't be necessary.

"The sheriff told us he had a limited force, but that he would ask Governor Murphy to provide him the aid of the National Guard to carry out the order of arrest," Brownell says. "I believe the union officials will ask the men to go out peacefully. Surely they will observe the order of the court."

The National Guard's only intention is to prevent a clash between the sheriff and the strikers. Guardsmen set up a "one pounder" cannon and two machine guns in front of Chevy Four and a machine gun on the roof of Chevy Five, across the street. The "military zone" on Chevrolet Avenue is guarded by another one-pounder, and guardsmen armed with loaded, bayonet-tipped rifles roam the street to prevent anyone from approaching Fisher Two.

Three o'clock comes and goes peacefully. The men don't walk out of the plant, and the sheriff doesn't try to evict them. Once again, Murphy refuses to settle the strike with force.

"I'm not going down in history as 'Bloody Murphy'!" the governor rails to a friend. "If I sent those soldiers right in on the men there'd be no telling how many will be killed. It would be inconsistent with everything I have ever stood for in my political life."

The next day—Thursday, February 4—GM obtains a writ of attachment from Judge Gadola for the restoration of its property and the arrests of the men inside. Sheriff Wolcott now sends a telegram to Murphy in which he formally requests the Guard's assistance: "Please advise me by wire whether you will place the national guard now on duty here at my disposal to carry out the orders of the court, or will it be necessary to deputize a substantially large group as deputies to uphold the court decree. Your immediate reply is respectfully requested."

Murphy does not reply immediately since he is busy negotiating with Lewis and Knudsen. If he were to reply, his answer would be no. Why would he break the strike, now that he has the two sides negotiating? Not only does he have them negotiating, he actually has proposals from both sides. The UAWA asks to be recognized as the collective bargaining agent for all employees in the twenty plants where its members are on strike. That's a slight retreat from its original demand of companywide recognition. The union also asks that "no discrimination should be made or prejudices exercised by either of the contracting parties against any worker because of his former affiliation, or activities in, any group or association of employees."

In other words, the union is demanding that no one be fired due to his actions in the sit-down. The UAWA also wants to represent its own members in the plants not affected by the strike, and it does not want GM to negotiate with any other organization until it signs a contract with the UAWA.

For its part, General Motors proposes to recognize the union's right to bargain for "those employees of the company who are members there in the plants above named"—that is, *only* UAWA members, and *only* in plants affected by the strike. GM also agrees not to form a competing company union, "but will give all its men free choice in the type of organization they may choose."

Even before embarking for Detroit, Lewis understands that preventing Murphy from evicting the strikers is the key to the negotiations' success. Lewis has observed the governor's "wobbling," as he attempts to talk these men out of the plants and to satisfy GM, the courts, and the conservative elements in his state. These include the former Republican governor, Frank Fitzgerald, whom Murphy defeated in 1936 and who plans to run again in 1938. It so happens that the state Republican convention is taking place in Detroit during the strike. Convention attendees cheer the news that Judge Gadola has issued a writ of attachment against the strikers. "It is beyond belief that the state permits wanton disregard of the law in connection with the strike," Fitzgerald declares from the podium, in a dig against his once and future opponent. "I do not believe the people want that sort of government."

During an evening discussion at the apartment Governor Murphy shares with his brother and sister, Lewis questions the legitimacy of Judge Gadola's injunction: "It is not the law, it is General Motors law. That injunction was written by John Thomas Smith in General Motors' offices and signed by Judge Gadola, in his court. That is General Motors' strikebreaking law. I am against strikebreakers. I don't care who breaks this strike, whether it is General Motors or Judge Gadola or the president or you, Governor Murphy. I simply say I am against strikebreakers."

Lewis, himself a national figure, senses Murphy's desire to raise himself to the same rank. He cannily plays on Murphy's aspirations for higher office—even the presidency.

"I had an impression," Lewis tells the governor during a later break in the negotiations, "that Frank Murphy was a man of ambition. You left an eighteen-thousand-dollar job in the Philippines, where you were living like a potentate with the cars and country palaces in the mountains to enter a precarious race here. President Roosevelt swept this state by nearly 200,000, you carried it by 40,000 because labor supported you. If you break this strike that washes us up and washes you up. General Motors fought you in the election and when we are gone you are gone. If you stand firm you will aggrandize your position enormously and there will be talk of Governor Murphy in 1940."

Publicly, Murphy stands firm. In response to Sheriff Wolcott's request for assistance, he reads a statement to reporters making it clear he will not unleash the National Guard on the strikers while negotiations are in progress: "I have directed the military early this morning to preserve order in Flint. I have asked them to see to it that mob rule does not happen and that no incident will be allowed to undermine peace negotiations. . . . The governor of the state and the military are not the agents of either side and never will be."

"Has the National Guard been ordered to assist the sheriff in enforcing the eviction writ?" Murphy is asked.

"You have just heard me answer," Murphy says, but then he adds, "Don't interpret this as an announcement that I'm refusing assistance to the sheriff. I'm keeping in touch with the situation in Flint half-hourly."

That coda is directed at Lewis, as a reminder that the governor retains the power to clear the plants and can use it at any moment. More than once Murphy takes Lewis outside the courtroom and tells him that if the men don't leave the plants peacefully, he will order the Guard to help the sheriff clear them out. But Lewis isn't fooled. Without the plants, the union's bargaining position will collapse. He calls Murphy's bluff, reminding him that if the National Guard enters the plants, bloodshed will result. The union men have vowed to die for the strike.

"I am not going to withdraw those Sit-Downers under any circumstances except a settlement," Lewis states. "What are you going to do? You can get them out in just one way, by bayonets. You have the bayonets. Which kind do you prefer to use—the broad double blade or the four-sided French style? I believe the square style makes a bigger hole and you can turn it around inside a man. Which kind of bayonets, Governor Murphy, are you going to turn around inside our boys?"

"I will do no such thing," Murphy concedes.

"Then why bellyache to me about my getting those boys out to save you?"

In Washington, President Roosevelt has been following the negotiations. He calls Murphy at the courthouse to tell him he thinks the two sides are close to a deal, and he will be glad to do whatever he can to push them closer.

"You are getting on the point where you are awfully close together," Roosevelt congratulates Murphy. "As I understand it, Knudsen has agreed they will give no more advantageous agreement to any other agency than they give to the union. They will not encourage or seek to develop further unions and they will give any guarantee to you or the Secretary of Labor to carry this out. This is a very good practice. I understand that Lewis late last night proposed the Toledo Agreement [which settled the 1934 strike at Electric Auto-Lite in Toledo, under which the company recognized the union's right to bargain for its members]. Also that GM here agreed to this and that the question is whether they will negotiate with other organizations on national issues, not local ones. These two things seem to me to be almost identical. I feel that you have a real chance to bridge the gap and if you want, but it is entirely up to you. I would be glad to say the same thing to both Knudsen and Lewis. Can't we get those friends together? Let me know. You are doing a swell job, Frank."

Murphy is finding Lewis a bigger pain in the neck than Knudsen. Perhaps Roosevelt has been misinformed, or perhaps he is overly optimistic—optimism is a vital feature of his personality, and his political appeal—but Lewis has not in fact surrendered on the idea of representing all workers in plants where the UAWA is recognized. First, he modifies his demand for companywide representation to the right to speak for workers in seventeen plants affected by the strike. Then he again retreats to a position of demanding representation in "between six and ten plants" where a majority of workers belong to the UAWA. But the company disputes that the union holds a majority in any plant and refuses to grant exclusive bargaining rights *anywhere.*

Lewis had hoped to place responsibility for settling the strike "in the lap of the president." Instead, it's in Murphy's lap, for which Roosevelt is grateful, but in these negotiations between America's largest company and its most obdurate labor leader, there are still some issues only the nation's most powerful man can settle.

On February 5, Roosevelt agrees to call Lewis and Knudsen. Frances Perkins types up another memorandum for the president, based on notes she has scribbled on Labor Department stationery during telephone conversations with the two men. Most of her advice concerns persuading Lewis to give up, at least for now, the principle of exclusive representation.

"Say to Lewis that you are not asking him to abandon his position on exclusive representation, just to postpone it," Perkins writes to Roosevelt.

Roosevelt should suggest that Lewis accept the Toledo Agreement and drop the exclusive bargaining demand for four months, Perkins advises. Those terms will certainly help the union build its membership in the plants. Workers will want to be covered by the UAWA's contract. And then the union can win representation elections, held by the National Labor Relations Board, under the terms of the Wagner Act. GM has been open to elections, but Lewis has rejected them. That suggests there may be some truth to the company's contention that the strikers represent only a radical minority of employees.

"Urge [Lewis] to consider that he will in effect have exclusive bargaining and an opportunity to organize his union on the basis of this partial victory, and that all of the agencies of the Government will assist in preventing discrimination and interference with the development of the union," the memo concludes.

Meanwhile, Murphy hears opposition to exclusive bargaining from an unexpected source: the labor movement itself. The governor receives a call from William Green, president of the American Federation of Labor, the organization from which Lewis's CIO seceded because it favored the interests of skilled tradesmen over assembly-line grunts.

Green's conversation with Murphy makes it clear why factory workers objected to the AFL: "We are deeply concerned about the news reports of your peace negotiations in Detroit," Green tells the governor. "They indicate that an exclusive bargaining agreement might be made with the Automobile Workers Union. We want the American Federation of Labor protected and preserved. An exclusive agreement would exclude our people. We are against it."

In Green's DC office, as he makes this phone call to Michigan, are representatives of the metalworkers and the building trades. Those workers also build cars. If only the UAWA is allowed to organize the plants, the trade unions will be frozen out.

"You must not yield to force and wrong," Green says. "We are willing to have this matter submitted to the National Labor Relations Board. We cannot yield to minority force or dictation."

Murphy replies that he's glad to hear Green's views, and that he doesn't represent either side in this dispute. He only wants a peaceful settlement.

Later, GM negotiators show Lewis telegrams from Green and the trade union leaders in an effort to convince the CIO chief that he does not represents a united labor movement. Lewis scoffs at the AFL chief's attempt to undermine his position. "Very well, gentlemen," he declares. "I'll walk out of these negotiations, and you can have Green and company in. Doubtless they can order our men out of the plants."

The strikers have faith in Murphy and Lewis, but they're also preparing for the worst in the event that negotiations break down. "Governor Murphy, Lewis and Knudsen are in conference," Francis O'Rourke writes in his diary. "Things look good on the outside. . . . I've got a blackjack braided. Hope I never have to use it. Some of the men are making knives and they are fancy ones, too."

The strikers have been fashioning even deadlier defensive weapons out of their work materials. They roll drums of an inflammable oil used in automobile paint to the windows. By attaching hoses and hand pumps, they discover they can spray the oil one hundred and fifty feet. Lighting trash aflame and tossing it on the oil will create a wall of Greek fire to repel any invader. The strikers are also hoarding muslin to hold over their mouths and noses in the event of another tear-gas attack.

Murphy is planning to issue a statement declaring that he plans to enforce Judge Gadola's order. An invasion of the plants is still out of the question, though. Even the National Guard officers in Flint are advising against it: their boys have no experience in putting down riots, and they don't have the stomach to shoot strikers. The National Guard's commanders advise Murphy to hold off on enforcing the writ of attachment. They're worried that in a confrontation with the strikers, the guardsmen will lose. If the Detroit talks fail to produce a settlement, they tell the governor, there is a nonviolent method of forcing the strikers to leave the plants: starving them out. The Guard can block food deliveries, as it did until the out-of-towners left Chevy Four. Then GM will have its property back in a matter of days.

Before drafting his letter, Murphy wants to speak with FDR again. The president gives him another pep talk. "Frank, you have been putting up a great fight," the ebullient voice from Washington blares through the receiver. "Stick to it! I know it is difficult, but eventually it will all work out all right. Don't be discouraged."

"Mr. President, I think I ought to make my position clear as chief executive of the state that the chief executive ought to be in a position to uphold the existing laws of the state," Murphy says to Roosevelt. "I will continue the conference, and they'll have to work out a solution, but in the meantime, I think I ought to make my position plain about the order of the court."

"You are absolutely right, Frank," Roosevelt says encouragingly. "You are justified in doing that. Go right ahead with it."

"When I make myself plain, Lewis can decide on the course he wants to take."

"Yes," Roosevelt agrees. "They will have to decide what they want to do."

After hanging up with Roosevelt, Murphy has a two-hour confab with Lewis, which he describes in his notes as "pleasant and interesting but fruitless." On the point of exclusive bargaining, Lewis is "unyielding." This is especially frustrating to Murphy, because the day before, GM gave him a letter agreeing not to bargain with any organization in the plants affected by the strike for ninety days without Murphy's permission. That's not good enough for Lewis. In this poker game, Lewis is bidding like a man who holds three aces and knows his opponent is trying to win with a pair of treys.

The next evening, Murphy thinks he has a breakthrough. After the parties return to the courtroom, Lawrence Fisher, negotiating on GM's behalf, tells him that the company will agree to the Toledo Agreement for three months. For three months, the company won't bargain with anyone but the UAWA.

Murphy thinks, "I can get this through if they extend it to six months."

Murphy pitches the six-month proposal to Lewis, assuring the labor leader that if he suggests it, GM will accept it: "You are the most persuasive man I have ever met in my life," Murphy says.

But Lewis demurs. "I don't want to make this offer unless I *know* it's going to be accepted," he says.

At 9:15 p.m., Murphy receives a call from Assistant Secretary of Labor Edward F. McGrady, who is monitoring the negotiations for Perkins. Excitedly the governor tells McGrady that he thinks a deal is imminent. The differences between the sides are down to three months. Three months of exclusive negotiations.

"We are experiencing the first ray of hope I have seen and I think we ought to crowd it through," Murphy says. "I have just had a grand talk with John Lewis alone. I asked the other men, who don't measure up to him at all, to leave and I am afraid they haven't told him the truth. It is just a three-month agreement extended to six on the same basis. If they agree to it for three months, with the Governor doing the arbitrating, on principle why won't they extend it to six? This includes the provision that they won't bargain with anyone until sanctioned by the Governor after a hearing. If it will settle this great strike I am willing to take a chance. The point is to get the strike settled which has the economy in Michigan and the nation terror-stricken. GM have agreed to do it for three months. John Lewis will take it if extended to six. There is no difference in principle and it takes the heat, so far as Washington is concerned, and puts it on my doorstep."

Murphy realizes that GM may require a little extra persuasion, so when he speaks to Frances Perkins a few moments later, he suggests to her, "You call or have someone else call Mr. Sloan," and tell him to order his men in Detroit to accept the six-month deal. Considering that their last conversation ended in a bitter shouting match, Sloan is unlikely to agree to speak to Perkins again, but he would have to talk to the president. In the next-to-last of his late-night calls with Washington, Murphy suggests to Roosevelt's secretary, Marvin McIntyre, that the chairman of GM and the president of the United States have a talk.

"The Boss has to get in touch with Sloan or the DuPonts, tell them this is okay," Murphy wheedles. "This strike has to go through tonight or we are done. I think GM ought to step up at this time. They agreed for three months and John Lewis wouldn't."

Finally, Murphy tells McGrady that he hopes to end the strike without threatening to expel the strikers. He's in a tough spot because law-and-order voters won't forgive him for ignoring the court order, but labor will never forgive him for enforcing it.

"Our only chance to settle this thing is tonight and I have got to make statements to protect my position," Murphy says. "One of two things ought to be done right away—the president should call Knudsen and tell him he thinks this is a good idea. No difference in principle—only three months—or the president should call Sloan or the DuPonts."

The president does not call Knudsen, or Sloan, or the DuPonts. It's nearly midnight when the courtroom empties and all the negotiators return to their hotel rooms, at the end of the strike's fortieth day, still without a deal.

John L. Lewis is in a bad mood, or at least he is pretending to be, to make the GM negotiators uncomfortable. That morning's *Detroit Free Press* carries a front-page report from the La Follette Committee hearings in Washington. A Pinkerton detective has testified that he visited Alexandria, Virginia, on a trip paid for by General Motors to gather information on the CIO. Lewis, the president of the CIO, lives in Alexandria. The detective claims not to know this. Lewis doesn't believe it—or at least he thinks that pretending not to believe it will place him on the moral high ground over GM, enabling him to extract some decisive concession.

During the afternoon negotiating session, Lewis interrupts the GM delegation to ask, "What's the basis for your statement? Some lousy Pinkerton?"

Glaring at his adversaries from beneath his famous gray eyebrows, Lewis growls, "I want to know who of you sent a Pinkerton bastard to spy on me and my home in Alexandria. I look on my home as my castle and I guard my privacy jealously. Who sent that Pinkerton? Was it you, Brown?"

Donaldson Brown, Sloan's right-hand man for finance, denies sending any detectives to spy on Lewis. So Lewis turns to GM counsel John Thomas Smith.

"Was it you, Smith?"

Smith insists he knows nothing about the Pinkertons, leading Lewis to grumble, "Well, how is this General Motors run, anyway?"

Finally, Lewis turns on Knudsen.

"What about the third one? You, Knudsen?"

"Well, I guess it must be my department," Knudsen concedes.

Lewis never finds out exactly who sent the Pinkerton man to Alexandria, but by the time he has exhausted his dudgeon, the train of the GM executives' arguments has been completely derailed. Lewis is following the advice of Bob Travis: "We've got 'em by the balls. Squeeze a little."

The strikers inside Chevy Four are also in a bad mood. In a letter to the governor, signed by Bud Simons, they have outlined a series of complaints directed at GM and the National Guard: the soldiers are preventing men from reentering the plants after trips home and are blocking friends and relatives from visiting at the gates; the heat and electricity are off; the water needs testing to prevent sickness. Murphy sends his state labor commissioner, George Krogstad, to investigate. After the National Guard allows him to pass through its lines, Krogstad presents himself to the steward at the door, who orders a truck to push aside the steel barricade. He finds a plant frozen to a standstill in an instant and prepared to resume running just as quickly. The machinery, shrouded in canvas, is regularly oiled. "Our police are constantly watching to see that the machinery is untouched and protected," the steward tells Krogstad, "We are going to win this strike and we want to be in a position to start at our jobs as quickly as we left them." All over the floors are paper plates sprinkled with sand for the men to spit in.

The steward relates to Krogstad that the strikers are bringing not only food through the windows in five-gallon jugs but water, too, because "we are afraid somebody might contaminate the city water." The strikers are also afraid the company will cut off the heat and electricity. To prepare for that eventuality they have laid in a supply of candles and built a stove in the recreation room. The rec room is where the strikers practice their only amusement—roller skating, although they "[enjoy] themselves to the extent of only three or four at a time, their skates being limited," Krogstad writes in his report to the governor

"What do you think of the governor's efforts to settle the strike?" Krogstad asks the steward.

"We are depending on him," the steward replies.

In his report, Krogstad tells Murphy that "the entire set up as far as discipline is concerned and so far as sanitation and safety are concerned is excellent. These boys are taking their strike very, very seriously. They maintain they have a definite grievance and are going to win. Those men are not sit-down strikers by any means. They are shut-down strikers. They have succeeded in absolutely stopping any production of Chevrolet motors and, by their organization in the factory, property is being protected, they are conscientiously protecting their jobs and their program, if it may be called such, is definitely well organized."

Murphy has one last card to play with John L. Lewis. On the evening of the ninth, he takes Lewis aside and reads him a five-page letter he has composed, dated February 8, in which he declares his intention to enforce Judge Gadola's order and clear the plants unless the strike is settled immediately.

"It has been and still is my earnest belief that matters in dispute should be settled by the peaceful methods of conference and negotiation," Murphy recites to Lewis. "Inasmuch, however, as the parties have thus far been unable after extended negotiations to find a basis of agreement, the time has come for all concerned to comply fully with the decision and order of the Court and take necessary steps to restore possession of the occupied plants to their rightful owner."

Lewis is unconvinced. To Murphy's further annoyance, Lewis thinks he has discovered another method of shaming him into ignoring the court order: appealing to his ethnic heritage.

"You talk of law," Lewis tells Murphy. "I believe you had a father, Governor Murphy, who went to prison because he defied British law in Ireland. He didn't like that law and British law and British judges put him in prison. I believe you had a grandfather and he didn't like British law and resisted it and he was hanged for it. Your grandfather was executed for resisting real law—law passed by the Lords Spiritual and Temporal and assented to by the Commons and sealed with the King's imprimatur. My compliments to your ancestors and I hope they will be able to look down and be proud of their Governor Frank B. Murphy, who was willing to resist not law but a General Motors injunction."

The argument is ineffective because it's entirely untrue. Neither of Murphy's grandfathers was hanged by the British. His father was imprisoned in Canada for three months during the Fenian raids, a series of attacks on British outposts in Canada in the 1860s by Irish Americans who were members of the Fenian Brotherhood, an organization agitating for Irish independence. Also, Murphy's middle initial is not B. His full name is William Francis Murphy. Lewis himself is the son of Welsh immigrants—his middle name is Llewellyn—so perhaps he is trying to bond with Murphy by inventing a shared sense of oppression by the English.

Murphy is offended by Lewis's rant. His pale face turning even paler with anger, he threatens that unless a settlement is reached that night, he will read the letter to the GM team, then give it to the newspapers, thus undercutting Lewis's negotiating position. Make a deal now, while you still have leverage, is the unspoken threat. The governor snatches the letter from Lewis's hand and storms out of the room.

As the Chevy Four steward told the labor commissioner, the strikers are "depending" on Murphy. He doesn't want labor to believe he's been anything less than an ally. He'll need union support in his reelection campaign next year. For those reasons, Lewis believes the letter is a bluff—and Lewis is right.

CHAPTER 11

EVACUATION DAY

JOHN L. LEWIS has a case of the grippe. On the morning of February 10, he awakens too ill to attend the negotiations—too ill, in fact, even to leave his bed. So Wyndham Mortimer represents the union in Judge George Murphy's courtroom, while Lewis stays in his hotel room at the Statler. There, Lewis and Martin hold a meeting of the UAWA's Board of Strategy, which has the authority to approve a settlement. The great labor chieftain directs the meeting in his pajamas, his belly swelling under the sheets.

Inside the courtroom, General Motors is giving in on the final two issues standing in the way of a settlement: the company agrees to rehire all workers, regardless of their actions during the strike, and it agrees to negotiate only with the UAWA for six months, as Governor Murphy has been urging.

Although President Roosevelt never fulfilled Murphy's request to call Alfred P. Sloan, his administration has been putting pressure on General Motors indirectly. Commerce secretary Daniel Roper has spoken to GM's Donaldson Brown. Perkins asks Roper to engage "an outstanding business leader" in the campaign to convince GM to capitulate. Roper enlists S. Clay Williams, chairman of the R. J. Reynolds Tobacco Company and an ardent New Dealer, who has served as head of the National Recovery Administration. Williams speaks with both Brown and Sloan, passing along the message that the White House wants this strike settled.

Brown tells Roper that GM wants only small changes in "the phraseology relating to a definition of the words 'exclusive bargaining agent.'" A clause in which the company and the union promise to negotiate in good faith "hereafter" is changed to "during the existence of the collective bargaining agreement."

However, no deal can be struck without Lewis's agreement, so late on the evening of February 10, Murphy adjourns the negotiations to the Statler Hotel. He installs Knudsen and Brown in Room 1236, where he has been staying during the negotiations so he can meet privately with the principals, then heads downstairs with Labor Department conciliator James F. Dewey to see the bedridden Lewis in Room 836. Murphy shuttles between the two rooms. Finally, in the wee hours of February 11, he takes the GM attorney, John Thomas Smith, to meet Lewis. The two men agree on the final language. Lewis pulls his blanket up to his chin and declares, "Now I can sleep for a while."

At 2:35 a.m., Murphy and Smith emerge from Lewis's suite to meet a throng of reporters in the hallway.

"*C'est fini*," Smith tells a newsman he recognizes.

"Come on up to my office," the governor tells the reporters, a grin deepening the lines of weariness on his face. "I have an announcement to make."

News of the settlement reaches the plants before dawn, while the morning newspapers are still in the delivery trucks. Good newsmen can't wait to break a story, so they simply shout it to the strikers before their own papers can scoop them. At four o'clock in the morning, a *Detroit News* photographer brings the tidings to Chevy Four. Using a military pass to get through the National Guard lines, he is met at the gates by union sentries, and taken inside to see Kermit Johnson. As the photographer is led to the back gate, where a truck barricaded with steel guards the entrance, plant police from nearby Chevy Nine overhear men talking about the settlement. They're just as thrilled as the strikers. No longer antagonists, the bulls and the sit-downers begin mingling and joshing like soldiers who have just crawled out of the trenches after the Armistice.

"Well, boys, it's sure fine," a guard says. "You are a nice bunch of fellows."

"You fellows are all right, too even if we did have to douse you with fire hoses in the last riot," a striker replies.

The National Guardsmen cheer. Strikers emerge from the factory to shake the hands and slap the backs of men they were prepared to do battle with a few days before. Inside Fisher Two, night sentries rouse sleeping strikers from their auto seat beds, urging them to join in a victory parade through the aisles between the assembly lines. Finally, a man carrying a *Flint Journal* makes his way past the guardsmen to deliver the story in black and white.

"Wish our van that carries the mail would come," writes Francis O'Rourke. "Hope the guard doesn't stop him today. Here he comes and he's smiling. He has a newspaper. Here's the headlines—STRIKE IS SETTLED! Thank God. The boys are dancing with each other, everyone is laughing. At last we go home. Home Sweet Home."

By the time the governor arrives at his brother's courtroom to oversee the signing ceremony at eleven in the morning, more than four hundred onlookers have crowded into the wooden pews. Governor Murphy seats himself at a clerk's table in front of the bench, between Wyndham Mortimer and William Knudsen, with his brother's gavel at his right hand. This isn't just a triumph for the union; it's a triumph for Murphy and for his new governorship—maybe the beginning of the "Murphy in 1940" presidential campaign. He wants to be front and center for the press photographers, who represent newspapers and newsreels from all over the country.

(There will be no Murphy in 1940 presidential campaign. The governor will lose reelection to Frank Fitzgerald, the man he defeated for the office, in part because of public dissatisfaction over his handling of the sit-down strike. Following Murphy's loss, FDR will reward his loyalty to the New Deal by nominating him as attorney general. Only then, during his Senate confirmation hearing, will Murphy make public the letter he read to Lewis, threatening to enforce the court order to evacuate the plants. As a candidate for the job of America's chief law enforcement officer, the letter will help Murphy demonstrate that he supports law and order. The Senate will confirm Murphy. Two years after that, it will confirm him to the US Supreme Court. The letter had been nothing more than a document designed to give Murphy political cover.)

"Well, the strike is ended, thanks to the courage and great faith of these men around me," Murphy says, gesturing also to GM's Donaldson Brown and John Thomas Smith and CIO General Counsel Lee Pressman, standing behind him. "I hope this peace will be a lasting one. It was brought about without force or violence. It was brought about through mutual trust and understanding."

Murphy signs the agreement with a flourish, using a fountain pen he received as a gift from President Manuel Quezon of the Philippines. There in the courtroom, the agreement is also signed by Knudsen, Brown, and Donaldson for the company, and Mortimer and Pressman for the union. The meeting then adjourns to the Statler Hotel, where the settlement receives its final signature from John L. Lewis, still confined to bed by his illness.

This is the document to which they affix their names:

> Agreement entered into on this 11th day of February, 1937, between General Motors Corporation (hereinafter referred to as the Corporation) and the International Union, United Automobile Workers of America (hereinafter referred to as the Union.)
>
> The Corporation hereby recognizes the Union as the Collective Bargaining Agency for those employees of the Corporation who are members of the Union. The Corporation recognizes and will not interfere with the right of its employees to be members of the Union. There shall be no discrimination, interference, restraint or coercion by the Corporation or any of its agents against any employee because of membership in the Union.

The Corporation and the Union agree to commence collective bargaining negotiations on February 16th with regard to the issues specified in the letter of January 4th, 1937, from the Union to the Corporation, for the purpose of entering into a collective bargaining agreement, or agreements, covering such issues, looking to a final and complete settlement of all matters in dispute.

The Union agrees to forthwith terminate the present strike against the Corporation, and to evacuate all plants now occupied by strikers.

The Corporation agrees that all of its plants, which are on strike, or otherwise idle shall resume operations as rapidly as possible.

It is understood that all employees now on strike or otherwise idle will return to their usual work when called and that no discrimination shall be made or prejudices exercised by the Corporation against any employee because of his former affiliation with, or activities in, the Union or the present strike.

The Union agrees that pending the negotiations referred to in Paragraph Two, there shall be no strikes called or any other interruption to or interference with production, by the Union or its members.

During the existence of the collective bargaining agreement contemplated pursuant to Paragraph Two, all opportunities to achieve a satisfactory settlement of any grievances or enforcement of any demands by negotiations shall be exhausted before there shall be any strikes or other interruption to or interference with production by the Union or its members. There shall be no attempts to intimidate or coerce any employees by the Union and there shall not be any solicitation or signing up of members by the Union on the premises of the Company. This is not to preclude individual discussion.

After the evacuation of its plants and the termination of the strike the Corporation agrees to consent to the entry of orders dismissing the injunction proceedings which have been started by the Corporation against the Union, or any of its members, or officers or any of its locals, including those pending in Flint, Michigan, and Cleveland, Ohio, and subject to the approval of the Court to discontinue all contempt proceedings which it has instituted thereunder.

From Washington, President Roosevelt sends Murphy a telegram offering his "heartfelt congratulations" for resolving "an acute situation which threatened serious disorder and dislocation, [but] has been amicably adjusted through negotiation." From New York City, Alfred P. Sloan praises Murphy for "the fairness with which he has handled a most difficult situation," and states that the agreement is "in complete accord with the principles upon which General Motors has stood since the beginning of this unfortunate controversy: It affirms the right of the representatives of any other group to negotiate in their own behalf, and we will continue our policy that any benefits extended in a settlement with any group will be accorded to all other employees in similar circumstances in the plants to which the settlement applies."

In Flint, the city's biggest celebration since Armistice Day is about to break out. One newspaper compares it to Mardi Gras, which took place in New Orleans just two days earlier. Mortimer drives straight from Detroit to Fisher One, where he reads the settlement to the strikers, who vote unanimously to accept it.

All day long, as the National Guard withdraws its barricade outside Fisher One, unionists who weren't part of the sit-down but hope to participate in the evacuation march have been trying to climb into the plant through the windows. Finally, the latecomers are told, "If you weren't willing to sit in with us, you can't come in to walk out with us."

Shortly after five o'clock, a half dozen bearded strikers—part of an unshaven crew who have dubbed themselves "the Beaver Boys of Flint"—walk out the front gate bearing bedding, clothes, an amplifier, and a heater. They drop it all off at strike headquarters across the street, then return to the plant with a delegation from the Women's Emergency Brigade, who have donned red and green berets. Up on the rooftop, a dozen men unfurl a banner declaring "Victory Is Ours." Now that the guardsmen are gone, the union sound car is driven through the north gate, past hundreds of supporters gathered on both sides of the driveway.

"Today is an exciting day," Homer Martin declares over the sound car's loudspeaker. "This evacuation marks the beginning of an era of better wages and better working conditions for workers. General Motors has at last recognized the rights of workers. We look forward to a great, united automobile workers' union. You have fought a great fight and the ends justified the means. The world pays you tribute."

When the strikers leave Chevy Four, the man at the head of the column, carrying an American flag, is Roscoe Van Zandt, an African American sanitation worker who was trapped in the plant during the takeover, then invited to join the occupation. His fellow sit-downers have voted to make him flag bearer.

At 5:42 p.m., Fisher One's factory whistle blows, signaling the end of the Flint sit-down strike—a forty-four-day shift. Four hundred men walk out of the plant and into the winter dusk behind the Stars and Stripes. They lead the march to the Pengelly Building for a celebratory rally. Showered with confetti and streamers, the strikers shout "Yea, Fisher!" and "What a day! What a day! We have won a great victory," before breaking into a rendition of "Hail! Hail! The Gang's All Here" that can barely be heard over the honking of hundreds of cars jamming Saginaw Street.

"Is there a question about who won the strike?" blares a voice from the sound car.

"No!" The crowd, which has grown into the thousands, sings a verse of "Solidarity Forever." Husbands seek out wives for their first kisses after lonely weeks apart. A mother hands an infant to the baby's long-absent father.

"Brothers and sisters, this is a historic occasion," Bob Travis announces from the sound car. "I want to congratulate the boys who were inside. Seventeen plants have been recognized by General Motors due to those boys."

Two thousand strong, carrying bundles of clothing in one hand and tiny flags in the other, the marchers stream north on Saginaw Avenue behind a flag bearer, two drummers, and a drum major—a patriotic vanguard resembling Archibald Willard's painting *The Spirit* of '76. Right behind them, litter bearers carry a stretcher bearing an effigy of George Boysen, the president of the Flint Alliance, whose role in prolonging the strike has not been forgotten.

As the marchers depart, GM plant police move in and bar the gates, exchanging civil farewells with the strikers, and even hurrying after them to return a bundle of clothing left behind in the watchmen's shanty.

When Travis arrives at Fisher Two, he meets with National Guard officers and persuades them to withdraw their troops across the Chevrolet Avenue bridge to allow a crowd waiting in front of Chevy Four to reach the plant. The guardsmen march away to the shouts of "Attaboy, soldiers" from men in second-story windows. The strikers file out the front door behind a guitarist plucking hillbilly tunes. When the Chevy Four crowd appears, it chants "Yea, Chevy! Yea, Chevy! Fight, fight, fight!," followed by "Yea, Fisher!" and then "Yea, Murphy!" in honor of the governor. The strikers fire flares into the deepening darkness, illuminating the march for newspaper photographers and newsreel cameramen.

Hundreds of strikers sporting union buttons march four abreast up Chevrolet Avenue, then Third Avenue, then Saginaw Street, where they halt to dump the Boysen effigy into the Flint River. The march ends at the Pengelly Building, where the victorious strikers jam inside to watch *The Strike Marches On*, a play put on by the Ladies' Auxiliary. They also break the temperance pledge they swore for the strike's duration. The celebration drags on until the wee hours of Friday morning, when tipsy couples drag themselves across the dance floor to the flagging strains of a weary band, every one of them drunk on booze and triumph.

After the evacuation, GM is building cars again within two weeks, despite complaints that the strikers trashed Fisher One by welding shut the doors, spitting tobacco on the floors, emptying the fire extinguishers, and cutting up upholstery to fashion blackjacks. The strikers are just as eager to get the plants running as the company, though. On the Saturday morning after the evacuation, Red MacAlpine packs his dinner pail and reports to Fisher One, where he spends the day picking up door hinges stockpiled as projectiles.

The workers immediately receive raises of five cents an hour. Then, on March 12, four weeks after the evacuation, the company and the union agree to a contract that applies to all the plants affected by the strikes. The contract establishes a grievance procedure, with shop committees to handle worker complaints. It specifies that in the case of necessary workforce reductions, workers will be laid off according to seniority. And it states, "The policy regarding speed of operations is that time studies shall be made on a basis of fairness and equity consistent with quality of workmanship efficiency of operations and the reasonable working capacities of normal operations."

The union doesn't get a thirty-hour workweek, and it doesn't get a minimum wage for all workers, in all plants, but the conditions that created so much exhaustion, anxiety, and resentment among the workers have now been banned, in black and white.

The Flint sit-down strike is the beginning of the United Auto Workers of America's rise to become the nation's preeminent labor union—the union that sets the standard for wages, benefits, and working conditions for industrial laborers everywhere. At the time of the May 1936 South Bend convention, when the strike was planned, the union had 30,000 members. By the end of the summer of 1937, membership had increased more than tenfold, to 375,000, as workers eagerly enroll to enjoy the benefits of belonging to the union that forced GM to the bargaining table. Less than a month after the Flint strike ends, workers at Chrysler's Dodge Main in Hamtramck, Michigan, sit down to force the company to recognize the UAWA. This time the strikers trust Governor Murphy enough to evacuate the plant, with the promise that it will not return to operations until an agreement is reached.

Walter Chrysler, who had counseled Sloan to compromise with the strikers, willingly signs a contract with the union. Henry Ford resists. On May 26, 1937, at Ford's River Rouge plant, forty guards batter and bloody four union organizers—including Walter Reuther—who attempt to cross a footbridge to distribute union literature (this becomes known in labor lore as the Battle of the Overpass). In 1941, Ford finally submits to a National Labor Relations Board election, in which its workers vote to join the UAWA. Eventually, the UAWA will represent all autoworkers at the Big Three: GM, Ford, and Chrysler.

Although he considers the Flint sit-down strike the worst setback of his career, even crusty, autocratic Alfred P. Sloan eventually comes to tolerate the United Auto Workers of America, rather than regarding the union as an antagonist. As Sloan writes in his 1964 memoir, *My Years with General Motors*:

> Our initial encounter with the CIO was . . . unhappy, for that organization attempted to enforce its demands for exclusive recognition by the most terrible acts of violence, and finally seized our properties in the sit-down strikes of 1937. I have no desire to revive the bitter controversies that arose over these early encounters with labor organizations. I mention them merely to suggest one of the reasons why our initial reaction to unionism was negative.
>
> What made the proposal seem especially grim in those early years was the persistent union attempt to invade basic management prerogatives. Our rights to determine production schedules, to set work standards, and to discipline workers were all suddenly called into question. Add to this the recurrent tendency of the union to inject itself into pricing policy, and it easy to understand why it seemed, to some corporate officials, as though the union might one day be virtually in control of our operations.
>
> In the end, we were fairly successful in combating these invasions of management rights. There is no longer any real doubt that pricing is a management, not a union, function. So far as our operations are concerned, we have moved to codify certain practices, to discuss workers' grievances with union representatives, and to submit to arbitration the few grievances that remain unsettled. But on the whole, we have retained all the basic powers to manage.

> The issue of unionism at General Motors is long since settled. We have achieved workable relations with all of the unions representing our employees.

(Unlike his contemporaries Henry Ford and Walter Chrysler, Sloan does not have a car named after him. His legacies are the Alfred P. Sloan Foundation, which provides scientific grants, and the Memorial Sloan Kettering Cancer Center, which he funded with a fellow GM executive, Charles Kettering.)

Now that they have a contract, no longer do workers have to bribe their foremen with food or favors in order to keep their names off a layoff list. No longer is a worker's career determined by the number of years he can keep pace with an assembly line tuned to the limit of human endurance.

When the sit-downer Henry Lorenz goes back to work at Fisher One, he feels, for the first time in his career at General Motors, that he and his fellow workers are "respected as human beings," which is all he was hoping for when he went on strike. "You didn't go to work and felt like you were a dog on a leash," Lorenz recalls many years later. "You were a little more freer. You could do your job."

After the strike, when a foreman turns the crank to speed up the line by two or three cars an hour, the shop steward can tell him, "Turn the line back to where it was before. Your schedule called for forty-four cars per hour, not forty-six or fifty or a hundred."

With his wages no longer dependent on a piecework bonus, Lorenz's pay rises from eighty-nine cents an hour to a dollar twenty-nine. Before the strike, when Lorenz begged a foreman for a bathroom break, he was often told, "You can wait; it's only another fifteen or twenty minutes until the shift ends." Now, a relief man is there to take his place if he needs to relieve himself, or go to the hospital, or gets a tack stuck in his finger.

Before the strike, Lorenz's foreman led him to a window and asked, "What do you see down there?"

"People," Lorenz replied.

"What do you think they are doing down there?"

"Looking for a job."

"You're smart. Now go back and get caught up or you will be standing in line looking for a job."

Lorenz's foreman can no longer threaten him with unemployment.

Before the strike, employees out of favor with the foreman were assigned to unpleasant jobs called "whipping posts" as a kind of hazing. Once, while working on the line, Lorenz was forced to cement parts to the bottoms of doors. He worked hunched over for hours, with no oleum to clean the cement off his fingers. Now that task is assigned to new employees, who are provided with oleum.

"[The struggle] was worth it tenfold," Lorenz later says. "Number one, when you walked into the shop and you went to do your job you didn't feel like you were being watched every minute by somebody. You didn't feel like when the line started that the foreman would come by and stand behind a post and watch to see if you worked to your full extent. Plus the fact that he didn't turn the crank at the end of the line to make the cars come faster. All these things stopped."

After the strike Lorenz works for General Motors for only nine more months, but many of his fellow strikers remain with the company for the rest of their working lives, retiring in the 1960s and '70s with pensions and lifetime healthcare benefits that were unimaginable to the autoworkers of the Depression—won in future contracts that would have been impossible without the sit-down strike.

It's a good place to work, General Motors.

EPILOGUE

EVERETT KETCHUM DIED IN 2013, at the age of ninety-eight. His ashes were buried in a grave beneath a tree outside a Presbyterian church in East Lansing that he helped found. Everett's funeral was a celebration of a prosperous and generous life, made possible by an event that took place over three quarters of a century before: the Flint sit-down strike, which historians have credited as the natal event of the modern American labor movement. The British Broadcasting Corporation dubbed it "the strike heard 'round the world." Ketchum was one of the last surviving participants. He was a fifty-cent-an-hour apprentice, just beginning his career. He signed on with the strike anyway, spending tense, idle nights on the shop floor playing euchre, watching movies, or listening to speeches by United Auto Workers organizers.

Everett not only participated in the battle that founded the blue-collar middle class but enjoyed all the rewards of the peace that it ushered in. There was never a better time to work for General Motors than the period from the 1940s through the 1970s. There was never a better time to be a factory worker, period. After GM recognized the UAWA, Everett received a pension plan and health insurance. During World War II, he stayed out of combat by building armored trucks for Chevrolet. Once the war was won, "Flint was booming. They even bused people up from the South, bring 'em up here to work. Everybody was working, everybody had a job, everybody had one or two cars, and you kept getting bigger homes. Oh, boy."

Widowed when his wife died in an automobile accident, Everett married a woman who ran the 4-H program at Michigan State College, and transferred to the Oldsmobile plant in nearby Lansing. As a tool-and-die maker, producing dies that stamped out fenders, he belonged to the shop-rat elite. Skilled tradesman at GM was the best job in town, blue or white collar. The tradesmen earned more money than the assembly-line workers, and when GM went bankrupt, in 2008, the retirees held on to their company health insurance, unlike the non-union salesmen and engineers. With another perk, his night-shift bonus, Everett bought houses near the campus and rented them to Michigan State students. In the early 1960s, around the time he began wearing the UAW twenty-five-year service ring that protruded from his fist like a pewter nut, he joined the company glee club, the Rocketaires, named after the Oldsmobile Rocket engine. Oldsmobile provided the Rocketaires' satin uniforms, gave them time off to rehearse, and paid them to sing at Christmas concerts in the company's two-thousand-seat auditorium. Every two years, Everett paid cash for a new Oldsmobile, getting an employee discount. When he retired in 1976, two years before the US auto industry hit its all-time high of 977,000 workers, the former four-bit apprentice was earning $27 an hour—more than fifty times his starting wage and certainly more than any of the budget analysts and wildlife biologists in Lansing's mazes of state government cubicles.

"The whole picture, to me, I was in the right place at the right time," he reflected. "I always had a job right from the time I was a five-year-old kid. I always had a job. My father was a small-town mechanic and he and another fella had a garage and my job was, after school, I come back and cleaned the tools up for the next day. I was twelve, fourteen years old. I got five dollars a day every day that I worked. For me, that was big money. At GM, I come in there at a good time. It was just the right era for a lot of things, and I appreciate that."

After he retired, he was guaranteed free health care for the rest of his life, which turned out to be thirty-seven more years, almost as long as he'd worked in the shop. Union wages made him well-to-do, and he shared his good fortune with others. He noticed that a hostess at his favorite pancake house always covered her mouth when she led him to a booth. He asked why. Reluctantly she revealed a mouth with two missing teeth and a cracked incisor. Soon after, Everett handed her a dentist's business card.

"Go there today and make an appointment," he ordered.

Dentures cost seven thousand dollars. Everett paid.

At the same restaurant was a bus girl who wouldn't smile because of her ruined teeth. Everett sent her to a dentist, too. Eventually Everett's generosity made him a minor celebrity in Lansing. Word got around about the Flap Jack Shack's tooth fairy. The *Lansing State Journal* called. Everett would not allow his name to appear in the newspaper because of his acts of charity, so the reporter referred to him as Dental Man.

Without the benefits the UAW won from General Motors, Everett would have lived his old age as an unwanted uncle, if he had lived his old age at all. After GM went bankrupt in 2008, I told him that his superannuation—both the cause and the result of his use of health benefits—was personally responsible for GM's financial crisis. Everett cackled.

"I don't know where I'd be living without it," he said. "I'd be living with one of my nephews or one of my nieces. My two sisters is gone. I really don't know where I'd be if I didn't have what I have. If I had to buy my insurance that I got, I wouldn't be living in this two-thousand-dollar-a-month apartment. But how long are my benefits gonna last, 'cause I'm not working? All the money that I've got is interest money that I saved through the years."

America's greatest twentieth-century invention was not the airplane, nor the atomic bomb, nor the lunar lander. It was the middle class. We won the Cold War not because of our military strength, but because we shared our wealth more broadly than the communists and, as a result, had more wealth to share. The communists boasted of creating a workers' paradise in the Soviet Union, but Michiganders lived in the real thing: two cars in every driveway, summer cottages and deer hunting trips Up North. So much of that, inside the auto industry and out, was the result of victories won by the United Auto Workers.

As the unions saw it, the labor movement overthrew an economic order in which the mass of humankind had been born with saddles on their backs, to be ridden by a booted and spurred aristocracy, an order in which the many toiled to provide pleasures for the few. Collective bargaining made obsolete the iron law of wages, which stated that labor could command no more than a subsistence living from capital. It made obsolete the notorious marketplace known as "bidding at the factory gate," in which workers offered their services for ten cents an hour, only to lose the job to a more desperate man who offered nine.

In September 1970, more than four hundred thousand GM workers went on strike and stayed out on strike for sixty-seven days, until GM gave them an annual cost-of-living increase and the right to retire with full benefits after thirty years on the job—the so-called "thirty and out" clause.

"We used to get stoned in the newspapers, every time we'd get something [new] in our contract," said Don Cooper, a Lansing autoworker who participated in that strike. "'Well, the autoworkers drove the price up because they got a raise.' But then everybody else would start getting raises, too, after we did."

For a city whose population peaked at just under two hundred thousand, Flint, Michigan, has played an outsize role in American history. As late as 1980, when General Motors employed eighty thousand workers in Genesee County, Flint boasted the highest median wage for workers under thirty-five in the country, thanks to union contracts that allowed new employees to start at the same wage as their more experienced line mates. The city's overall median income for young workes was higher than San Francisco's. Flint was the model of a community whose wealth was shared broadly, rather than concentrated among an elite. Flint's only true aristocrat was Charles Stewart Mott, who in 1907 accepted a 5 percent share in GM to move his wheel manufacturer from Utica, New York, to Flint. Mott died in 1973, leaving his fortune to a foundation that has spent more than $1 billion on civic projects.

Flint, the middle class, the union movement, and the auto industry are none of them as prosperous as they were in the twentieth century. The decline of all four is intertwined. In the early 1980s, the American auto industry began losing customers to Japanese and German manufacturers. Motorists responded to gasoline shortages by purchasing fuel-efficient vehicles, which foreigners built well (the Toyota Corolla, the VW Beetle) and Americans built like crap (the Ford Pinto, the Chevy Chevette). The term "Rust Belt" became synonymous with the industrial Midwest. GM's layoffs and factory closings hit its hometown particularly hard, resulting in what locals call "the pull out."

On December 10, 1987, almost exactly fifty-one years after the sit-down strike began there, GM closed Fisher One, putting 2,550 employees out of work. After the plant was sold to a Detroit developer, a few of the remaining sit-downers picketed in protest. They believed the company was exacting belated revenge for the sit-down strike.

"I don't think they ever liked us since the sit-down strike," said an eighty-two-year-old strike veteran as pickets chanted "Union In, Scabs Out" at contractors hired to maintain the plant for the new owners—the UAW wanted its own members doing the work.

"The pride and heritage of the Sit Downers demands that we do not cave in to GM now or ever," declared the president of Local 581, which represented the plant. "Local 581 will not give up on the fight for justice and representation in our plant that the retirees organized so long ago."

In fact, GM closed Fisher One because it was building Buick City, an eight-factory, 235-acre, $280 million complex on Industrial Avenue, which employed 28,000 workers. Instead of building bodies on the South End of Flint and trucking them to the North End, GM built the entire car in one location. On November 22, 1997, GM announced it was closing Buick City, an announcement a local UAW official called "some Thanksgiving bad news that will cripple our community for years to come." The Fisher One building is now the headquarters of Diplomat Pharmacy, a drug distributor.

The militancy that inspired the Flint sit-down strike was passed down to the next generation of Flint autoworkers, and to the generation after that. The sons and grandsons of the sit-downers believed that their labor had built GM, and that the company owed them good wages and benefits in return. Strikes in Flint took twice as long to settle as strikes in other GM towns, but they were so effective that the company's local nickname was Generous Motors.

Today, GM's Flint-area workforce is down to 6,500—less than a tenth of what it was in the 1970s. That's consistent with the overall decline of GM's hourly employment, which has fallen from 511,000 to 50,000, as a result of automation and the loss of market share. It's easier to argue that Flint suffered because it was a one-industry town, where two-thirds of the workforce depended on an auto factory paycheck, than to argue that GM singled it out for disinvestment as revenge for the sit-down strike.

Flint, the city that once boasted the nation's strongest middle class, now has the nation's highest poverty rate, with nearly half its residents unable to pay for basic needs. Besides being the nation's poorest city, in some years Flint has been its most violent. In 2010, sixty-six people were murdered in Flint, breaking a record set when the city had twice the population and establishing a murder rate so high that New York would have needed five thousand murders to match it. In 2011, Michigan governor Rick Snyder appointed an emergency manager to oversee Flint's distressed finances. To save money on water costs, the manager withdrew Flint from Detroit's water system and arranged to pipe water from Lake Huron instead. While the pipeline was being built, Flint drew its drinking water from the Flint River, but failed to treat it to prevent corrosion of lead pipes. State officials were accused of lying that Flint's water plant was employing sufficient corrosion controls, and of altering water quality reports to falsely lower lead levels. The Flint water crisis caused twelve deaths from Legionnaires' disease, introduced lead into the blood of thousands of children, and landed Flint on the cover of *Time* magazine under the headline "The Poisoning of an American City."

Were the victories of the sit-down strike ephemeral, not just for Flint but for the entire middle class? Did they benefit only the generation that won them, and the generation that followed? American workers are back to where they were before the strike happened. Between 1970 and 2014, the share of the nation's income that went to the middle class—defined by the Pew Research Center as households that earn from two-thirds to double the median income—fell from 62 percent in 1970 to 43 percent in 2014. Meanwhile, the wealthiest 1 percent claimed 19 percent of the nation's income—their highest share since 1928. From 1947 to 1973, hourly earnings increased an average of 2.2 percent a year. Since then they've been stagnant, barely keeping up with inflation even as productivity has boomed. Was the middle class just a moment, an interlude between two gilded ages that more closely reflect the way most societies have structured themselves economically, with an aristocracy and a peasantry?

The middle class's decline in the United States is coterminous with the decline of the labor movement. At the 2019 White Shirt Day, a commemoration of the sit-down strike held each February 11 in Flint (union members wear white shirts, reflecting their view that they're just as good as management), UAW vice president Cynthia Estrada noted that the union no longer represents a majority of workers who build vehicles in the United States. Foreign manufacturers here, such as Volkswagen, Toyota, and BMW, have resisted unionization by building their plants in the South, a region traditionally hostile to labor unions. When the UAW tried to organize a Volkswagen plant in Chattanooga, Tennessee, in 2014, a group of anti-union workers calling itself Southern Momentum invoked cultural, regional, racial, and political resentments to persuade VW employees that a union was a threat not just to their livelihoods but to their way of life. Billboards labeled the UAW "the United Obama Workers" and presented images of the derelict Packard Motors plant alongside the slogan "Detroit: Brought to You by the UAW." A pamphlet compared the union's campaign to a Civil War campaign by the Union Army: "One hundred and fifty years ago . . . the people of Tennessee routed such a force in the Battle of Chickamauga." The UAW lost the election, 712–626. In fact, manufacturing workers are now less likely to be represented by unions than the workforce as a whole.

Shortly after losing that organizing vote in Tennessee, the UAW won a campaign to represent graduate students employed as teaching assistants at New York University. In 1983, around the time the term "Rust Belt" entered the public consciousness, 30 percent of factory workers were still unionized. Today, it's around 9 percent. According to the Bureau of Labor Statistics, the most unionized job category is "education, training and library occupations."

The anti-labor movement has succeeded not only in busting industries traditionally organized by labor but also in preventing the unionization of jobs that have replaced well-paying industrial work. In the 1970s, General Motors was the largest private employer in the United States. In the twenty-first century, that title is shared by Walmart and Amazon, two companies that have staunchly resisted unions and whose owners are among the ten wealthiest Americans. Given the billions in profits these companies generate, there's no reason their employees can't be as well compensated as autoworkers. The reasons given for the low pay—that retail work and package handling are unskilled, entry-level jobs not meant to support a family or lead to a career—are ex post facto justifications made possible by the reality that Walmart and Amazon can get away with paying low wages because they don't fear unionization.

The shrinking of the middle class is not a failure of capitalism. It's a failure of government. Capitalism has been doing exactly what it was designed to do: concentrating wealth in the ownership class, while providing the mass of workers with just enough wages to feed, house, and clothe themselves. That's the natural drift of the relationship between capital and labor, and it can only be arrested by an activist government that chooses to step in as a referee—as Frank Murphy, Frances Perkins, and Franklin D. Roosevelt did in 1937.

Free-market conservatives, though, consider unions cartels that restrain trade and raise wages above market rates. They've been at war with the labor movement since just after World War II, when a wave of strikes led to the passage of the Taft-Hartley Act, which outlawed the closed shop, making so-called "right-to-work" laws possible. Ronald Reagan's firing of the striking air traffic controllers in 1981 was considered the most decisive signal that the federal government would henceforth take the side of employers rather than unions.

Collective bargaining is inimical to the conservative ideal of the rugged individual. The labor movement, whose byword is solidarity, seemingly has less of a place in modern America, which is a more individualistic society than it was during the heyday of unions. In the 1950s, America was a Common Man's country, an economically liberal, socially conservative nation that enforced restraints on both personal and economic behavior: it was considered wrong to amass an enormous fortune at the expense of workers, like the robber barons whose greed was blamed for the Depression, still a living memory for most adults. In 1950, the average CEO earned twenty times as much as his employees; that factor is now more than 300. The United States is a freer country now than it was then, but that freedom has, arguably, been bad for the labor movement.

In *Capitalism: Its Origins and Evolution as a System of Governance*, Bruce Scott of the Harvard Business School describes how the dismantling of social and political strictures in the 1960s eventually resulted in demands for the dismantling of economic strictures:

> I trace the rise of deregulation to the emergence of social, political and economic instabilities in the United States in the 1960s, starting with the instabilities associated with societal protests against segregation or institutionalized racism. The notion of self-regulation, or the removal of traditional standards of behavior (which were seen as tools of racial prejudice, sexism, elitism, and/or protection of privilege) in favor of market-based standards of behavior became popular in the social, then the political, and finally, the economic realms.

Can the middle class rise again? During the coronavirus crisis of 2020, workers at an Amazon delivery center in Chicago organized a movement that led to the company's granting paid time off to all employees, both full and part time. Amazon workers also walked off the job to demand that the company shut down the facility after an employee tested positive for covid-19. During the crisis, workers deemed "essential" such as grocery clerks, waiters, baristas, and package handlers were among those who generally receive the lowest pay and fewest benefits. Indeed, Amazon hired a hundred thousand new package handlers to handle the surge in online shopping that resulted from stay-at-home orders.

The crisis was a radicalizing experience for many of those workers. It taught them that their labor is worth more than their employers have been paying them. Could it have been a step toward another sit-down strike? Amazon's services are as essential to twenty-first-century life as the automobile was to life in the twentieth. The company's founder, Jeff Bezos, is wealthier than Henry Ford was. If workers were to occupy Amazon fulfillment and delivery centers to demand greater safety and job security—the same causes that motivated GM workers in Flint in 1936—they could shut down American commerce. A sit-down strike is not an obsolete tactic. The blueprint for better working conditions, and for a revival of the middle class, is in this book.

In the words of Olen Ham, a sit-down striker who died a year before Everett Ketchum, at the age of ninety-five: "We created the middle class." It may take another sit-down to recreate it.

ACKNOWLEDGMENTS

I SPENT A LOT OF TIME in Flint to research this book, and I benefited from the help and hospitality of a lot of Flintstones.

On my first trip there, I met with Steve Dawes, who is now director of UAW Region 1D. Steve showed me the sit-down strike memorial outside region headquarters, which features bronze representations of some of the strike's most important events. He also invited me to White Shirt Day, a ceremony commemorating the strike, held every February 11 in Flint.

Colleen Marquis was new to the job of archivist at the Genesee Historical Collections Center at the University of Michigan–Flint's Frances Willson Thompson Library. Nonetheless, she was able to direct me to oral histories, newspaper clippings, and scrapbooks that helped me tell this story. The staff at Wayne State University's Walter Reuther Library in Detroit also guided me toward a wealth of material on the strike. So did the late Greg Miller at the Kettering University Archives.

Jan and Ted Nelson allowed me to stay at their home whenever I visited Flint, and introduced me to Elizabeth Perkins-Harbin, the daughter and niece of the Perkins brothers, who are the subjects of chapter 2 in this book.

Thanks also to former UM-Flint professor Neil Leighton, who conducted dozens of oral history interviews with strikers in the late 1970s and early 1980s. Not only were those interviews invaluable resources; so was Neil. We met for lunch at Coral Gables in East Lansing while I was still researching the book, and he read the manuscript for accuracy.

In writing this book, I tried to combine the storytelling skills of a journalist with the research skills of a historian. To that end, I earned a master's degree in history from the Harvard Extension School. Two instructors in particular, Doug Bond and Don Ostrowski, taught me the archival research methods I used in this project. My agent, Jonah Straus, and my editor, Joanna Green, believed I could write a history book.

Finally, of course, I want to thank my family: Kristen, Lark, and Birch. I love you all. I hope this makes you proud of me.

A NOTE ON SOURCES

In writing a narrative account of the Flint sit-down strike, I tried as much as possible to recreate interactions and conversations between the participants. The most useful resource in this endeavor was an oral history project conducted in the late 1970s and early 1980s by the University of Michigan–Flint Labor History Project. A team of interviewers overseen by a political science professor, Neil Leighton, and a history professor, Kenneth West, interviewed more than a hundred surviving strikers and Women's Emergency Brigade members. Most of the interviews—along with boxes of files, scrapbooks, and memorabilia from the strike—are archived in boxes at the Genesee Historical Collections Center at the university's Frances Willson Thompson Library. There are no strikers left to tell the story of the Flint sit-down, but their voices and reminiscences have been preserved in the university repository. (Some of the interview transcripts are available online, at www.umflint.edu/archives/labor-history-project.)

Also useful were two memoirs of the strike: *Organize! My Life as a Union Man*, by Wyndham Mortimer, and *The Many and the Few: A Chronicle of the Dynamic Auto Workers*, by Henry Kraus. Both include detailed reconstructions of important events, such as the takeovers of Fisher One and Chevy Four. Secretary of Labor Frances Perkins shared her recollections of the strike in her memoir, *The Roosevelt I Knew*, and in a series of oral history interviews with Columbia University. Perkins recreated her conversations with some of the era's most important figures, including John L. Lewis, Frank Murphy, Alfred P. Sloan, John Nance Garner, and Franklin D. Roosevelt. Finally, I spent a lot of time in the archives of the *Flint Journal*, whose anonymous reporters wrote the first draft of every Flint sit-down strike history.

NOTES

ABBREVIATIONS

GHCC Genesee Historical Collections Center, Frances Willson Thompson Library, University of Michigan–Flint

FMP Frank Murphy Papers, Roll 108, Bentley Historical Library, University of Michigan–Ann Arbor, online at https://quod.lib.umich.edu/b/bhlead/umich-bhl-86734

FJ *Flint Journal*, U of Michigan–Flint Library, Flint Public Library, and Library of Michigan

INTRODUCTION: VEHICLE CITY

(1) *Durant, the man who would one day found General Motors:* Bernard A. Weisberger, *The Dream Maker: William C. Durant, Founder of General Motors* (Boston: Little, Brown, 1979), 39–59.

(2) *"Flint is the most natural center for the manufacture of autos":* Lawrence R. Gustin, *Billy Durant: Creator of General Motors* (Ann Arbor: University of Michigan Press, 2008), 60–61.

(2) *The buyers asked Durant to run Buick:* Gustin, *Billy Durant*, 40–110.

(3) *In the 1900s, Flint's population tripled:* Blake Thorne, "See How Flint's Population Has Changed over 150 Years," MLive.com, May 23, 2014.

(3) *The plants were so desperate for workers:* Frank Rodolf, "An Industrial History of Flint," unpublished manuscript, 1949, Flint Public Library, Automotive History Collection.

(4) *"Saginaw Street was a sight":* Rodolf, "An Industrial History of Flint."

(4) *Whole families filled the streets:* Rodolf, "An Industrial History of Flint."

(5) *As the new century began its second decade:* Terry B. Dunhan and Lawrence R. Gustin, *The Buick: A Complete History*, 5th rev. ed. (Princeton, NJ: Princeton Publishing, 1980), 59–60.

(5) *"When Buick was closed for inventory"*: Rodolf, "An Industrial History of Flint."

(5) *Flint more than doubled in population:* Thorne, "See How Flint's Population Has Changed over 150 Years."

(6) *The company established a dummy developer:* Tomlison, Harburn, York & Associates et al., Civic Park Home Preservation Manual (City of Flint: Flint Neighborhood Preservation and Improvement Project and City of Flint, 1981), www.thelandbank.org/downloads/1cphomepresman1981.pdf, 1–15.

(6) *General Motors did not control just its employees' working hours: I.M.A. News.*

(7) *As long as General Motors was growing:* Rodolf, "An Industrial History of Flint."

(7) *"There was a lot of sharp sheet metal"*: Ken Malone, "Even Fainting of Workers Wouldn't Stop Line," FJ, December 28, 1986.

CHAPTER 1: A STRANGER IN TOWN

(9) *The gauges filled:* Mark Torregrossa, "Recent Heat Doesn't Even Compare to 1936 Heat Wave," MLive.com, July 10, 2018.

(10) *one of the toughest jobs at General Motors:* Gilbert Rose, interview by Bill Meyer, Flint, August 13, 1979, transcript, GHCC.

(10) *At the beginning of a shift:* William Genske, interview transcript, GHCC.

(11) *"The man was so driven by the speedup"*: Genora Johnson Dollinger, in *With Babies and Banners: Story of the Women's Emergency Brigade*, dir. Lorraine Gray, New Day Films, 1979.

(11) *A man named Neil Yaklin:* Neil Yaklin, interview by Raymond Yaklin, 1982, transcript, GHCC.

(12) *Presses chop off fingers:* Orvel Simmons, interview by Kenneth B. West, February 28, 1980; Robert Breedlove interview, 1978, transcript, GHCC; Grant Ricks, interview by Kenneth West, March 13, 1980, GHCC.

(12) *That sweltering summer:* Wyndham Mortimer, *Organize! My Life as a Union Man* (Boston: Beacon Press, 1971), 103–22.

(13) *Mort, as he is known:* Mortimer, *Organize!*, 1–68.

(14) *"To organize Flint"*: Mortimer, *Organize!*, 51.

(15) *Another obstacle, as Mortimer sees it:* FJ, October 1930; March 1934.

(15) *"foreign agitators and communists from Detroit, Pontiac and Chicago"*: FJ, March 1930.

(16) *The AFL chartered 183 federal auto unions:* John Barnard, *American Vanguard: The United Auto Workers During the Reuther Years, 1935–1970* (Detroit: Wayne State University Press), 47.

(17) *John L. Lewis, the president of the United Mine Workers:* Melvyn Dubofsky and Warren Van Tine, *John L. Lewis: A Biography* (New York: Quadrangle/New York Times Book Company, 1977), 203–47.

(18) *"Not until the workers in the automotive"*: "Lewis Committee for Industrial Unionism Is Asked to Disband," *Cedar Rapids Tribune*, January 24, 1936.

(19) *Almost immediately after Lewis spoke:* Barnard, *American Vanguard,* 59; Mortimer, *Organize!,* 101–8.

(21) *Among Mortimer's first recruits is Berdine Simons:* Bud Simons, interview, 1978, GHCC.

(23) *Most of the four thousand African American autoworkers:* Mortimer, *Organize!,* 110.

(25) *Surreptitiously, Clark approaches his fellow foundry workers:* Henry Clark, interview by Neil Leighton, 1978, GHCC.

CHAPTER 2: THE PERKINS BOYS

(27) *Wyndham Mortimer starts the campaign:* Mortimer, *Organize!,* 116–18.

(27) *Bob Travis, an organizer from Toledo:* Bob Travis, interview by Neil Leighton, Los Angeles, December 13–15, 1978, GHCC.

(29) *"Flint was a GM town to the bone":* Victor Reuther, *The Brothers Reuther and the Story of the UAW: A Memoir* (New York: Houghton Mifflin, 1976), 143.

(29) *Among his hideouts:* Leo Connelly, interview by Bill Meyer, Flint, March 6, 1980, GHCC.

(30) *Lenz is aware of the organizing drive:* David Farber, *Sloan Rules: Alfred P. Sloan and the Triumph of General Motors* (Chicago: University of Chicago Press, 2002), 192.

(30) *"How come," Roy Reuther asks:* Reuther, *The Brothers Reuther,* 145.

(31) *"If I can only feel, when my day is done":* Sidney Fine, *Frank Murphy: A Michigan Life* (The Clarence M. Burton Memorial Lecture 1984), pamphlet (Lansing: Historical Society of Michigan, 1985), 2.

(31) *The 1937 model year:* Raymond Zink, interview by Kenneth West, March 4, 1980, GHCC.

(32) *In 1934, the National Industrial Recovery Administration:* National Industrial Recovery Administration, *Hearing on Regularizing Employment and Otherwise Improving the Conditions of Labor in the Automobile Industry* (Washington, DC: 1934), 97–98.

(32) *Another worker lists his earnings:* National Industrial Recovery Administration, *Hearing on Regularizing Employment,* 144–47.

(33) *Wildcat strikes break out:* Bud Simons interview.

(33) *"Honest to God, Bob":* Henry Kraus, *The Many and the Few: A Chronicle of Dynamic Auto Workers* (Urbana: University of Illinois Press, 1985), 42–45.

(34) *Laborers have been sitting down:* Joel Seidman, *Sit Down* (New York: League for Industrial Democracy, 1937), 1–6.

(35) *"Sit-downs do not occur":* Seidman, *Sit Down,* 1.

(35) *Thus, when Bill and Frank Perkins:* The following account draws on Kraus, *The Many and the Few,* 47–54; Bill and Frank Perkins, interview, August 1988; Bruce Malott, interview by Kenneth West, August 21, 1979.

(39) *"The dark clouds of fear":* Mortimer, *Organize!,* 124.

(39) *Everett Ketchum is a twenty-one-year-old:* Everett Ketchum, author interview, East Lansing, Michigan, summer 2011.

(40) *The simplest way to satisfy a foreman:* Cloyse Crane, interview by Neil Leighton, Flint, February 27, 1980, transcript, GHCC.

(40) *One night-shift Chevy foreman:* Grant Ricks, interview by Kenneth West, March 13, 1980, transcript, GHCC.

(40) *Even religion plays a role:* Adlore LaRose, interview by Andy Grantham, Flint, October 1978, transcript, GHCC.

(40) *Gibbs is no militant:* Robert Gibbs, interview by Bill Meyer, Grand Blanc, Michigan, May 29, 1980, GHCC.

(42) *Roy Reuther and Travis are so concerned:* Kraus, *The Many and the Few*, 62–68.

(43) *Wyndham Mortimer considers Murphy:* Mortimer, *Organize!*, 124–25.

(44) *emboldened workers begin sitting down:* Barnard, *American Vanguard*, 83.

(45) *On the first day of winter:* Kraus, *The Many and the Few*, 76–77.

CHAPTER 3: "THIS IS WHERE THE FIGHT BEGINS"

(47) *The great Flint sit-down strike actually begins in Cleveland:* Mortimer, *Organize!*, 125–27.

(48) *On the evening of the thirtieth:* Joe Devitt, interview by Jay Flowers, July 1978; William Genske, interview by Mary Hempsall; Kraus, *The Many and the Few*, 86–90.

(52) *Bud Simons walks up and down:* Bud Simons Papers, Walter Reuther Library, Wayne State University.

(54) *That morning, Francis O'Rourke:* Francis O'Rourke, "Flint 1936–7: Diary of a Sitdowner," GHCC, available online at https://libcom.org/history/flint-1936-7-diary-sitdowner.

(54) *"Send over some cigarettes at once":* Bud Simons Papers, Walter Reuther Library, Wayne State University.

(55) *Down at GM headquarters in Detroit:* "Here Is Complete Text of Knudsen's Statement Outlining Attitude on Collective Bargaining," *FJ*, January 1, 1937.

(55) *Outside the militant Fisher Body plants:* "Bitter Labor Battle Looms as A.F.L. Orders Craft Unions Back to Work," *FJ*, January 10, 1937; "Strike Situation at a Glance," *FJ*, January 5, 1937.

(56) *Judge Edward D. Black issues an injunction:* General Motors Corporation v. United Auto Workers of America, Genesee County Circuit Court, 1937.

(56) *Despite the authority of his office:* Kraus, *The Many and the Few*, 108–9; "Sheriff Fails to Serve Papers Although He Talks to Committee," *FJ*, January 4, 1937.

(57) *Next, the sheriff visits the Pengelly Building:* Kraus, *The Many and the Few*, 110–11; "Sheriff Fails to Serve Papers."

(58) *Martin is not quite finished with Judge Black:* "Martin Urges Judge Black Be Impeached," *FJ*, January 7, 1937.

(58) *Before leaving Flint:* "G.M. Turns Down Demands Made by Automobile Union," *FJ*, January 4, 1937.

(60) *The strikes are spreading:* "Strike Situation at a Glance," FJ, January 4, 1937; Barnard, *American Vanguard*, 87.

CHAPTER 4: THE SIEGE

(61) *"Well, Diary, Fisher #2":* O'Rourke, "Diary."
(62) *To organize life inside Fisher One:* Bud Simons interview.
(62) *"I ate so much damn bologna":* Cecil Hendricks, interview, GHCC.
(62) *So the union sets up a canteen:* Ralph Orr, "How Cook Saved UAW," *Detroit Free Press*, January 9, 1972; Joe Fry, interview, 1980, GHCC.
(63) *Eventually, the food committee approaches the Hamady cousins:* Elmer "Red" McAlpine, interview by Bill Meyer, July 2, 1980, GHCC.
(63) *The "Hillbilly Orchestra," made up of strikers:* Timothy P. Lynch, "'Sit Down! Sit Down!' Songs of the General Motors Strike, 1936–1937," *Michigan Historical Review* 22, no. 2 (Fall 1996): 1–47.
(64) *"Little Group Perils 40,000 Jobs":* I.M.A. *News*, January 7, 1937.
(65) *Josiah Jordan sneaks out:* Kay McCall, author telephone interview, 2019.
(65) *Bud Simons appreciates the pressure:* Simons interview.
(65) *The strikers allow the journalist Mary Heaton Vorse inside:* Mary Heaton Vorse, *Labor's New Millions* (New York: Modern Age, 1938), 59–71.
(66) *the number of relief cases in Genesee County:* Sidney Fine, *Frank Murphy: The New Deal Years* (Chicago: University of Chicago Press, 1979), 301; "Welfare Applications Mount As Jobless Families Increase," FJ, January 8, 1937.
(67) *So the strikers set up a loudspeaker:* "March on Flint City Jail Climaxes Labor Outbreak Thursday," "Crowd Fails to Free Two Held for Breach of Peace," both in FJ, January 8, 1937.
(69) *They direct their deepest anger:* "Boysen Drafted to Direct Drive," "Thousands Join Alliance as Strike Paralysis Closes Another Factory," both in FJ, January 7, 1937.
(70) *A GM employee, Leo Schwesinger:* Leo Schwesinger, letter to Labor Department, January 8, 1937, GHCC.
(71) *A Buick employee writes to FDR:* Inar Gothold, letter to Franklin D. Roosevelt, January 9, 1937, GHCC.
(72) *A sympathetic worker writes to Perkins:* Michael Toth, letter to Frances Perkins, January 11, 1937, GHCC.

CHAPTER 5: THE BATTLE OF THE RUNNING BULLS

(73) *But some have been preparing for the confrontation:* Fred Ahearn, interview by John DeYonker, July 1978, GHCC.
(74) *Every evening at six o'clock:* Kraus, *The Many and the Few*, 125–45.
(74) *One of the sit-downers, Roscoe Rich:* Maynard "Red" Mundale, interview by Neil Leighton, Otter Lake, Michigan, July 22, 1980, GHCC; Roscoe Rich interview, 1978, GHCC.

(75) *At 8:15, Victor Reuther arrives:* "Militia Starts for Flint After Rioting Injures 28," FJ, January 12, 1937.

(75) *With instructions from Red Mundale:* Mundale interview; Rich interview.

(76) *Striker William Connolly is standing:* William Connolly, interview by Neil Leighton, Sarasota, Florida, March 4, 1980, GHCC.

(77) *Meanwhile, a team of strikers:* Mundale interview.

(77) *"It was bad enough they turned my car over":* Cloyse Crane, interview by Neil Leighton, Flint, February 27, 1980.

(77) *Fred Ahearn tears an ashtray:* Ahearn interview.

(77) *Halfway through their retreat:* Mundale interview.

(78) *Police gunfire wounds fourteen strikers:* "List of Injured," "Militia Starts for Flint After Rioting Injures 28," "Reporters, Photographers Duck Bricks and Stones During Riot," all in FJ, January 12, 1937.

(78) *Nearly three thousand spectators:* "Militia Starts for Flint."

(78) *Genora Johnson, who has rushed over:* Genora Johnson Dollinger, interview by Jack W. Skeels, July 31, 1960, Genora and Sol Dollinger Collection, Walter Reuther Library, Wayne State University.

(79) *the wife of the wounded Hans Larson:* Elsie Larson, interview by Kenneth West, April 11, 1980, GHCC.

(80) *"We got them on the run again":* O'Rourke, "Diary."

(80) *Fifty miles to the southwest:* "Militia Starts for Flint"; "Murphy Here to See Crisis," FJ, January 12, 1937.

(81) *During a meeting of President Roosevelt's cabinet:* Albertson, "Reminiscences of Frances Perkins."

(83) *Roosevelt is conflicted:* Frances Perkins, *The Roosevelt I Knew* (New York: Viking Press, 1946), 321–22.

(84) *"If the Fisher Brothers never make another nickel":* Fine, *Frank Murphy: The New Deal Years*, 299.

(84) *After an all-night conference:* FMP.

(85) *That day, Michigan National Guardsmen:* "1,200 Troopers Arrive to Serve as Military Aides to City Police," FJ, January 13, 1937; "More Than 2,000 Troops Due in Flint Tonight; Five Military Stations Set Up," FJ, January 14, 1937.

(85) *An artillery officer from Kalamazoo:* Martin Japinga, interview, GHCC.

(86) *"We men are pleased":* O'Rourke, "Diary."

(86) *A lieutenant from Holland:* Japinga interview.

(87) *A double-stacked headline:* "Heroism Defeats Police Brutality," *Flint Auto Worker*, January 15, 1937.

(87) *but the Flint Journal . . . praises the police department:* "Two Issues Here Must Not Be Confused," FJ, January 14, 1937.

(87) *The battle even inspires a ballad:* Lynch, "Sit Down! Sit Down!"

(88) *a fed-up governor sends letters:* FMP.

CHAPTER 6: THE WOMEN'S EMERGENCY BRIGADE

(89) *Genora Johnson is no ordinary factory wife:* Genora Dollinger, Skeels interview; Genora Dollinger, speech, 50th Anniversary Pioneers Reunion, Flint, August 2, 1987; Genora Dollinger, interview by Sherna Gluck, Genora and Sol Dollinger Papers; "Women's Brigade Gives Militant Aid to Auto Strikers," *Socialist Call*, February 13, 1937; Mary Heaton Vorse, "What the Women Did in Flint," *New Republic*, February 17, 1937; "Women Give Their Views of Strike Controversy," FJ.

(91) *At the meeting is twenty-year-old Nellie Besson:* Nellie Besson Hendrix interview, 1975; interview by Gary Freeman, July 5, 1978.

(92) *the Ladies' Auxiliary prints up a leaflet:* Ladies' Auxiliary, "Womenfolk of Automobile Workers," leaflet text printed in *Flint Auto Worker*.

CHAPTER 7: "GENERAL MOTORS HAS DOUBLE-CROSSED US"

(99) *Frank Murphy thinks he has a deal:* FMP; "Agreement Reached," "Corporation and Union Leaders Join Murphy Trying for Solution," "Michigan Democrats Launch Murphy's Presidential Boom at Capital Dinner," all in FJ, January 15, 1937.

(101) *Once the truce is announced:* "Strike Extra. Victory Is Ours," *Flint Auto Worker*, January 15, 1937.

(102) *"It having been agreed":* "Three Statements Announce Truce," FJ, January 15, 1937.

(102) *the governor summons:* "300 Accused In Riot Writs; Murphy Asks Them Withheld," FJ, January 15, 1937; "Arraign 4 Leaders in Riot," "Prosecutor Says Governor Sought Dismissal Action," both in FJ, January 16, 1937.

(104) *At the same time, Murphy:* "4,000 Flint Workers Assail Outside Agitators at I.M.A. Mass Meeting," FJ, January 15, 1937.

(105) *Boysen fires off a telegram:* "Flint Alliance Seeking a Voice in GM Parley Opening Monday," FJ, January 16, 1937; "Bargaining Parley for Flint Non-Union Workers Is Asked of General Motors," FJ, January 17, 1937.

(106) *"Extra! Extra! Men are to evacuate plants":* O'Rourke, "Diary."

(106) *On the Sunday morning of the evacuation:* Kraus, *The Many and the Few*, 160–65.

(108) *Ten minutes after the evacuation:* "Strikers Still Hold Plants; Peace Conference Imperiled," FJ, January 18, 1937.

(109) *The following morning, Monday, January 18, Martin is back in Detroit:* "Strike Conference Breaks Up; Series of Daily Negotiations Is Called Off," FJ, January 18, 1937.

(110) *"With reference to the Flint Alliance":* "General Motors Statement Explaining Company's Position on Strike Parley," FJ, January 18, 1937.

(110) *Murphy, who is at home in Detroit:* "Strike Conference Breaks Up."

CHAPTER 8: MISS PERKINS AND MR. SLOAN

(113) *After graduating from Mount Holyoke College:* Kristin Downey, *The Woman Behind the New Deal: The Life and Legacy of Frances Perkins* (New York: Penguin Random House, 2010), 11–137.

(116) *"For years, labor never had a chance"*: Downey, *The Woman Behind the New Deal*, 202.

(116) *Murphy steps off the train:* "Federal Intervention in Motor Strike Now Distinct Possibility," FJ, January 19, 1937.

(117) *Perkins thinks she can broker a settlement:* "Reminiscences of Frances Perkins," interviews with Dean Albertson, 1951–55, 1957, 1960, 1961, Oral History Archives at Columbia, Rare Book & Manuscript Library, Columbia University, New York.

(119) *Sloan, on the other hand, is a finance guy:* David Farber, *Sloan Rules: Alfred P. Sloan and the Triumph of General Motors* (Chicago: University of Chicago Press, 2002).

(120) *his nemesis, John L. Lewis, gives a press conference:* "Here's the Statement Issued by John L. Lewis Following Conference with Secretary of Labor," FJ, January 21, 1937; Farber, *Sloan Rules*, 203–4; Dubofsky and Van Tine, *John L. Lewis*, 263–64; "Lewis Demands Put Roosevelt on the Spot," FJ, January 23, 1937.

(122) *Andrew Jackson Transue:* Andrew Jackson Transue, interview by Dale Cyran, July 9, 1978.

(123) *In fact, Perkins believes:* Downey, *The Woman Behind the New Deal*, 210.

(124) *So many strikers defect:* Ellis Carver interview, 1980.

(124) *Sensing the city's strike weariness:* "Workers Plan Program of Action as Company Prepares to Reopen Plants," FJ, January 24, 1937.

(125) *GM's lawyers return:* "G.M. Asks Showdown by Seeking Injunction Against Flint Strikers," FJ, January 29, 1937; *General Motors Corporation*, filed January 25, 1937.

(125) *The Flint Alliance does not share:* "These Resolutions Were Adopted at Mass Meeting in Auditorium," FJ, January 27, 1937.

(125) *Murphy refuses their request:* "Alliance Is Refused Protection Guaranty to All Flint Workers," FJ, January 28, 1937.

(129) *More than any other executive:* Farber, *Sloan Rules*.

(132) *Perkins isn't giving up on Sloan:* "Reminiscences of Frances Perkins."

(138) *"Mr. Sloan breaks his promise"*: O'Rourke, "Diary."

CHAPTER 9: CHEVY FOUR

(139) *Travis drives his Willys-Overland:* Travis interview; Kraus, *The Many and the Few*, 209–26.

(144) *The next day's* New York Times: "Women's Brigade Uses Heavy Clubs," *New York Times*, February 2, 1937.

(144) *The Flint Journal writes:* "30 Women Make Flint History by Taking Active Part in Riot," FJ, February 2, 1937.

(144) *Meanwhile, inside Chevy Four:* Connelly interview; Charles Reed interview, GHCC; Ken Malone, interview by Henry Kraus, 1978, GHCC; Travis interview; Leo Robinson, interview by Michael Kukla, July 13, 1978, GHCC; Henry Lien interview, 1979; Rose interview.

(148) *Genora Johnson takes this taunt personally:* Genora Dollinger, Skeels interview.

(148) *From city hall and the county jail:* FMP.

(149) *a tactic he later tells Secretary Perkins:* Perkins, *The Roosevelt I Knew*, 323.

(149) *At one-thirty in the morning:* Kraus, *The Many and the Few*, 220–26.

(151) *Judge Gadola issues his decision:* *General Motors Corporation*, February 3, 1937.

CHAPTER 10: MURPHY'S LAW

(153) *Franklin Delano Roosevelt has a cold:* Perkins, *The Roosevelt I Knew*, 323.

(153) *John L. Lewis is already on his way to Detroit:* Dubofsky and Van Tine, *John L. Lewis*, 267.

(153) *Murphy meets with Knudsen and the GM executive Lawrence Fisher:* FMP.

(154) *Perkins types up a brief memorandum:* Frances Perkins Papers 1865–1965, Archival Collections, Columbia University Libraries.

(154) *"Is that you, Bill?":* Perkins, *The Roosevelt I Knew*, 323–24.

(154) *The next morning at nine-thirty, Knudsen and Lewis sit down:* "Knudsen and Lewis Meet to Discuss Strike at Invitation of Governor," FJ, February 3, 1937.

(155) *"The irreconcilable anti-unionism":* Walter Lippman, "Today and Tomorrow," February 1937.

(156) *they send a desperate telegram to Murphy:* FMP; "Text of Telegrams by Strikers Appealing to Governor for Aid," FJ, February 3, 1937.

(156) *But from Fisher One, strike leader Bud Simons writes:* Bud Simons Papers, Walter Reuther Library, Wayne State University.

(156) *Yet even as Knudsen and Lewis talk:* "Knudsen and Lewis Meet to Discuss Strikes at Invitation of Governor," FJ, February 3, 1937.

(157) *In response to the union's show of force:* "Sheriff Appeals to Governor for National Guards," FJ, February 5, 1937; "Drastic Steps Taken Here to Safeguard Citizens," FJ, February 5, 1937.

(158) *"I'm not going down in history as 'Bloody Murphy'!":* Irving Bernstein, *The Turbulent Years: A History of the American Worker, 1933–41* (New York: Houghton Mifflin, 1970), 541.

(158) *Sheriff Wolcott now sends a telegram to Murphy:* FMP.

(159) *the state Republican convention:* "Sheriff Appeals to Governor for National Guards," FJ, February 3, 1937.

(159) *"It is not the law"*: Sidney Fine, "John L. Lewis Discusses the General Motors Sit-Down Strike: A Document," *Labor History* 15, no. 4 (Fall 1974): 563–70.

(161) *"I am not going to withdraw those Sit-Downers"*: Fine, "John L. Lewis Discusses."

(161) *In Washington, President Roosevelt has been following*: FMP.

(162) *On February 5, Roosevelt agrees*: Frances Perkins Papers, 1865–1965, Archival Collections, Columbia University Libraries.

(163) *The governor receives a call from William Green*: FMP.

(164) *"Governor Murphy, Lewis and Knudsen"*: O'Rourke, "Diary."

(164) *Murphy is planning to issue a statement*: FMP.

(164) *Before drafting his letter*: FMP.

(165) *Murphy thinks he has a breakthrough*: FMP.

(167) *John L. Lewis is in a bad mood*: Fine, "John L. Lewis Discusses the General Motors Sit-Down Strike."

(168) *The strikers inside Chevy Four are also in a bad mood*: FMP.

(169) *"You talk of law"*: Fine, "John L. Lewis Discusses the General Motors Sit-Down Strike."

CHAPTER 11: EVACUATION DAY

(171) *John L. Lewis has a case of the grippe*: Dubofsky and Van Tine, *John L. Lewis*, 270; "Strike Peace Hopes Rising," *FJ*, February 10, 1937.

(171) *Commerce secretary Daniel Roper*: FMP; Fine, *Frank Murphy: The New Deal Years*, 313.

(172) *However, no deal can be struck*: "Strike Settled," *FJ*, February 11, 1937; "GM Announces 25 Million Pay Raise as Strike Peace Agreement Signed," *Detroit News*, February 11, 1937; "Long Day of Bickering Precedes Announcement by Murphy of Strike's End," *FJ*, February 11, 1937.

(174) *Only then, during his Senate confirmation hearing*: Fine, *Frank Murphy*, 199.

(174) *This is the document to which they affix their names*: "The First UAW-GM Agreement, February 11, 1937," reprint document (Detroit: UAW Education Department, 1995).

(176) *From Washington, President Roosevelt sends Murphy a telegram*: "Governor Praised for Peace Efforts," *Detroit News*, February 11, 1937.

(176) *In Flint, the city's biggest celebration*: "Thousands See Demonstration After G.M. Plants' Desertion," *FJ*, February 2, 1937.

(180) *Although he considers the Flint sit-down strike the worst setback*: Alfred P. Sloan Jr., *My Years with General Motors* (New York: Doubleday, 1964), 405–6.

EPILOGUE

(183) *Everett not only participated in the battle*: Ketchum interview with author.

(186) *In September 1970*: "GM Strike End of an Era," Michael Barone, Creators .com, October 1, 2007.

(186) *"We used to get stoned in the newspapers"*: Don Cooper, author interview, Grand Ledge, Michigan, 2011.

(186) *As late as 1980*: "The Richest Cities for Young People: 1980 vs. Today," Derek Thompson, *Atlantic*, February 15, 2015.

(187) *On December 10, 1987*: FJ.

(188) *the overall decline of GM's hourly employment*: David Welch, "GM Now Has Fewer UAW Employees Than FCA, Ford," *Bloomberg News*, August 29, 2019.

(188) *Flint suffered because it was a one-industry town*: "What General Motors Did to Flint," Ryan Felton, *Jalopnik* (online magazine), April 28, 2017.

(188) *In 2010, sixty-six people were murdered in Flint*: Mark Brush, "A Violent Weekend in Flint, Michigan, Homicides Hit 50," Michigan NPR, September 17, 2012, https://www.michiganradio.org/post/violent-weekend-flint-michigan-homicides-hit-50.

(189) *Between 1970 and 2014*: Pew Research Center, *The American Middle Class Is Losing Ground*, report (Washington, DC: December 2015).

(189) *From 1947 to 1973*: Lawrence Mishel, Elise Gould, and Josh Bivens, *Wage Stagnation in Nine Charts* (Washington, DC: Economic Policy Institute, January 2015), 221.

(189) *When the UAW tried to organize*: Edward McClelland, "Why White Men Hate Unions," *Salon*, September 1, 2014.

(191) *"I trace the rise of deregulation"*: Bruce R. Scott, *Capitalism: Its Origins and Evolution as a System of Governance* (New York: Springer, 2011), 528.

(192) *In the words of Olen Ham, a sit-down striker*: Nick Carey, "As UAW Fades, So Does a Path to U.S. Prosperity," Reuters, May 31, 2009.

PHOTO CREDITS

1. Knudsen, Sloan, Mott, and Barth standing in front of car. From the collections of Kettering University. Kettering Archive.
2. Green, Perkins, and Lewis. Library of Congress, Prints & Photographs Division, photograph by Harris & Ewing, LC-DIG-hec-39083. Harris & Ewing Collection (PD).
3. Striker handshake: Walter P. Reuther Library, Archives of Labor and Urban Affairs, Wayne State University. Reuther 4004.
4. Children protesting: Walter P. Reuther Library, Archives of Labor and Urban Affairs, Wayne State University. Reuther 4715.
5. Men reading newspapers: Walter P. Reuther Library, Archives of Labor and Urban Affairs, Wayne State University. Reuther 45976.
6. Strikers at windows with effigy: Walter P. Reuther Library, Archives of Labor and Urban Affairs, Wayne State University. Reuther 4003.
7. Crowd of strikers. Walter P. Reuther Library, Archives of Labor and Urban Affairs, Wayne State University. Reuther 3889.
8. Four National Guardsmen: Walter P. Reuther Library, Archives of Labor and Urban Affairs, Wayne State University. Reuther 3920.
9. National Guard with machine gun. Walter P. Reuther Library, Archives of Labor and Urban Affairs, Wayne State University. Reuther 3935.
10. Strikers' band: Walter P. Reuther Library, Archives of Labor and Urban Affairs, Wayne State University. Reuther 3907.
11. Strike calendar. Walter P. Reuther Library, Archives of Labor and Urban Affairs, Wayne State University. Reuther 3882.
12. Solo shot of Sloan: *Alfred P. Sloan*, 1937, Agence de presse Meurisse. Accessed 2020 from http://commons.wikimedia.org/. Public domain.
13. Women's Emergency Brigade marches. Walter P. Reuther Library, Archives of Labor and Urban Affairs, Wayne State University. Reuther 3995.

14. UAW signing agreement. Walter P. Reuther Library, Archives of Labor and Urban Affairs, Wayne State University. Reuther 3977.
15. End of strike. Walter P. Reuther Library, Archives of Labor and Urban Affairs, Wayne State University. Reuther 3925.
16. Strikers and flag: © 1937 MLive/The Flint Journal. All rights reserved. Used with permission. Mlive 37.

INDEX